FINDING
STRENGTH
IN WEAKNESS

FINDING STRENGTH IN WEAKNESS

Help and Hope for Families Battling
CHRONIC FATIGUE SYNDROME

Lynn Vanderzalm

Foreword by Dr. David S. Bell
Leading CFIDS Researcher

ZondervanPublishingHouse
Grand Rapids, Michigan

A Division of HarperCollins*Publishers*

Finding Strength in Weakness
Copyright © 1995 by Lynn Vanderzalm

Requests for information should be addressed to:

ZondervanPublishingHouse
Grand Rapids, Michigan 49530

Library of Congress Cataloging-in-Publication Data
Vanderzalm, Lynn.
  Finding strength in weakness : help and hope for families battling Chronic
Fatigue Syndrome / Lynn Vanderzalm.
      p.   cm.
  ISBN: 0-310-20004-0
  1. Chronic fatigue syndrome. I. Title.
RB150.F37V36 1995
616'.047—dc20   95-20166
                                                                    CIP

---

*The Doctor's Guide to Chronic Fatigue Syndrome: Understanding, Treating, and
Living with CFIDS*, ©1994 by David S. Bell, M.D. Reprinted by permission of the
author and Addison-Wesley Publishing Company, Inc.

"Up Close," quoted from *Today's Christian Woman* (Sept./Oct. 1993). Copyright
1993, *Today's Christian Woman*, published by Christianity Today, Inc.

Edited by Mary McCormick
Interior design by Sue Koppenol

Printed in the United States of America

---

95 96 97 98 99 00 01 02 /❖ DH/ 10 9 8 7 6 5 4 3 2 1

To my husband, Bas:
Your unending love gives me the security
and strength to walk the valley.
Your commitment, compassion, and humor help Alisa
to blossom despite CFIDS.

To our son, Matt:
Thank you for allowing me to depend on you
in so many ways.
You have forged a balanced path as the healthy child
in a CFIDS family.

To our daughter, Alisa,
my precious companion in the struggle with CFIDS:
You exhibit great courage and faith in persevering
through the pain, losses, and challenges of living
as a child and teenager with CFIDS.

To our comforter, Christ:
Your all-sufficient strength is revealed in our
all-encompassing weakness.

Contents

Foreword

More than a decade ago the small town in which I practiced pediatrics was rocked by a strange illness that would later be called chronic fatigue and immune dysfunction syndrome (CFIDS). Mystified by the complexity of CFIDS and moved by the devastation the illness has on families, I have devoted much of my skill and energy to treating children with CFIDS and to conducting research that will help us better understand and treat CFIDS in the coming decades.

In the past ten years I have learned a great deal from countless CFIDS children and their families. I have watched as this illness has robbed these children and adolescents of years of health, social interaction, development, hopes, and dreams. I have seen their courage and endurance in the face of a skeptical medical community. These children and families struggle on the edge of despair while the medical community debates whether or not CFIDS is a "real" disease—as if human suffering has ever been imaginary. CFIDS is a real disease that happens to real people, even children.

Science has been reluctant to approach CFIDS. In the early part of the century, medical science was concerned with fatal infectious diseases—the plague, smallpox, tuberculosis, even the flu. With the revolution in technobiology and the conquering of infectious disease, medicine has lost its insight and has been reduced to a series of laboratory formulae. And CFIDS, lacking easy laboratory description, has been missed. Yet just as infectious disease became the definition of twentieth-century medicine, CFIDS is the key to medical understanding in the twenty-first century.

With most diseases, science educates the public. But with CFIDS, the public has educated science. This book is a marvelous contribution to our understanding of CFIDS. By examining the stories and insights of people with CFIDS, including those within her own family, Lynn Vanderzalm teaches us all. This book tackles an important topic: the impact of CFIDS on the family and particularly on children with the illness. I congratulate Vanderzalm on her faith, patience, and knowledge in translating a family's experience and pain so that others may benefit.

Most of all, I congratulate Vanderzalm's daughter, Alisa, an adolescent who struggles with CFIDS. Adolescence is a time of great turmoil—the developmental issues for healthy children are difficult at best. When adolescents have a chronic illness, both psychological development and identity formation are affected, creating for them a crisis of who they are and who they will be. The long-term injury caused by CFIDS may be worse for children than for adults.

Children who come to my office often face the confusion of whether their symptoms are because they are sick or crazy. They experience a constant "flu-like" illness, yet many physicians have told them that they look healthy, that there is nothing wrong with them, and that they should "snap out of it." In a sense, physicians accuse adolescents of throwing away their lives. Over a period of time, identity formation becomes affected as these teens must decide whom to trust: their own subjective experience or the advice of their physician. Choosing the former may alienate them from professional help; choosing the latter may cause their illness to become worse.

The greatest harm to children with CFIDS is not the ravages of the disease; it is the loss of knowing who they are, of knowing who they might become. For many it is the loss of faith, encouraged by disbelieving and skeptical medical professionals who seem unwilling to listen to their patients.

CFIDS is a complex illness that lies on the cutting edge of immunology, virology, neurology, and psychiatry. Oversimplification of the illness is a form of rejection and is a disservice to children with this condition. CFIDS is like wisdom: It is obvious to those who have it and elusive to those who don't.

I urge physicians, scientists, politicians, educators, and employers to listen and respond to the CFIDS community. Compassion is the first step in the healing process.

David S. Bell, FAAP
Harvard University
Cambridge, Massachusetts

Acknowledgments

The writing of this book was truly a group effort. Any book is, I'm sure, but because I am debilitated by CFIDS, I needed more help than normal. The greatest help came from the seventy people I interviewed for the book: men, women, and children who either have CFIDS or love someone who does. Listening to their stories gave me deeper insight into the unique struggles of families living with CFIDS. Hearing their pain made me more determined to invest energy in writing this book. Hearing of their faith polished my own window into the character of God.

Thank you for your vulnerability, your honesty, and your inspiration: Jeff and Margaret Beaird; Sam Banner; Evelyn and Dan Beecher; Janet Bohanon; Carla and Dave Crosby; Linda Moore Driscoll; Jorge Estrada; Candy and Leah Feathers; Gregg and Shawn Fisher; Dick Fritz; Mark and Nancy Fuller; Sharon Gray; Helen and Don Gruelle; Kurt and Sue Hedlund; Susan Haggerty; Jim and Lynn Hekman; David and Wendy Hill; Ruth Huizenga; Jody Hurst; Janet Ireland; Deborah Lynn and Timen Jansen; Diane Lamont; Karen Lang; Dave and Debi McAdoo; Ann McErleane; Donna and Jeff McCullough; Britta and Ruth Magnuson; Barbara, Dave, and Nancy Masoner; Craig Maupin; Darla and Jerry Montague; Becky Moore; Sherry Nace; Winona Offray; Sharon Postma; Robin Ralston; Mary Ryken; Bob Scrudato; Becky Turner; Brian and Jane Vander Ploeg; Alisa Vanderzalm; Laura van Vuuren; Cyndi and Steve Volkers, and their children, Amanda, Brooke, Christina, Steven, and Timmy; Sharon Walk; Beth and Linda Waysek.

Thank you also to the family members and friends who prayed through this process. All of us who have CFIDS know that taking on a long-term commitment is risky, but the prayers of many people have bolstered me through the writing process. Special thanks to Carla Crosby, who called weekly to hear of answered prayers and to ask for new requests, and to Dave, Barbara, and Nancy Masoner and Jody Hurst, who covenanted to pray together regularly for this project.

Thank you to my friends and family members who agreed to read through the book and add their insights; your responses are invaluable to me. To Cherie Ewings, Candy Feathers, and Karen Schultz I give deep thanks for your help in typing interview transcripts and other quotations; you have been angels.

All of us with CFIDS thank the specialists and researchers who have devoted their energies to understanding and treating CFIDS. We know you work against tremendous odds as you face resistance from government agencies, misunderstanding from the medical community, and little recognition for your efforts. Please persevere. We all need you.

Thank you to other friends who have encouraged me along the way: Candy Feathers for your continual flow of encouraging cards and notes; Bruce and Dori Wine for opening your lake home to us so that I could write without distractions for several weeks; Sue Anderson for your unflagging support and your ability to help me test my wings.

Final thanks to the Zondervan people who caught the vision of how God would use this book to heal and comfort people. Mary McCormick and Sue Koppenol, bless you for all your efforts to make this a useful book. Special thanks to my editor, colleague, and friend, Sandy Vander Zicht; you are an exceptional person.

Introduction

A dozen times I have talked myself out of writing this book. After all, I'm a sick person, and sick people, I told myself, shouldn't be using their energy to write books. If that didn't convince me, I would remind myself that I am the parent of a child who has been debilitated with a chronic illness for nearly half of her life and who needs her mother's energy.

Three reasons finally compelled me to take my laptop computer to the couch and begin to write. The first is the people with whom I have talked about their struggle with the mysterious viral, immune-system illness known as chronic fatigue syndrome (CFS), or perhaps more accurately known as chronic fatigue and immune dysfunction syndrome (CFIDS, pronounced *see-fids*). As I listened to their stories, to the agony they have experienced, to the loneliness they feel as they battle with an illness that much of the medical community would like to ignore, to the rejection and misunderstanding they have faced not only from the medical community but also from their friends and families, I knew I needed to share their stories.

These are stories of men and women who have battled CFIDS for years, several of them for nearly two decades. They are stories of children who have been robbed of years of childhood and adolescence by this debilitating illness. They are stories of husbands and wives who have remained faithful and supportive while their spouses are reduced to being dependents rather than companions. They are stories of parents who have altered their lives to care for their children with CFIDS. They are stories of courage and tenacity, of love and sacrifice, of faith and perseverance.

The people I talked with are not malingerers. They are intense people, most of them engaged in thriving ministry all over the world. Most of them are high achievers, leaders, people who burned the candle at both ends. They were busily involved in satisfying work and ministry when they were struck down by a crippling immune-system disorder that left them bedridden and unable to function.

I have seen the impact that CFIDS has had on them as individuals. The adults ask probing questions: Of what value am I now that I can't work anymore? How will my illness affect my marriage, my children, my own worth and self-esteem? How will my illness affect my ability even to *consider* marriage or having children? How do I glorify God in the midst of a debilitating illness and pain? The children ask haunting questions: Will I ever be normal again? Why is God doing this to me? Will I ever be able to go to school again? Will my friends leave me now that I'm sick? Will I be able to attend college or get married?

I have seen the impact that CFIDS has had on families. Marriage vows to love each other in times of sickness and in health are tested to the limit as husbands and wives make daily choices to love and nurture sick spouses. Children live in the void left by parents who are unable to be involved actively in their children's lives because of CFIDS. Parents give up their own goals to care for bedridden children who normally would be involved in school, social activities, sports, youth groups, dating. Single men and women wonder if anyone will ever marry them now that they are ill.

I also have seen the impact that CFIDS has had on the church. Many of the people I spoke with have seen their ministries threatened and altered by this illness. Most of them served the church in several capacities; they were often leaders. Now they are the needy ones who need meals and basic help from the church. Many of them have experienced painful disappointments as their churches try to minister to families struggling with a long-term, disabling illness.

But it is more than the stories that have compelled me to write. The second reason I write is the thousands of other people who have CFIDS, people whose stories are not in this book, who don't understand the illness that ravages their bodies, who have never talked with another Christian who has CFIDS, who feel alone, some on the edge of despair.

Introduction

People who have CFIDS walk an uncharted path. Before 1988, people knew very little about chronic fatigue and immune dysfunction syndrome. Even now the research community neither understands the cause nor knows of many successful treatments for the illness. People with CFIDS need pathfinders, people who have walked before them and who can tell them what is ahead. Several excellent books published in the past few years help people understand the complexities of CFIDS and offer coping strategies, but none of these books offers durable answers to the many emotional and spiritual issues raised by trying to cope with CFIDS.

The final thing that compelled me to write this book is my very own argument for *not* wanting to write it: I have CFIDS, and I'm the parent of someone who has CFIDS. In the end, I decided that a healthy person could not write this book. Only someone who is in the valley with CFIDS and only someone who has watched a family member in the valley with CFIDS can speak with credibility.

And that is the wonder of God. He takes our years in the valley, the valley we thought to be the wasteland, and turns them into useful tools.

I hope this book is helpful to several groups of people. The first group, obviously, is the men, women, and children who have CFIDS; you stand on the front lines of the battle. The second group, the family members of people with CFIDS, is equally important. Even though you don't have the physical symptoms of CFIDS, you "have the illness" too: You face many of the same questions, adjustments, losses, emotional pain, and discouragement. The third group is those who are newly diagnosed with CFIDS or those who think they may have CFIDS; I hope this book lights your path into the valley and gives you hope. A fourth group is the children with CFIDS; no other book allows the children to speak or discuss their special needs. The fifth group is the variety of people who interact with people with CFIDS—medical professionals, employers, church leaders, educators, school officials, and friends; may you grow in your understanding of CFIDS so that you can respond with deeper compassion and support.

In preparing this book I interviewed over seventy people: men, women, and children with CFIDS as well as their spouses, parents, and children. I talked with people who have severe cases of CFIDS, some who have been bedridden for over a decade. I also talked with people who have milder cases of CFIDS; many of them are able to work part-time, but that's all their bodies will allow. The good news is that I also talked with people who have recovered from CFIDS. My interviews confirm that CFIDS is no respecter of persons. I spoke with students and school administrators, doctors and counselors, educators and engineers, homemakers and high-powered executives, missionaries and mechanics, Caucasians as well as Hispanics and African-Americans—all of whom have CFIDS.

All the stories shared in this book are true. Some names and a few details have been changed to protect the privacy of people sharing deeply personal stories. Sometimes I chose not to mention names because people wanted to be honest about their painful experiences without hurting the other people or organizations involved.

In one sense these stories are "snapshots" taken at various places in the CFIDS valley. Some snapshots find people wrestling with painful questions and doubt. Other snapshots show people who have stumbled and can't seem to get their balance. Still other snapshots reveal people at a place of acceptance and growth. Each snapshot gives an honest glimpse of people forging their faith in the crucible of physical, emotional, and spiritual suffering. They offer no easy answers, but their words have power because they have been tested.

If you struggle with CFIDS, you may find these stories are mirrors revealing parts of your story. I suspect you will see yourself in these stories. And that, I think, is comforting. Just knowing that someone else has experienced what you experience, has felt what you are feeling, has asked the questions you are asking is encouraging. The people in these stories hope that their experiences will make your way through the CFIDS valley more understandable and less frightening.

If you are hoping to find cures or miracle treatments for CFIDS in this book, you will be disappointed. I made a conscious decision not to discuss treatments in this book, in part because I am not qualified to do that, in part because success with treatments varies widely from person to person, and in part because new treatments probably will be available by the time this book is published. This is not at all to suggest that treatment is unimportant. You will find treatment options discussed in the books and periodicals listed in the final section of this book.

My deep prayer is that each of you who walks in the CFIDS valley will find that Christ is in the valley with us, comforting us, giving us hope, standing with us. I hope that you see and hear him offering you strength through the pages of this book.

Let me say a few words about the names CFS and CFIDS. In many ways they are synonyms. I chose to use *chronic fatigue syndrome* in the title of this book because that is the name most people recognize. However, I try to use the term *chronic fatigue and immune dysfunction syndrome* in the book because that name more accurately describes the illness.[1] Researchers as well as people with the illness feel that *chronic fatigue syndrome* is a misleading term because it limits the perception of the illness to only one of its symptoms: fatigue. While fatigue is certainly a major symptom of the illness, it is in no way either the only symptom or the worst symptom. One doctor said of the name *chronic fatigue syndrome*: "Calling this chronic fatigue syndrome is like calling . . . a stroke 'chronic slurred-speech syndrome.'"[2]

The term *chronic fatigue and immune dysfunction syndrome* suggests that the illness goes beyond fatigue to a disruption in the immune system, a disruption that affects many of the body's interdependent systems. While many people have suggested another name change, such as chronic fatigue immune activation syndrome, no change is forthcoming. It's also important to realize that this illness is called by several other names as well: chronic Epstein-Barr viral syndrome (CEBV), Epstein-Barr viral syndrome (EBV), myalgic encephalomyelitis (ME), to name only a few. To avoid confusion, this book will refer to the illness as chronic fatigue and immune dysfunction syndrome or CFIDS unless other names are used in quotations.

Part 1

Face the Illness

CFIDS is a devastating and elusive illness that afflicts millions and poses a major public health threat. It is a serious disease of immune dysfunction and neurological impairment.

MARC M. IVERSON, PRESIDENT OF THE CFIDS ASSOCIATION OF AMERICA, INC.

- What is wrong with me?
- Understand CFIDS
- Grieve your losses

Chapter **1**

What Is Wrong with Me?

*At one point I could hardly lift my head off the pillow. I
felt as if I was going to die. Everything was wrong in
my body. I had already seen all kinds of doctors, and I
do mean all kinds of doctors. No one could tell me
what was going on in my body.*

BECKY TURNER, TEACHER WITH CFIDS

The third weekend in October 1988 forever changed my life. Everything that happened before that weekend is B.C.—before chronic
fatigue and immune dysfunction syndrome. Everything that happened
after that weekend is colored by a frightening, debilitating illness.

In many ways the weekend was normal, except that our son,
Matt, and I both had the flu. We were achy, had fevers, felt drained of
all energy. In two days Matt recovered and returned to school. I got
worse. Seven years later, I have still not recovered.

Not one to rush to doctors, I waited several weeks before I went
to our internist. By that time I had a swollen throat, sore ears, a persistent fever, and extreme fatigue. Fairly confident that he would have
some answers for me, I went to my doctor's office. That day I came
home with ten days' worth of antibiotics. I dutifully took the medication, fully expecting to feel better in two or three days. When I felt
even worse after completing the ten-day regimen, I returned to my
doctor, less confident than I had felt on the first visit.

By this time even traveling to my doctor's office was a struggle.
I became increasingly weaker, feeling much more pain when I walked

or moved. During this second visit, my doctor and I explored other explanations for my symptoms. I had traveled with my husband, Bas, to both Bangladesh and remote areas of Thailand six months earlier. Perhaps I had picked up a parasite or other illness there. A few weeks before I had become sick, World Relief, the Christian relief and development organization for which Bas works, had had its international conference, and staff members from Asia, Latin America, and Africa were in our home. Perhaps I had caught something they had carried. My doctor, who had lived overseas, was not new to foreign and tropical diseases. But as we explored the various options, we came up empty-handed. Since a number of my symptoms seemed to be respiratory, he decided to try a stronger antibiotic, and he referred me to an ear-nose-throat specialist. When I left my doctor's office that day, he said to me, "I hope this works. If not, I'll see you in two weeks."

I thought to myself, *Two more weeks! Why can't he find out what's wrong with me? I'm not sure I can hang on emotionally for another two weeks.* Little did I know at the time how foolish those thoughts would seem seven years later.

That two weeks seemed interminable. I felt no better as a result of the stronger antibiotics. I also was experiencing more symptoms. I had night sweats that left my nightgown and sheets wet. I developed head pain unlike any other headache I had experienced before. When I tried to walk, I felt as if my body was incredibly heavy. It was hard for me to move it from one room to another. I began to spend most of my day on the couch.

Strong nausea awakened me in the morning and persisted throughout the day. Maybe I was pregnant. That was an unnerving thought for a forty-year-old, but at least it would explain a few of my symptoms. A trip to the gynecologist confirmed that I was not pregnant.

Sleep soon became a problem. Although I was deeply exhausted all the time, I couldn't fall asleep when I went to bed. I would toss and turn for hours, finally going into a light sleep, only to awaken again in an hour.

Several times during that period, I wondered if I was losing my sanity. I felt trapped inside a body I didn't understand. I knew I was sick, yet nothing in the tests the doctor had done explained my symptoms.

What is Wrong with Me?

I returned to my doctor's office for more tests to rule out lupus, Lyme disease, multiple sclerosis, hepatitis, leukemia, and other illnesses that could explain some of my symptoms. I began to feel alarmed.

While I waited for results of these tests, something happened to increase my alarm. One afternoon after school our nine-year-old daughter, Alisa, returned home almost an hour late from her neighborhood paper route. When I questioned her about why it took her so long to deliver her twenty newspapers, she sighed, "Oh, Mommy. I was so tired. Every time I brought a newspaper to a house, I had to sit on the steps for a while before I could go to the next house. I don't know what's wrong with me."

Bas and I exchanged knowing glances. What was happening? This was not our bouncy, effervescent daughter. Rather than jump to any conclusions, we said nothing, not even to each other, and merely watched her for several days. She was too sick the next day to go to school. We could hear from her speech how swollen her throat had become during the night. She had a fever, and she was weak.

After several days with no improvement, we took Alisa to the pediatrician, who was sure she had a strep infection or mononucleosis. However, both tests came back with negative results. The pediatrician put her on antibiotics and assured us she would be fine. This was beginning to sound like a familiar pattern.

Bas and I had lots of questions as we watched Alisa get sicker with symptoms remarkably similar to the ones I had. What *was* this illness? Was it contagious? Should we quarantine our house from outsiders? We had a graduate-school couple who lived in our house with us; were they in any danger?

We continued to ask those questions as we regularly returned to our doctors during the next months. On one visit the pediatrician said something about the Epstein-Barr viral syndrome. I didn't even hear the rest of his comment. I had heard about Epstein-Barr virus before. Dana, a friend of ours, had had the Epstein-Barr virus for four years at that point. She had been working for World Relief in Africa when she became sick with a strange and harrowing illness. I didn't remember all the details about Dana's illness, but I knew it had drastically disrupted her immune system and forced her to return to the U.S. for medical treatment. After eleven specialists had evaluated her, one doctor in Seattle finally laid out all her tests on a boardroom table and began some intensive detective work. That doctor finally diagnosed her condition as Epstein-Barr viral syndrome. Dana returned to her parents' home, where she was bedridden for the first four years, unable to take care of herself.

Was *this* what our pediatrician thought Alisa had?

After doing all he could for us, the pediatrician referred us to an infectious-disease specialist at the Children's Memorial Hospital in Chicago.

About the same time our internist decided that he had done all he knew to do for my symptoms, so he referred me to an infectious-disease specialist who also had experience in tropical illnesses. I saw the specialist in February. After the doctor finished asking me an extensive set of questions, reviewing the previous months' test results, and examining me, he said he thought I had chronic fatigue syndrome.

Rather than feel relieved to hear a name for the illness I had been battling for months, I felt myself getting angry. *Chronic fatigue syndrome—what kind of name is that?* I thought.

"Are you telling me I have a psychosomatic illness?" I blurted out. "Is chronic fatigue syndrome a euphemism for hypochondria?"

He sensed my anger and defensiveness. "No, it's not a euphemism. Chronic fatigue and immune dysfunction syndrome is an illness that affects your immune system and disturbs many of the chemicals normally produced in your brain. I'm going to prescribe a very low dosage of an antidepressant to treat your sleep disturbance."

At this point I was frustrated to the point of tears. First, he told me the illness is not psychosomatic; then he told me he was going to put me on an antidepressant. I had a fever and swollen throat; I wasn't depressed. Could I trust this guy?

Again he sensed my frustration and went on to explain. "At this point CFIDS is not curable. I can treat only symptoms. Your sleep disturbance is significant at this point. Because your body has not been in deep sleep for months, parts of your immune system are not functioning well. I'm using low doses of an antidepressant not because I think you're depressed but because it will help regulate some of the sleep-inducing chemicals in your brain. If I were treating you for depression, I would be prescribing a dosage several times greater than what you will be taking." He went on to prescribe some medication, telling me I might not feel any effect from the medication for another four to six weeks. I grimaced at the thought of more waiting.

On the way home from the doctor's office, I reviewed my emotions. I was both relieved and troubled. I had never before heard of CFIDS, and the doctor's description of it sounded like so much mumbo-jumbo. The illness had such an evasive name; the treatment didn't seem to fit the symptoms. I felt confused and very alone.

Eager to hear how the doctor's appointment had gone, my friend Sue came to see me after I returned home. She sat on the other end of my couch while I cried, partly out of relief to have a name for the force that was crippling my body, more out of anger that the illness was so nondescript, so mysterious. I wanted a diagnosis of a recognized disease, not some illusive illness whose name suggested that maybe I was a little tired occasionally. Sue listened to my feelings, then handed me an article she had clipped from the *Chicago Tribune*. The article was about chronic fatigue and immune dysfunction syndrome. It was the first time I had seen the name in print.

Sue did not know I would come home with this diagnosis. In fact, the article she gave me was three months old. She had read it the night before from a stack of old newspapers she had kept by her bed, waiting for free time to read them. Sue did not know I would need that article, but the Lord did.

As I read the article, I felt some relief. The people quoted in that article understood what was going on in my body. Perhaps the most important piece of information in the article was the address and phone number of an information network about the illness: the Chronic Fatigue and Immune Dysfunction Syndrome Association in Charlotte, North Carolina. I immediately phoned the number and requested information about the illness. That connection to a reliable source of information would become a lifeline for me in the next seven years.

Meanwhile, Alisa became sicker. She was able to attend school only a few hours a week. I coordinated her schoolwork with her teacher and tried to help her keep up with her class.

Finally Bas and I were able to take Alisa to Chicago to see the infectious-disease specialist at the children's hospital. Alisa and I could barely walk through the corridors of the hospital; the one-hour car ride had worsened our nausea and head pain. We were weak, dizzy, feverish, and achy. Although Children's Memorial Hospital treats thousands of children from the Chicago metropolitan area and several surrounding states each year, the doctor who examined Alisa had never before seen her cluster of symptoms. He ordered several tests to rule out polio, lupus, multiple sclerosis, allergies, Lyme disease, lead poisoning, and other illnesses that might explain her bizarre symptoms. It would be several months before he excluded the other illnesses and told us that he thought Alisa also had chronic fatigue and immune dysfunction syndrome.

Although we didn't think so at the time, the road to a diagnosis for Alisa and me was fairly smooth. We benefited from a working case definition for CFIDS released by sixteen researchers and clinicians under the direction of the Division of Viral Diseases of the Centers for Disease Control (CDC) (see chart on next page).[1]

The road to a diagnosis for Alisa and me seemed smooth by comparison to the road for Jim Hekman, who became ill in 1983. Not having the benefit of a published working case definition, Hekman spent years traveling from one doctor to another, trying to find out what was wrong with him.

Because Hekman wanted to find doctors who would be on the cutting edge of medical awareness, he went first to a university teaching hospital. After carrying out extensive and expensive tests, the doctors said to Hekman, "We know you're very sick. We know something is definitely wrong, but we don't know what it is. If we don't find out soon what it is, it probably will kill you."

CDC Working Case Definition, 1988

Physical criteria:

- Chronic or recurring fatigue that reduces activity level by at least 50 percent, does not go away with bed rest, and lasts for six months or more.
- Other obvious causes of fatigue, including significant depression, must be ruled out.

Symptom criteria:

Person must have at least 8 or 10 of these symptoms persist or recur over a six-month period:
- Low-grade fevers
- Sore throat
- Swollen or tender lymph nodes in the neck or under arms
- Unexplained general muscle weakness, discomfort, or pain
- Headaches that differ in type, severity, or pattern from previous headaches
- Prolonged (24 hours or greater) generalized fatigue after levels of exercise that would have been previously tolerated
- Joint pain without redness or swelling
- Mental problems, including light sensitivity, confusion, forgetfulness, excessive irritability, difficulty thinking, inability to concentrate, depression
- Sleep disturbance, both inability to sleep and needing too much sleep
- Abrupt onset of symptoms over a few hours or days

Disheartened and deeply discouraged, Hekman went back to his hometown, hoping to find some different answers from his family physicians. They did routine tests on Hekman and found no unusual test results. Having run out of answers, the doctors said to him, "Nothing shows up on the tests. Nothing is wrong with you. It must be in your head. You must be emotionally or mentally disturbed."

27

"At this point I was nearly despondent," Hekman recalls. "Something was desperately wrong with my body. The professionals had poked and prodded, tested and retested. In the end they could find nothing to explain my symptoms. I remember leaving the house one morning at six o'clock, and instead of going to work, I drove to a nearby park. I spent three hours wrestling with what was going on in my life. I kept hearing the medical people say, 'There's nothing wrong with you. We can't find anything wrong.' But a voice inside me kept screaming, *Something is desperately wrong with my body, but no one will listen!*

"That morning I determined to end my life. What good was I to my family? We had exhausted our options as well as our money. Maybe they were better off with me dead.

"The Lord in his mercy kept me from taking my life. Instead, my wife, Lynn, and I decided I needed some help. I went to a Christian mental hospital for an evaluation, thinking that maybe what I was experiencing was psychological. If that were the case, the mental-health professionals could treat me and we could get on with our lives. The evaluation indicated that I was suffering from anxiety, but we agreed that the anxiety was caused by my illness and the uncertainty it produced in my life and my family's life.

"In the end, professionals had told me they could find nothing wrong with me physically, emotionally, or spiritually. I was at a dead end. Months went by. I stumbled through as many days as I could at work. I slept most of the time I was home.

"But Lynn and I refused to let this illness get to us. Even though all the doors seemed to close in our faces, we were determined to find some answers. We went to see a doctor in Detroit, four hours away. He was the first person who thought I might have chronic fatigue syndrome. Even though he was sure that's what was debilitating my body, he knew of no successful treatment. I returned home, worsened, and needed to leave my work. I eventually obtained a full and permanent disability status with the Social Security Administration."

Many people who became sick with CFIDS in the early or mid-1980s share Hekman's frustration and desperation. For six years Debi McAdoo was shuttled from specialist to specialist, resulting in many false diagnoses, lots of medical bills, unbearable strain on her marriage, but no recovery. She saw fifteen different doctors before she was diagnosed with CFIDS in 1989.

The medical community is more than perplexed by this mysterious illness. Some medical professionals find it hard to live with the ambiguity of an illness that is hard to diagnose, and they resort to telling their patients that nothing is wrong with them. The fear, confusion, frustration, and isolation that results from that approach is devastating to families.

Fear

Steve and Cyndi Volkers know that fear all too well. In 1986, their nine-year-old daughter, Christina, became severely fatigued, had daily fever, and developed allergies. In the first few months she had almost continuous infections, most of them in her ears and throat. The glands under her arms and on her neck swelled to alarming size. In the beginning the doctors thought Christina had leukemia. But a second set of immune-profile tests showed no leukemia. The doctors said she definitely had an immune-system problem, but they didn't know what it was. They put her on an allergy-treatment plan.

After seeing a hematologist and several more pediatricians, the Volkers grew weary of the routine. "None of the specialists could find the basis for Christina's illness. Some said it was chronic Epstein-Barr viral syndrome. Some said it was mononucleosis, and it would be fine in six weeks. By this time Christina had been sick for two years. We were beside ourselves with fear and frustration. What was wrong with our daughter?

"Christina had severe head pain that would not lessen with medication. One doctor told us she had chronic repetitive migraines. We finally took her to a chiropractor who helped alleviate some of the pain. He was the one who gave us an article from a medical journal about CFIDS. That was the first time we had ever heard of it. That was in 1988, shortly after the CDC published the working case definition. As Christina deteriorated and developed many neurological problems, a chiropractor referred us to a neurologist, who admitted

Christina to a hospital. At that point she was totally bedridden and often couldn't remember her name or how old she was. They ran MRIs and all the other neurological tests.

"This neurologist did not believe in CFIDS, but his nurse called me later and said she had a friend with CFIDS. The nurse had a lot of information about the illness and was convinced Christina had it. She gave us the names of a team of doctors—a husband and wife. After Christina was discharged from the hospital, we made an appointment with these doctors. After seeing all of Christina's test results, one of the doctors diagnosed her right away as having a classic case of CFIDS. We've been with these doctors since then."

The Volkers' nightmare did not stop with Christina's diagnosis. In fact, their nightmare was just beginning. During the past eight years their other four children also have been diagnosed with CFIDS. Cyndi now has it as well.

Confusion

Many people also feel overwhelmed with confusion. Linda Moore Driscoll was teaching at a seminary in Guayaquil, Ecuador, when she first became ill with what she calls the "flu that never went away." She had a debilitating fatigue, fever, severe headaches, as well as muscle and joint pain. The Ecuadorian doctors tested her for toxoplasmosis, caused by a parasite. Her hair started to fall out, and the fatigue worsened to the point that she had to spend inordinate amounts of time in bed.

"I felt miserable," Driscoll recalls. "I was unable to maintain my schedule and had to cut back to the bare minimum. I taught my classes, but it took a lot just to do that. My teaching was suffering, and my body was getting worse. I had frequent throat infections, staph infections, and yeast infections. My doctors began to treat me for rheumatoid arthritis and Lyme disease, in case either of those illnesses was the root of my problem.

"I felt emotionally drained by the process. First, the doctors would tell me I had one thing and treat me for whatever that was. Then for a month I would live with some hope: Maybe this is what I have; maybe this treatment will bring an end to this horrible debilita-tion. But by the end of a month or two, I felt no better, and often I felt worse. Month after month, I had this test and that treatment. But in the end I was no better. In fact, I was beginning to have significant sleep disturbance. I had trouble concentrating, which affected my ability to teach. I was losing emotional reserve. I became irritable. Lit-tle things took on huge dimensions for me. Finally my doctors said they had done all they could. I would have to return to the States for further tests and treatment. The mission board agreed and granted me a medical furlough. It was a real roller coaster."

Frustration

Dick Fritz lived with CFIDS for over ten years before he received a CFIDS diagnosis in late 1992. Frustrated by doctors who had no clue about what was wrong with him, Fritz plodded on, try-ing to earn income for his family of four children. He knew he was ill; he knew something was robbing him of the ability to function as an accountant and businessperson. But he was left for ten years with no answers. "I remember the relief I felt when I received the diagnosis. Just to realize that other people knew what I was experiencing. I felt such a change inside to have a name for this illness."

When I listen to people like Dick Fritz, people who have lived with CFIDS for so many years before they obtained an accurate diagnosis, I am amazed at their courage and perseverance. Looking back, some of them feel that living with the uncertainties, the fear of the unknown, the self-doubt, the misunderstanding from other people before they had a diagnosis was almost more difficult than living with the illness itself.

Isolation

Evelyn Beecher, who has had CFIDS for four years, voices the isolation she felt. "When I first became ill, I felt so alone. I wondered if I was the only Christian with this awful disease. What had I done to contract it? One day I wrote to Focus on the Family to ask them to do a radio broadcast about Christians with CFIDS. In response, a man called to encourage me and prayed that I would be able to accept and endure this disease victoriously. I cried as God touched my heart by his prayer." Winona Offray feels a similar isolation. She knows of no one else in the black community who has CFIDS. Until she met another person with CFIDS, Linda Moore Driscoll felt total isolation. "I felt so alone. My doctors didn't understand me. *I* didn't understand me. Then I spoke to someone who had CFIDS. What a relief! I knew I wasn't making up this illness, but just talking with someone else who *knew* what I was feeling helped me tremendously."

Finding a diagnosis is the first important step to coping with the CFIDS. Dr. David Bell, one of the country's leading CFIDS researchers, says, "I feel that the single greatest treatment [for CFIDS] offered by the physician is an accurate diagnosis. . . . Only with an accurate diagnosis can patients begin to learn about their illness . . . Anxiety begins to fall, and the process of accommodation begins. Without an accurate diagnosis, everything becomes more difficult, and it is possible that because of the added stress and fear of the unknown, the symptoms and disability become worse."[2]

If you have CFIDS, you may recognize the feelings the people in this chapter describe. If you think you may have CFIDS, persevere in your attempts to find an accurate diagnosis. Make sure that doctors have ruled out the other illnesses that could explain your symptoms. It may take a while, but don't be satisfied until you have a diagnosis that explains your symptom cluster. Find a doctor whom you trust, a person who will work with you for the long term. Don't let medical professionals tell you CFIDS is not real or not a valid diagnosis. The CFIDS Association of America has compiled a "Physician's Honor Roll" of physicians who have diagnosed and treated CFIDS in their patients. For a copy of that honor roll for your state, contact the CFIDS Association of America, Inc. at the address listed in the "Find the Help You Need" section at the back of this book.

⌒

I agree with Dr. Bell. Once we knew what Alisa and I had, we could put aside the questions of what was wrong with us and begin to take the next important step: understanding the complexities of the illness that was taking over our bodies.

Chapter *2*
Understand CFIDS

I am doing so much better, even though my symptoms haven't changed that much. Just to know what I have and to understand what CFIDS does in my body has helped me to change my focus from confusion to coping, from fear to hope. As I learn even more about CFIDS, I feel my situation will become more manageable. Armed with books and journals about CFIDS and supported by a doctor who will work with me long distance, I'm planning to return to southern Africa to see if I can resume some of my work there.

LAURA VAN VUUREN, NEWLY DIAGNOSED WITH CFIDS

When I left my doctor's office with a name for the illness that had hijacked my body, I felt some relief. But I soon realized that I had more questions than my doctor was able to answer: What causes chronic fatigue and immune dysfunction syndrome? What is happening in my body? Will these symptoms ever go away? How long will it last? Will it get worse? Will I ever be able to return to normal life? Will these pills make me better? Is CFIDS contagious?

In the weeks that followed, I began the process of learning about CFIDS. My first step was to contact the information source listed in the newspaper article my friend had brought to me the day I received a diagnosis: The CFIDS Association of America, Inc., in Charlotte, North Carolina. When the first packet of information came, I devoured it and immediately sent for other educational materials listed in the back of their journal, *The CFIDS Chronicle*.[1] Then I called our public library to order magazine and newspaper articles about CFIDS.

Learning about CFIDS was an important first step in helping me accept the illness. Knowing became a comfort to me, a protection against the fear of the unknown. I remember that when I first showed my parents the articles about CFIDS, my mom commented, "I don't think it's good for you to be reading this. It will only scare you."

I responded, "No. If I *don't* read this stuff, I will be scared. I need to know what I can."

Learn About CFIDS

I am so grateful for the information that was available to us in early 1989. As I've listened to the stories of the many people who became ill in the early eighties, before the CDC's working case definition was published, before the first books about CFIDS were published, I realize the anguish they endured because they had nowhere to turn. Today when I talk with people who are newly diagnosed with CFIDS, I can point them to several reliable sources of information about CFIDS: The CFIDS Association of America, Inc. and *The CFIDS Chronicle*, which publishes articles highlighting the most recent research findings about CFIDS as well as articles written by people with CFIDS; David S. Bell's book *The Doctor's Guide to Chronic Fatigue Syndrome: Understanding, Treating, and Living with CFIDS*; and Katrina Berne's book *Running on Empty*. These are excellent places to start. The "Find the Help You Need" section of this book lists dozens of other sources of information and help in the process of understanding CFIDS.

This chapter does not pretend to explain the complexities of CFIDS. It is merely an overview of basic information about the illness and its characteristics. Because I am neither a medical professional nor a CFIDS researcher, I rely on the wisdom of those who are. The main voice in this chapter is that of Harvard University Medical School researcher Dr. David Bell. I chose Dr. Bell because he has an unusual ability to cut through the jargon and explain complex issues in ways that make sense to nonmedical people. I have seen this ability demonstrated not only in his books but also in his office and on the phone as he has treated our daughter, Alisa.

Understanding CFIDS is no easy task. In some ways the list of questions about CFIDS is longer than the list of answers.

What We Don't Know

Researchers do not know what causes CFIDS. Although they are in the process of testing various hypotheses and models for understanding CFIDS, at this point they do not know what causes the illness. And until they understand the causes of CFIDS, they will not find a cure. The medical profession also does not know how to treat CFIDS; health-care professionals can treat some CFIDS symptoms, but they cannot treat the illness. Researchers have seen the destructive tracks of the illness in the immune system, the neurological system, the endocrine system, and the muscular system, but they do not know exactly how CFIDS affects these systems.

In many ways CFIDS research is like dozens of skilled men and women who are examining a separate square foot of the proverbial elephant. Some concentrate on the immunologic aspects, some on the possible viral agents, others on neurological damage, still others on the dysfunctions seen in other body systems. Each researcher has made enormous strides in understanding his or her square foot, but it will take years before these researchers will be able to step back enough, pool their knowledge, and see the elephant for what it is.

What We Do Know

This is not to say that the effort of dozens of researchers around the globe is of little value. Quite the opposite. CFIDS research represents a new medical frontier. One medical professional compared solving the mysteries of CFIDS to discovering bacteria: It will revolutionize medical science. We can take great hope in the progress researchers have made. These men and women labor in a hostile environment with very little financial backing from the government and other health agencies. We who struggle with CFIDS owe them our continuing respect and support.

At this point researchers believe that CFIDS is a complex and debilitating illness that involves the interaction between an immune-system dysfunction and trigger agents, possibly various viruses. The illness causes incapacitating fatigue, neurological problems, pain, and a constellation of symptoms that can resemble other disorders, including mononucleosis, multiple sclerosis, fibromyalgia, AIDS-related complex (ARC), Lyme disease, post-polio syndrome, and autoimmune diseases such as lupus.[2]

Because CFIDS is incurable, difficult to diagnose, and difficult to treat, people who have the illness find it a frightening and confusing experience. Symptoms wax and wane from day to day, and even moderate exertion can bring on a devastating physical crash or collapse. Unexplained relapses can cause people to become more debilitated for weeks, months, or years. Adults and children with this invisible illness often face skepticism and misunderstanding from medical professionals, family members, friends, co-workers, and school personnel.

In an attempt to understand CFIDS, let's examine the various components of the definition of the illness.

Chronic

CFIDS is a chronic illness, one that does not resolve itself in a given period of time. People have referred to their illness as "the flu that never went away" or "the ten-year case of mononucleosis." Most of us have dealt with acute illnesses before, even severe acute illnesses. But it takes a very different set of coping skills to deal with a chronic, unending illness. Along with chronic pain and unrelenting symptoms come chronic emotions—fear, anger, despair, grief, frustration—which will be discussed more fully in another chapter.

With CFIDS we see very little change from day to day. In my case, it is only as I look back three or six years that I can see the gradual increases in my ability to function.

Fatigue

Many illnesses cause fatigue, even chronic fatigue: cancer, diabetes, renal failure, and others. Some medications even cause chronic fatigue. But the chronic fatigue in CFIDS is anything but generic. *It is a distinct kind of fatigue.*

Most of us have a hard time finding words to describe the fatigue in CFIDS. I feel drained, as if someone pulled the plug on my energy source. Sometimes it feels as if my blood aches throughout my whole body. Sometimes it takes effort just to breathe. One person described his fatigue as "having lead in my veins." Another person used an analogy: "The CFIDS fatigue is to normal fatigue as a forest fire is to a spark." The closest I've ever come to describing the physical, mental, and emotional exhaustion is comparing it to the jet lag I have felt after returning from Asia—except that the jet lag of CFIDS never ends, not even with sleep.

As I interviewed people, I heard a common refrain: The CFIDS fatigue is the greatest threat to our marriage, our sexual life, my spiritual life, my emotional stability, our family life, my ability to consider marriage, our ability to have children, my friendships. This is serious fatigue.

Immune Dysfunction

Researchers agree that the immune systems of people with CFIDS function improperly in two ways. First, the system's shut-off valve doesn't work properly, leaving the immune system in an overactive state that dumps excessive amounts of chemicals, known as *cytokines*, into our bodies. When healthy bodies fight any infection, cytokines enter the bloodstream, causing the person to feel feverish, achy, and tired. But in CFIDS, the level of cytokines becomes almost poisonous, perhaps causing many of the debilitating symptoms we feel. The second dysfunction in the immune system is that natural-killer-cell production is low, leaving the immune system underactive. Natural killer cells, another component of the immune system's line of defense, are replenished in our bodies in the deepest level of sleep. Bodies robbed of deep sleep by the sleep disturbance so common in CFIDS do not produce adequate numbers of natural killer cells. As a result, a suppressed immune system allows other viruses to replicate more easily and roam the body unchecked.

Dr. David Bell comments on the seriousness of these immune dysfunctions: "The immune system does not become activated by itself; there are too many checks and balances. . . . Whatever activates the immune system is important enough for the body to risk serious overreaction, and the consequent problems, to try to fight it. The presence of IL-2 and/or its receptor [Interleukin-2 is a specific cytokine produced in abnormal amounts in people with CFIDS] means that something very serious is going on."[3]

Syndrome

The designation *syndrome* simply means that this illness is characterized by a group of signs and symptoms that appear together.

Debilitating

CFIDS robs people of their ability to function as they did before they became ill. The level of debilitation varies from person to person. Some people are mildly debilitated and can work full-time or attend school full-time, but the CFIDS symptoms appear after activity. Some people are moderately debilitated and have symptoms even when they rest; they are able to work or attend school part-time. Others are severely debilitated and have strong symptoms even when they rest; they are able to function at light work only a few hours a day. Still others are completely bedridden, always have severe symptoms, and are unable to care for themselves.

The debilitation is caused both by physical symptoms like head pain, joint pain, the extreme fatigue, nausea, abdominal pain as well as by neurological symptoms like distorted vision, memory loss, and the "brain fog" that limits the ability to think clearly, quickly, or sequentially.

Pain

People with CFIDS have head pain as well as pain in their joints, lymph nodes, throat, abdomen, and eyes. The pain varies from searing and untreatable to bearable and treatable. Tim Kenny, author of *Living with Chronic Fatigue Syndrome: A Personal Story of the Struggle for Recovery*, says, "My dominant sense of the world is pain. Pain is my sixth sense; at times it is my only sense."[4]

Constellation of Symptoms

CFIDS has many symptoms. Each person with CFIDS has a unique combination of symptoms, but they all fit into a specific symptom constellation that forms a recognizable pattern. My symptom cluster is similar to our daughter's in most ways, but she has some symptoms I don't have, and I have some she doesn't have. As I interviewed people for this book, we realized that the same dynamic existed: We had some symptoms in common and some that were unique to each of us. Dr. David Bell lists the following forty symptoms as the ones he has found most consistently in the CFIDS constellation of symptoms.[5] The percentage following each symptom indicates a rough estimate of what percentage of patients report that particular symptom.

I have arranged this from highest to lowest percentages.

fatigue or exhaustion	95%
headache	90%
lack of restful sleep	90%
fever or sensation of fever	85%
blurring of vision	80%
malaise	80%
sensitivity to bright lights	80%
short-term memory loss	80%
light-headedness	75%
muscle pain	75%
difficulty concentrating	70%
abdominal pain	70%
depression	65%
joint pain	65%
allergies	60%
bloating	60%
numbness/tingling in extremities	60%
scratchiness in eyes	60%

palpitations	55%
diarrhea	50%
lymph-node pain	50%
night sweats	50%
sore throat	50%
constipation	40%
fainting spells	40%
flushing rash of the face and cheeks	40%
weight gain	40%
balance disturbance	30%
chills	30%
dizziness	30%
eye pain	30%
insomnia	30%
muscle weakness	30%
panic attacks	30%
shortness of breath	30%
bitter or metallic taste	25%
chemical sensitivities	25%
burning on urination	20%
hair loss	20%
sexual dysfunction	20%
swelling of the extremities or eyelids	20%

Part of understanding CFIDS is understanding not only *your* particular cluster of symptoms but also how your body responds to these symptoms. In the first few years, I was aware of every symptom because it was new. My body tuned in to new pain and sensations, registering the appropriate alarm that something was not working well in my body. After many years and many tests to rule out other possible causes for my symptoms, I've been able to turn off the alarm bells. I still feel the symptoms with their pain and discomfort, but I am no longer alarmed by them. It's the "same old head pain," even though it sometimes feels as if a fist is trying to push its way out of the base of my skull. It's the "same old joint pain," even though it causes me to limp at times. When I feel a new symptom, I make sure to check it out with my doctor. Sometimes it signals a separate infection; other times the symptom is added to my list of CFIDS symptoms.

Learn your particular cluster of symptoms. Find relief from any symptoms that are treatable. Although I have chosen not to discuss the various treatment options in this book, you can find information about a wide spectrum of treatments in the Physicians' Forum in back issues of *The CFIDS Chronicle* and in several of the books listed in the "Find the Help You Need" section at the end of this book.

Trigger Agents

Researchers believe certain viruses play a role in CFIDS. Before 1988, the Epstein-Barr virus (EBV) had been implicated as a cause of CFIDS, hence the early name Chronic Epstein-Barr Viral Syndrome. However, EBV has since been discounted as a viral cause of CFIDS. Researchers are studying other viruses, such as herpes viruses, like human herpes virus 6 (HHV-6); enteroviruses, like the Coxsackie B virus; and retroviruses, which are viruses that invade human cellular DNA and hide from the body's normal immune responses.[6]

But the presence of the viruses does "not imply separate illnesses; [the viruses] imply that the primary problem is the immune dysfunction that permits them. . . . The emphasis in research is shifting from the details of specific viruses to the cause of the immune dysfunction."[7]

People whose onset of CFIDS was acute can point to a specific event or infection that started the CFIDS cycle in their bodies. For many people it was an infection. I had the flu. Some people point to a case of mononucleosis or pneumonia that never resolved itself. Others, especially people who lived overseas when they became ill, feel that CFIDS spiraled off from a case of malaria or hepatitis. However, CFIDS can be triggered by other events, like surgery, exposure to toxic chemicals, stress, physical injury, or an accident. Jim Hekman wonders whether the solvent reclamation station in the factory he worked in played a part in his CFIDS. Paul and Juli Grose wonder whether the quinine drugs they had taken to prevent malaria when they traveled overseas suppressed their immune systems to the point that the CFIDS cycle began. Bob Scrudato traces the origin of a relapse to the hepatitis-B shots he needed as a volunteer fireman.

Difficult to Diagnose

One of the great frustrations, both for the ill person and the medical professional trying to help the ill person, is that CFIDS is difficult to diagnose. At present, the medical community has no test or combination of tests to diagnose CFIDS. The diagnosis must be based on symptoms and on the exclusion of other illnesses that could cause the same symptoms.

In 1994 the *Annals of Internal Medicine* published new guidelines for the evaluation and study of CFIDS, which state that chronic fatigue cases can be classified as chronic fatigue syndrome if the patient meets both of the following criteria:

1. Clinically evaluated, unexplained persistent or relapsing chronic fatigue that is of new or definite onset (i.e., not lifelong), is not the result of ongoing exertion, and is not substantially alleviated by rest, and results in substantial reduction in previous levels of occupational, educational, social, or personal activities.

2. The concurrent occurrence of four or more of the following symptoms: substantial impairment in short-term memory or concentration; sore throat; tender lymph nodes; muscle pain; multi-joint pain without joint swelling or redness; headaches of a new type, pattern, or severity; unrefreshing sleep; and post-exertional malaise lasting more than 24 hours. These symptoms must have persisted or recurred during six or more consecutive months of illness and must not have predated the fatigue.

As I interviewed people, I heard over seventy litanies, each with a common theme: "When my test results came back normal, my doctor told me my illness was all in my head." I could fill the rest of this book with stories of disappointment, frustration, hurt, fear, and humiliation people suffered because of false diagnoses or the refusal of medical professionals to admit that something was wrong with them.

"The key to diagnosis of CFIDS is an understanding of the under-lying pattern of symptoms rather than an emphasis on the most promi-nent symptoms. The physician must return to sound clinical medicine, taking a complete medical history and listening to the entire range of symptoms in order to observe the underlying pattern. This is a throw-back to the grand old days of clinical medicine when the symptoms of an illness were studied in detail. The mark of modern medicine is to jump to the lab test that will give the answer in the least amount of time. We practice 'game show medicine': The patient begins to relate symp-toms, and the first doctor to ring the buzzer with the correct answer wins. This approach simply does not work with the CFIDS patient."[8]

People with CFIDS symptoms need to learn to communicate clearly with their doctors. Give your doctor a sense of your level of ability before you became sick, then explain your level of debilitation: "Before I became ill, I was a very fast-moving mother of three kids, and I was a competitive athlete. I was nationally ranked as a distance freestyle swimmer. I had a very stringent workout schedule and com-petitive-meet schedule. Now I can barely walk around the block." Tell your doctor your complete list of symptoms, even if the symptoms sound bizarre or seem to be unrelated. State them objectively and con-fidently; only *you* know what has been going on in your body. If your doctor implies that you are making up the symptoms or exaggerating them, hold your ground. Your symptoms are your only clues to what is going on in your body.

If you don't understand something, ask. Say, "Are you telling me that you think these symptoms are all in my head?" If I had not asked that of the infectious-disease specialist, I might have gone home and resented him, fanning the flame of my growing fire of fear and doubt. Give your doctor freedom to say that he or she doesn't know the answers to your questions. However, if your doctor does not respect your symptoms or refuses to take you seriously, find a doctor who will.

Incurable

At this point, CFIDS is an incurable illness. When researchers understand the causes of CFIDS, they will be closer to finding a possible cure. That is not to say that people do not recover. The majority of people with CFIDS, as many as 80 percent, are functioning well after two years of illness.[9] If you are newly diagnosed with CFIDS, take heart. You may be in that group. I've spoken with a missionary who, although he was severely debilitated in the first year, has been able to return to full functioning. A friend who was debilitated with CFIDS for three years now is free of his symptoms and has returned to a full schedule of teaching, speaking, and global travel. A third friend has just finished her master's degree and is working full-time— and that's after eight years of CFIDS, including two years of total debilitation.

However, for those who have not recovered, CFIDS can be manageable. Many treatments are available, although not all people respond to the treatments. In an interview on the *Good Morning, America* television show, Dr. David Bell said, "I don't think treatments are causing people to get better. I feel they are getting better on their own as the illness resolves itself, sometimes in three to five years. A number of treatments can improve the symptoms during that time, but I don't feel the treatments are causing the cures."[10]

Along with various medications I have taken for specific symptoms, one of the most important management tools I have found is "active rest therapy"—intentional rest that is aimed at allowing my body to rebalance itself so that I can function at a future point. If I have a high-symptom level, I may manage my life from a couch for three days so that I can be well enough to go out for an evening; if my symptom level is moderate, I may need to stay quiet in the afternoon so that I can have energy to spend some time with my husband at night. When I rest, I don't always sleep. I make sure I'm off my feet and not exerting physically, mentally, or emotionally.

Hallmarks of CFIDS

In addition to understanding the basics about CFIDS, it's also important to be aware of several unusual hallmarks of this illness.

Waxing and Waning Symptoms

Unlike an acute illness, where the symptoms build at a fairly constant level and then gradually taper off, the CFIDS symptoms wax and wane; they can vary from day to day or hour to hour. I see my symptoms as a kind of barometer. Altogether I have a range of about fifteen symptoms, which come in clusters. The first cluster is the "constant" cluster; I have these symptoms all the time. For me, that cluster includes five symptoms, including the unrelenting fatigue. The second cluster is the "varying" cluster; I get these symptoms (in addition to the first cluster) after I've exerted, when my body is fighting another infection, or when I'm headed for a crash. For me, that cluster includes another five symptoms. The third cluster is the "crash" cluster; I get these five symptoms (in addition to the other ten) when I crash and am the sickest.

The second cluster is the "varying" cluster because I don't always experience the same combination of symptoms. On Monday the head pain may be fairly strong. On Tuesday the head pain may have subsided, but the pain in my joints may have increased. On Wednesday I may get a fever in addition to the joint pain. Although the combination varies, the symptoms I experience are always within the same cluster of fifteen. When I get a new symptom, I explore it to decide whether it's part of CFIDS or indicative of another illness.

This fluctuation is understandably frustrating not only for people who have CFIDS but also for the people who interact with them, like doctors, friends, and family. When we are sick with an acute illness, we stay home and people accept that we're sick. But with CFIDS we may feel too sick to be in church on Sunday, but on Wednesday we may feel well enough to do an errand. When people see us out of the house, they often conclude we're well again. What they don't understand is that even if we are well enough to be at the grocery store on Wednesday, we may not be well enough to be out again for the next five days.

The CFIDS Crash

The second hallmark is the CFIDS crash—the feeling of being hit by the ten-ton truck, a feeling of total collapse. The crash usually

45

comes after some sort of exertion or as the result of an infection. Carla Crosby can go for weeks with a mild level of symptoms; then if her sleep has been disturbed for a few nights or if she has been too active, her body will crash. She never knows whether it will be a two-day crash, a two-week crash, or a long-term relapse.

Some people can anticipate a crash and avoid it by resting and conserving energy. Others "plan for the crash." One businessman with CFIDS knew that going to a sales conference would probably lead to a crash, but he assessed the benefits of attending the conference and decided to go to the conference and plan for the crash. He scheduled three days working at home after the conference. When his body crashed, he had the option of working from his laptop computer in bed.

Relapses

A third hallmark of CFIDS is the frequency of relapse, when people lose the level of functioning they had been able to maintain and return to a more debilitated state or even become sicker than they had been in the beginning. While most people with CFIDS experience a slow but steady improvement or a plateau with very little fluctuation in their level of illness, others experience the CFIDS roller coaster marked by relapses and remissions. These relapses can last for a few months or for several years. After two years of a CFIDS plateau, Britta Magnuson points to a flu shot she had in her sophomore year in high school as the beginning of a two-year relapse.

One of the difficulties about dealing with crashes and relapses is we never know how long they will last. Two years ago our daughter, Alisa, had a two-week crash that turned into a six-month relapse. Other times she will bounce back from a crash in four or five days. When I talk with Alisa's teachers after she's been out of school for three days in a row and they ask how long she'll be out, I often don't have a clue. We have learned to take things one day at a time and not to plan too far ahead.

The Invisible Illness

A fourth hallmark is that CFIDS is an invisible chronic illness. That's a good-news, bad-news thing. It's good news that we don't look as bad as we feel. But it's bad news that people mistake our "looking healthy" for feeling healthy. "People who don't have this illness think because we may look okay on the surface that we are fine and we just get tired sometimes as they do. People ask me what is wrong, and when I tell them, they say, 'Oh, I have that!' They don't know the pain. They don't see me when I am in bed, so sick that I can't get up or eat or drink. People judge us on the way we look."[11]

The Misunderstood Illness

The preceding paragraphs have already described several common misunderstandings about CFIDS: "If I can't see this illness in a lab test, it must not exist"; "CFIDS is just feeling tired all the time"; "If you look good and are in the grocery store, you must have recovered." Let me briefly describe a few other common misconceptions.

CFIDS is another form of AIDS. Although AIDS and CFIDS have several common characteristics, the two syndromes have significant differences. First, AIDS is usually fatal; CFIDS is not. Second, HIV is present in AIDS; HIV is not present in CFIDS. Third, with AIDS the immune system is severely suppressed; with CFIDS the immune system is overactive. Fourth, AIDS patients are generally more mobile and functional for longer periods of time; CFIDS patients are generally debilitated by fatigue and neurological symptoms for much longer. Fifth, while AIDS is transmitted by blood-to-blood contact, CFIDS is not.

People with CFIDS are lazy and are malingerers. I appreciate CFIDS specialist Dr. Daniel Peterson's reply to this response. "Chronic fatigue syndrome is not a quick and easy way to wealth and happiness, or to Social Security disability. While you may qualify for Social Security disability with great effort, you are certainly not going to get wealthy on $292.10 a month. I have been impressed over the last few years by how few patients are malingering, attempting to imitate this disease, or attempting to seek secondary gains."[12]

Healthy people would have a hard time dealing with the kind of rejection and misunderstanding that people with CFIDS deal with from their families, friends, co-workers, and medical professionals.

But when you're ill and need to use all your physical and emotional strength just to get through the day, the misunderstanding becomes a crushing blow.

Understanding CFIDS is an important step in coping with the illness. Read reliable books. Talk with medical professionals knowledgeable about CFIDS. Understand how the illness affects your body. Talk with other people who have the illness. Find a CFIDS support group in your area. Commit yourself to an ongoing process of learning.

Once you've come to understand more clearly what CFIDS means for you, you can move on to grieving the losses and making the life changes that will help you manage the illness and find a meaningful life in spite of CFIDS.

Chapter *3*

Grieve Your Losses

> *Any death must change us. Grief is, first, the raw*
> *awareness of that change, but then it becomes a*
> *terrific struggle: a violent disputing of the facts, a*
> *striving for life again, a revising of the terms by which*
> *we know ourselves, a sometime surrender to despair,*
> *and finally a conscious acceptance of the change—*
> *in which we change. This is a labor, burdensome,*
> *aching, and painful. But it can accomplish a blessed*
> *rebirth in the griever.*
>
> WALTER WANGERIN, JR., *MOURNING INTO DANCING*

Once I began to understand the complexities of CFIDS and what it did to my body, the reality began to hit me: Life as I knew it was over; lots of things would have to change. Although those two realizations seemed to happen simultaneously, they were in some ways two separate processes. Before I could make changes in my life, I needed to grieve the loss of the way things had been before I became ill with CFIDS. Admitting that I couldn't do certain things or be certain things meant I was facing many little deaths: the death of who I was.

Brian Vander Ploeg expresses a similar realization. "I can say that I'm acquainted with death. I felt myself die over a multi-year period of time. Parts of my life shut down, parts of my being shut down, my *sense* of being shut down. It was more painful to wake up again than it was to die because it took longer. I realized what I lost, and the indignity of it was beyond comprehension."

And as with any death, we grieve.

We often think grieving is a painful process that we should try to avoid—that only weak and unstable people grieve. Yes, grieving is a painful process, but it is also a constructive and necessary process, one that ultimately leads to acceptance and the ability to move on. In the case of CFIDS, grieving the losses allows us to accept the illness so that we can make the physical, emotional, relational, and spiritual changes necessary not only to survive CFIDS but also to thrive in the midst of CFIDS.

The first step in grieving the losses is recognizing them. The following examples will help you become aware of some of your specific losses. Don't be afraid to admit that you've lost things. Admitting them is not dwelling on them; it's looking them in the face so that they no longer have the power to discourage you. Listing your losses is essential to helping you move *beyond* those losses to acceptance and redefining your life.

External Losses

"Probably the worst emotional impact of CFIDS for me is all the loss," reflects Debi McAdoo, who has battled CFIDS for over a decade. "Not only did I lose my health, but I also lost control, success, career, financial stability, esteem, social life, friends, fun, church—and the list goes on." Some of the most obvious losses we must face and grieve are the external losses.

Loss of Health

Obviously CFIDS robs us of good health. And with that loss comes the realization that we can't rely on our bodies to allow us to do things. Brian Vander Ploeg comments, "I could always count on my body. I have pushed it to every physical limit imaginable—mountain climbing, white-water kayaking, aerobatic flying, all sorts of grueling wilderness excursions—and never had to pay a price for it. That old me died when CFIDS hit. My physical exertion now consists of walking from room to room, and that I do with a lot of pain."

Nancy Masoner was in high school when CFIDS robbed her of her ability to read. "I used to consume books, but now when I read for only five minutes, my head hurts and the back of my eyes begins to burn. I call it 'brain burn.' Reading makes me very tired in my head and totally wears me out."

Sharon Postma, music director in her church, lost her ability to sing and direct. "When I am sickest, I have trouble breathing. For over a year I couldn't sing because I didn't have enough air. Directing the choir became impossible because my arms felt as heavy as two-by-fours. I was forced to take a leave of absence."

Other people have lost their ability to remember simple things like their addresses, which toothbrush is theirs, how to get back to their houses from the library, or how to add a single column of figures in their checkbooks.

Loss of Financial Security

CFIDS has cost many people their jobs. Some have had to leave their jobs; others continue at a reduced physical and mental capacity. Leaving a job means not only losing the satisfaction, identity, and relationships a job brings but also losing income, insurance coverage, and financial security for the future.

The financial pressure can become overwhelming. One couple estimates that in the twelve years since one spouse became ill with CFIDS, they have spent thirty-six thousand dollars on medical expenses not covered by their insurance plan. In addition to medical bills, many people with CFIDS have to pay for services they once were able to do themselves, like housecleaning, car maintenance, yard work, food preparation, and child care, to name a few.

Loss of the ability to provide for their families is a particularly significant loss for many men with CFIDS. Before his illness, Dick Fritz, a take-charge entrepreneurial type, envisioned himself in his own business, able to provide the best education for his four children and household help for his wife so that she could be involved as a team member in their business. When CFIDS struck, Fritz was reduced to working only two to three hours a day. His wife has had to work outside the home to provide the basics for his family, and his children have had to choose colleges that they can afford on their own resources. This is not what Fritz had planned.

The financial drain forces people to work beyond the limits their health would allow. Deborah Lynn Jansen and her husband, Timen, both have CFIDS. "I kept working temporary jobs, and each time I did, I got worse and worse physically, and in turn emotionally, mentally, and spiritually. I lost all faith. I was worn out and frustrated, discouraged, and physically killing myself just to help provide the basics for Timen and me."

Although some people still have a job, CFIDS has affected their ability to do their work. One woman, a high school special-education teacher, finds it hard to concentrate on her task. "I graduated with honors and was on the dean's list, but now I feel as if I'm dyslexic or something. I will write a word on the board, and my students will tell me it's the wrong word or it's backward. Often I will lose my train of thought. One of the ironies of this experience is that I understand my students better now that I am impaired too. My school is offering early retirement, which I would like to consider, but I'm worried about what insurance coverage I will have."

Loss of Ability to Attend School

Most children with CFIDS lose their ability to attend school; some attend only a few hours a week, and others can't attend at all. While many children would be only too eager to miss school, the CFIDS children with whom I talked deeply grieve their inability to be in school. Before they became ill with CFIDS, they were actively involved in their schools' academic, social, and sports programs. Missing all that is a painful loss of a major part of their lives. Many of the children I spoke with are gifted in academics, sports, music, or drama—all things they can no longer do.

Like many CFIDS high school students, Sharon Gray missed a lot of school in the early days of her illness. As a result, she couldn't graduate. Several of the teachers believed Gray was missing class for inexcusable reasons, and one refused to let her make up her assignments, wanting to make an example of Gray in order to discourage other chronic skippers. The day before graduation Gray was told she wouldn't graduate with her class. Although she was devastated by the injustice of the school's decision, she did not let that deter her. A week later she took the general education diploma (GED) test so that she will be ready to start college whenever her body is ready.

Loss of Relationships

Relational losses are staggering for people with CFIDS. One man said, "My wife and I feel as if we don't have any friends. We've had to cancel plans so many times that some people tend to avoid us, and we withdraw from social situations. Since we used to spend so much time with other people, the lack of social involvement has been a real stress on our marriage."

Candy Feathers feels she lost her *ability* to be with people. "I've lost all my friends. That's been very hard because I was very much a people person before I got sick. I loved people. CFIDS has almost changed my personality. I experienced so much pain from people's insensitivity to CFIDS that now it doesn't matter to me if I'm around people or not. I feel as if I have lost my ability to trust many people."

These relational losses—losses not only of specific relationships but also of how we relate to people—are so significant that we will explore them more fully in a later chapter.

Loss of Faith in the Medical Profession

Many people with CFIDS have lost faith in the medical profession, to which they had always looked for answers and understanding. "I now laugh at my own naïveté about doctors," Becky Turner comments. "I had always thought that when I was too sick to take care of myself, doctors would take care of me and make me well. In the early months of CFIDS, I would drag myself to a doctor, wait two or three hours, tell my story, and wait in anticipation for those wise words that would bring about a diagnosis, a treatment, and a cure so that I could get on with my life. How I longed for a doctor to say, 'I know you are sick, and I'm going to take care of you.' But that never happened. Because I am a single parent, the doctors often wrote off my symptoms as depression about not having a man in my life. I could never understand how loneliness could cause fever, swollen lymph glands, or many of my other physical symptoms."

A recent letter from one woman interviewed for this book illustrates that people continue to have devastating experiences with medical professionals. She reports that her doctor, who diagnosed her CFIDS and has treated her for the past four years, has just "dumped" her. He says he no longer believes in CFIDS as a valid diagnosis and doesn't know of another primary-care physician who does. He calls CFIDS a "throw-away" diagnosis, which makes her feel like a "throw-away" person. She wonders whether he is laughing about her to his colleagues. People with CFIDS need so much energy just to survive the illness itself that to deal with medical professionals who refuse to treat them or who dismiss their illness as nothing only adds to the grief. If the medical profession can't help ill people, then who can?

In an article in the *Journal of the American Medical Association,* Dr. Tom English, another physician with CFIDS, addresses his medical colleagues, asking them to imagine that they are the patient with CFIDS. "You catch 'a cold' and thereafter the quality of your life is indelibly altered. You can't think clearly . . . or follow the plot of a television program. . . . You inch along the fog-shrouded precipice of patient care, where you once walked with confidence. . . . You are exhausted, yet you can sleep only two or three hours a night. You were a jogger who ran three miles regularly; now a walk around the block depletes your stamina. Strenuous exercise precipitates relapses that last weeks. *There is nothing in your experience in medical school, residency, or practice with its grueling hours and sleep deprivation that even approaches the fatigue you feel with this illness. 'Fatigue' is the most pathetically inadequate term.* . . . I have talked with scores of fellow patients who went to our profession for help, but who came away humiliated, angry, and afraid. Their bodies told them they were physically ill, but the psycho speculation of their physicians was only frightening and infuriating—not at all reassuring."[1] English urges his colleagues to take CFIDS seriously, listen to their patients, keep an open mind, and apply their intellectual skills to the complexity of the illness.

Loss of Independence

Most of us who have CFIDS are competent, able, independent people, sometimes fiercely independent people. CFIDS robs us of that independence. Suddenly we need to depend on family and friends to do basic things for us, like laundry, meal preparation, shopping, balancing our checkbooks. It's not easy for us independent types to ask for help, to be needy.

The single men and women with CFIDS find losing their independence especially hard. Ann McErleane had just gone off to college when she became severely debilitated by CFIDS. "I've always been independent. I *need* my independence. But when I became so sick, I returned to my parents' home and became completely dependent on them. Completely."

Another single woman in her thirties feels a lot of stress because she has lost her financial independence. Although she is able to live in her own apartment, she needs to depend on her parents for help with paying medical expenses, including several hospitalizations. While her parents have offered the money, they have also expressed resentment about her illness and impatience that she doesn't recover.

Loss of Control

"The most difficult thing about having this illness is that I no longer have any control in my life. I go to bed every night having to trust the Lord for the next day, not knowing whether I'm going to wake up in the morning and be able to get out of bed or whether I'll have lots of symptoms." Many people with CFIDS echo these words from Carla Crosby. Accustomed to setting goals, devising an action plan, and making things happen, many of us have lost the ability to plan even four or five hours ahead. We are unable to make commitments or to schedule events. Things that were once basic assumptions about life are now up for grabs. Everything becomes tentative.

Brian Vander Ploeg has always thrived on taking risks, not only in the physical world but also in the business, social, and spiritual world. He never saw problems—only challenges. For most of his life he responded to those challenges with energy and intellectual curiosity, finding himself successful in nearly everything he attempted. He approached CFIDS with the same determination and expectations: Jump in, study the problem, find a solution, do what it takes, and move on. Except this time it didn't work. For the first time in his life he confronted something that did not yield to intellect, personality, spiritual forces, or medical science. CFIDS was out of his control.

Loss of Dreams

Jeff McCullough grieves the loss of the dream he and his wife, Donna, had to become a team that would help people strengthen their marriages. Months before they were married, Donna became ill with CFIDS. For over a decade their dream has been on hold. Not only has the illness left Donna bedridden for years at a time, but it also has placed surprising strain on their own marriage. "I shake my head at the irony of it. Here we were going to be a pastoral team and help other people with their marriages, and instead, CFIDS has nearly ruined our own marriage. We have had tremendous struggles coping with this illness. It has changed us forever. Living with CFIDS is like going through a war or being in a concentration camp. It has been devastating."

Dan and Evelyn Beecher also have grieved the loss of many of their dreams. "We have faced very real losses. We miss *the way it used to be* in our marriage, or we hurt for *the way it will never be.* We mourn the dreams we have had as a couple for our marriage."

When Evelyn became ill with CFIDS, she and Dan had just begun what they thought would be a long-term project as missionaries in Puerto Rico, but Evelyn became severely ill and had to return to the States for medical treatment. Their dreams crashed hard. "The biggest struggle was having to deal with the crash of a vision," said Dan. "Three years later I can still feel the shock of coming to realize this illness was going to threaten our ability to stay in Puerto Rico.

First, I felt the threat and then the reality of an aborted dream in a mission setting I was finding very fulfilling. Then I wrestled with the possibility that my youthful wife could have a long-term, debilitating disease. The crash was intensified by the fear of not being able to find a job back in the States. When the men in my former Sunday school class learned that we were returning to the area, they said, 'Don't come back here. Unemployment is high, and there are no jobs.' Our dreams were gone."

Several single people with CFIDS have had to face the loss of their dreams for marriage. One of the men recounts, "I was in a relationship heading toward marriage when I became ill." A single woman expressed similar losses. "Because I have to support myself, I use all of my energy on my job. When I get home, I am so sick that I collapse on the recliner and sleep, sometimes for the rest of the night. On the weekends I have to do errands. I have no energy or time for any kind of meaningful relationship. Sometimes I wonder if I will ever be able to marry. Who would want to marry someone who is as debilitated as I am?"

As parents of a child with CFIDS, Bas and I have felt a loss of our dreams for our daughter. We see in her abilities that have no opportunity to be expressed or tested. She has rich talents in drama, music, speech, art, and writing, yet she is unable to be in the choir, on the speech team, on the drama team—any extracurricular activities that would help her develop or even recognize those abilities. As a result, she has had very limited ways to discover who she is. It's also hard for us to watch her grieve as her friends excel in the very areas in which she would love to be involved and in the very areas in which she would find great joy and satisfaction.

Loss of Roles

Before we became ill with CFIDS, most of us were the givers, the doers, the caretakers. Now we have lost the ability to do much of that. Barbara Masoner grieves the loss of her role as the giver of hospitality, of having guests in her home for dinner and special gatherings. Like many parents with CFIDS, Jody Hurst grieves the loss of her ability to be the kind of parent she would like to be.

Many of the men with CFIDS grieve the loss of roles as family provider and protector. It has been hard for them to see that their wives need to work full-time outside the home to help care for their families.

Internal Losses

Some of the internal losses are harder to recognize and harder to face. As you examine some of the internal losses described here, try to identify what your specific internal losses have been.

Loss of Identity

As the months ticked by and I realized I was not getting any better, I had to face the reality that I was losing some of my identity. For the past two decades of our lives, my husband and I have focused our energy on the needs of the poor—for eight years with alcoholic and homeless men and women in the inner city of Boston, and for the past twelve years with the Third World poor in famine areas, refugee areas, and disaster areas. Our lives were focused outward. When I became sick, I could no longer do those things. I resented needing to pull inward and take care of my body and be much more self-centered than I had been before CFIDS. My resistance came from two misunderstandings: that my identity is tied up in what I do and that my faith was vital only if it expressed itself in outward ways. I had to do a lot of changing, as subsequent chapters will reveal.

When CFIDS showed up in Brian Vander Ploeg's body, he and his wife, Jane, had just moved into a new community. "No one here knew me before I got sick. My past is obliterated. Some people think of me only as a spaced-out person who can't function very well. They know nothing about the guy who hung by his teeth at the top of a mountain or flew his own aircraft into the crater of Mount St. Helens. I can't even remember that guy some days. CFIDS has stripped away all my strengths. All that I have left are my areas of weakness, and even they are hardly available."

Gregg Fisher, author of *Chronic Fatigue Syndrome: A Victim's Guide to Understanding, Treating, and Coping with This Debilitating Illness*, looks back on thirteen years of living with CFIDS and says, "I have lost who I am, or at least who I want to be. These past thirteen years have been nothing close to what I had expected life to be. I no longer have high aspirations; I just want to be the type of husband I long to be, the type of Christian I want to be, to be a father, a friend, active in the church—the basic minimum requirements of what I thought life would be. CFIDS has taken that away."

Loss of Self-worth

Tied closely to our sense of identity is our sense of worth. When CFIDS strips us of the ability to do what we have always considered to be meaningful things, we question whether we are worth anything. "Not only have I lost my job, which I *loved*, and my ministry in the church, but I don't feel I contribute anything as a person. I feel like a burden to family and what friends I have left." These words of a person with CFIDS express what many of us feel when we think of the losses we have suffered.

"I felt my self-worth drop," says Evelyn Beecher. "I have always perceived myself as an intelligent person: I was in the National Honor Society in high school, and I've handled many confidential and important materials in my jobs. Now I often have trouble doing simple jobs, completing a simple errand, or remembering the names of friends. When my husband and I are with friends, my mind often fogs out, and I have trouble following a conversation and framing an intelligent reply. Usually people look at me as if I am a little retarded."

In my own case, as I became increasingly debilitated, I feared becoming housebound, an invalid. That word bothered me. Was I an invalid, an *invalid*—non-valid—person? What was I worth to my family if I couldn't cook meals, attend school functions, attend church with them, travel with them, be an effective wife and mother? What was I worth to my friends if I couldn't be involved with them on committees or in other group situations? What was I worth to God if I needed to spend most of my time on a couch rather than behind a podium or in a classroom? As I faced these questions, I realized that I needed to redefine my sense of worth and value.

Loss of Self-confidence

As a seminary professor in Ecuador, Linda Moore Driscoll always had confidence in her ability to handle a heavy workload as well as many responsibilities in the church and the community. Then she battled with CFIDS for four years. Now, even after she has recovered to the point that she can again work full-time, she says, "I no longer have the confidence to face stressful situations or a work overload or having too many commitments all at once. I never know how my body will respond."

Before becoming ill with CFIDS, our daughter, Alisa, had always been an extroverted, confident child who participated in classroom discussions. During her middle-school years we watched her crawl into a shell and become insecure and almost reclusive. We attribute her extreme loss of confidence in part to three teachers who doubted the reality of her illness and made insensitive remarks to her. Even though the rest of her teachers were understanding and supportive, the presence of the three insensitive teachers stripped her of her self-confidence.

Jody Hurst, a charge nurse with responsibility for a hospital staff before she became ill with CFIDS, found herself unable to drive or to do simple math problems with her five-year-old daughter, Olivia. Trying to help her daughter understand, Hurst explained that CFIDS had done some damage to the parts of her brain that helped her work with numbers. Although Hurst has lost confidence in her ability to do basic things, she has not lost her sense of humor. She was able to laugh when her husband told her he had overheard Olivia telling the older women at church that her mother couldn't be in church because she was brain-damaged.

Loss of Confidence in God

One of the most frightening losses for people with CFIDS is their ability to feel or to sense God's presence or comfort. Brian Vander Ploeg says, "I lost my ability to relate to God. That was baffling and offensive to me. I used to enjoy sensing him. But now I realize that my inability to sense his presence is merely a function of my illness. I patiently wait for him to re-enable that capacity."

Jeff McCullough, whose spouse has been debilitated for over a decade with CFIDS, has felt great disappointment with God. "I considered myself a very strong Christian. Before Donna got CFIDS, I was headed for seminary. However, this illness threw me a curve that I never learned how to handle. God and I sparred off, and I basically said, 'You need to help me.' But he hasn't helped me. I don't feel his comfort. All I get is pain and emptiness and no answers. I've just kind of given up. I feel as if I'm wandering in the wilderness. I'm totally lost in that area of my life. And that adds to the pain."

Sharon Postma remembers when she had been sick for so long that she couldn't sing "Great Is Thy Faithfulness." She would get stuck on the line, "Morning by morning new mercies I see." "I didn't *feel* that mercy," Postma remembers. "I would cry during the whole song. I was quite sick at the time and everything looked very bleak. That's when I questioned, 'Are you there, Lord?'"

Loss of Confidence in the Church

When I asked people with CFIDS how their churches have been able to support them during their illness, I was surprised at the amount of hurt many people have experienced. As a result, many people with CFIDS have lost their confidence in the church's ability to be compassionate.

One woman said, "The church that we were attending when I first got ill gave us no acceptance or support. No one ever brought our family a meal. The pastor never came to visit me. He never prayed with me. When he called our house, it was always to ask my husband for something. His wife called two or three times over the period of the first three years. And the last time she called me, she asked me if Satan was keeping me from coming to church. It's not that we didn't try to educate them about the illness. For some reason they were unable to respond with any kind of compassion or understanding. That hurt because I had been very active in the church's life before I became ill. A year ago my family changed churches, and although I have not been able to attend any church services, I feel relieved that I am no longer in contact with our former pastor and his wife."

Grieving

From these few descriptions of losses people have experienced because of CFIDS, you can begin to recognize what things you have lost. But what does it mean to *grieve* those losses?

As we know from studies about grief, people go through various stages in the grieving process: shock, denial, bargaining, anger, depression, and acceptance. Grief is never that tidy or sequential. Often we find ourselves in two stages at once or moving back and forth between stages. The ultimate goal of grief is acceptance, an ability to live with the realities of our new situation. But again, life is not always predictable. As we face new losses or see our losses in a new way, we may feel as if we lose our ability to accept. One person with CFIDS comments, "The grieving process seems never to end. As I recover, I begin setting goals, making plans, only to have a relapse yank them from me again when I least expect it."

Let's review how the various stages of grief reveal themselves in the lives of people with CFIDS.

Shock

The week I was working on this chapter, I listened to a friend go through this initial stage. Laura van Vuuren had just received a diagnosis of CFIDS, and she was not happy about it. She has seen what the illness has done to Alisa and to me, and her gut cry was, "No. I don't want that illness! I know I'm sick, and I know I've been debilitated for three months, but *not* CFIDS! Lynn, I can't believe this. I don't like this at all."

Ann McErleane was in college when she got her diagnosis of CFIDS. "I was bedridden, hardly able to move. My ability to read was affected, and I couldn't concentrate in class. I fell severely behind in my classes. When one of my friends suggested that I might have

CFIDS, I immediately rejected that possibility. *I* could never get a chronic illness. That couldn't happen to *me*. But the inevitable happened. My doctor told me I had CFIDS. I remember feeling an overwhelming sense of shock. What was this disease? How and when would I get better? I had no answers, and neither did the medical profession. I felt completely alone."

Denial

Another stage of grief is denying the reality of CFIDS in our bodies and denying our need to change. Debi McAdoo, a high-energy person who spent most of her early adult life addicted to work, sees how she denied her illness at various points in her thirteen-year battle with CFIDS. "As soon as I felt well enough, I would go back to work. At one point my health had improved enough that I was working sometimes more than forty hours a week, at a great cost to my body, which was in pain most of the time. I was taking painkillers on a daily basis to keep up with the new pace I had set for myself. I am still recovering from this mistake four years later."

One health-care professional with CFIDS said, "I've always lived my life at 130 percent and never had to pay a price for it. When I first started to feel sick, I didn't want to acknowledge the symptoms. I just kept pressing on." When we deny the reality of CFIDS in our bodies and try to appear normal, we often revert to our old pattern of doing things: push ahead, take charge, keep going, ignore our bodies' signals, get the job done at all costs—the formula for a crash and possibly a relapse.

Some people express their denial in their hesitance to tell people they are sick. Certainly, not everyone needs to know that we are sick. But the people closest to us—family members, friends, colleagues, employers, teachers, and some classmates—need to know some details about our illness. An Ethiopian proverb reminds us, "He who conceals his disease cannot expect to be cured."

Bargaining

Dr. Sam Banner remembers bargaining with God in the early years of his CFIDS. "My drive to get well was so strong, but I had to come to grips with the idea that I might not get well. I found myself trying to make deals with God. I wanted information. 'God, just let me know if I'm going to get well.' He has not told me the answer to my question, so I have to grab on to what I know about him and to any stability that I have in my life."

Anger

Anger is one of the most powerful grief emotions. We feel angry with our bodies, with the pain, with what we can't do. We feel angry that we can't *be* who we are. We feel angry that we can't work and our medical expenses are so high. We feel angry with people who think we're weak, with media that trivialize our illness, with doctors whose ignorance turns to arrogance. We feel angry that we can't be with people. We feel angry as we watch the rest of the world go by. We feel angry with God. Jorge Estrada comments, "When CFIDS hit me, I didn't have the physical endurance, the mental tenacity, or the emotional stability to keep up my spiritual disciplines. So I suffered spiritually. I went through a three-year period where I didn't understand what was going on, and I was very angry with God. I started to withdraw from him and from other people." Remember that the anger itself is a normal and understandable response. Anger itself is not bad. It becomes destructive when we stuff it, misdirect it, or indulge in it.

First, when you feel anger rising, express it constructively. I found that the journals I kept in the beginning years of my illness were a safe place to vent my anger. On the pages of my journals I would write it all. I addressed each entry to God so that my outpouring of feelings became a conversation with him. I was never worried that he would reject me because of my anger. Somehow I felt that he was the best person with whom I could share my anger.

Walter Wangerin, Jr., in his book *Mourning into Dancing*, agrees. "If the anger does rise within you, name it, accept it, and send it to God! Why? First, because we think God is responsible. Even when we fear to admit it, God is our final antagonist. . . . But second, because God can take it! God, who understands us better than we understand ourselves, will not be destroyed by our most passionate rages. In fact, he sees already the fury and its intended object before we confess either one. And it hurts the Lord when our anger hurts his people. Better, then, to give it to God."[2]

Second, when you feel anger rising, direct it at the appropriate object: the illness, not people. It's very easy to lash out at people around us: doctors who don't or won't understand, a friend who expects too much of us, a spouse who doesn't pull his or her own weight, church members who ignore our needs. We need to remember that CFIDS is a difficult illness for *everybody* to handle. Medical professionals who treat us insensitively don't do so out of malice as much as ignorance. Our spouses don't mean to burden us; they often don't understand how we feel from day to day. Most people don't intend to be insensitive or rude or flippant with us; they are uncomfortable with illness, and they don't know appropriate responses. That doesn't mean we dismiss these responses, but we can express our anger in ways that don't hurt others in return.

Third, remember that the intensity of your anger often is related to how sick you feel. One woman was surprised at what an angry person she became during her sickest years. As she gradually recovered, she discovered that her anger subsided too. Looking back, she now realizes that the emotional energy it took to deal with excruciating pain and severe debilitation sapped her of any emotional energy she needed to respond in positive, loving ways or to process her anger constructively.

Depression

Great controversy surrounds the depression associated with CFIDS. While many people with CFIDS have had their doctors dismiss their illness as depression, CFIDS is not caused by depression, and it is not synonymous with depression. "Depression is not what we have. We have a serious disorder that disrupts the immune system, degenerates muscle tissue, destroys normal metabolism, robs our memory and thinking abilities, and causes severe brain damage, among other things. This is real—it is not imagined. It does not begin in our minds."[3]

However, many people with CFIDS have experienced depression. Most of the depression is caused by the circumstances involved in the illness. After battling CFIDS for thirteen years, Gregg Fisher says, "CFIDS isn't depression, but you'd have to be superhuman not to struggle with depression while enduring years of chronic debilitating illness."

After one of her doctors told her that her symptoms were caused by depression, Laura van Vuuren responded, "I really don't think I'm depressed. I was not depressed when this thing hit me. Quite honestly, I am now becoming depressed out of frustration of not being able to function normally and do my job, of not knowing what's wrong with me, and not knowing when I'll be back to normal." A month later a doctor diagnosed her with CFIDS.

Acceptance

As we noted before, the ultimate goal of grief is to come to a place of acceptance. I remember that after I wrestled with the realities of what CFIDS was doing to my life and our daughter's life, after I cried and argued with God, after I tried everything I knew to get over this illness, I came to my first point of acceptance. I remember having a conversation with God.

"Lord, I don't know what you are doing. I don't like this illness. I don't like seeing Alisa suffer and lose so much. We have done everything we know to do. We have confessed our sin, prayed for healing, consulted doctors, asked our family and friends to pray for us. The elders of our church have prayed with us and anointed us, according to New Testament instructions. I must assume that for today you have chosen not to take this illness from us. When I gave myself to you and when Bas and I gave Alisa to you when she was born, we gave you everything: our minds, our souls, our gifts, our relationships, and our bodies. They are yours to do with as you please. You know what we are capable of doing when we are well. And you know what we can't do because we are ill. What you do with us is your business. It no longer matters whether or not we get well. What matters is that you are free to do what you need to do in and through us. It's your choice. If you choose to reveal yourself to us and to others through this illness, then that's your choice. And I choose to believe that that is a good choice. I do not want to be well one hour before you want me to be well."

That was the beginning of a series of surrenders that were the stepping-stones to acceptance. In surrendering, I have not given up. I have not resigned myself to this illness. Resignation is passive. This is an active surrender that still carries with it a fighting spirit: a fight for health, a fight for strength, a fight for restoration. But recovering from this illness is no longer the driving force, no longer the major issue for me.

Some people have misunderstood this acceptance and think we no longer want to get better. I choose to see it as the pathway to getting better, from the inside out.

Robin Ralston remembers the day her counselor helped her along the path to accepting her life with CFIDS. "I decided that I either had to fight this or give in to it. My counselor suggested a third option: acceptance. That's when I first realized that I could accept the illness without giving in to it. That was very freeing for me. I still hate the illness, and I can be angry about it and cry over it, but I have taken the first step to acceptance. It's something I struggle with daily. On the days when I only have ten symptoms, I can handle things. But the next day I may have twenty symptoms. When no one is around, I get depressed and scream inside, *I can't stand this. I hate this disease, I hate you, God. I can't do this anymore.* I go back and forth. My goal is to come to a point that I can live with this illness without all the emotional turmoil, but I'm certainly not there yet."

Coming to a point of acceptance is a journey that continues through the entire course of CFIDS. It's important to remember that just as CFIDS symptoms wax and wane from day to day and week to week, our ability to accept the impact of CFIDS will also wax and wane. We may feel a sense of acceptance one day, only to be ambushed by denial or bombarded by anger the next. That doesn't mean we've lost all acceptance. It means the journey continues, even though we vacillate.

"Grief is a process. It involves honesty about the loss, time to experience sadness and renewal, and responsibility to take action."[4] No matter where we are in the grief process, we must allow ourselves to *feel* these various feelings and not just say, "I was angry for a while, but now I am over that." It is common for people with CFIDS to intellectualize their feelings, and when we do this, we only prolong the various stages of grief. We may try to push them under the surface and pretend they are gone, but they will either resurface at another, perhaps inappropriate, time or fester like an unclean wound and hinder our recovery. "When we allow ourselves to *feel* these painful feelings and when we *share* the grief with safe and supportive others, we are able to *complete* our grief work and thus be free of it."[5]

Celebrate the Gains

As important as it is to grieve the losses, it is also important to learn to celebrate the gains. Last week as I walked from the car to the grocery store, I thought, *This is incredible. I can do my own grocery shopping this year. For many years I was too sick to walk up and down the aisles of the store, but this year I can do it. It feels so good.* Or I celebrate that I can now walk up a flight of stairs without stopping several times to gather strength.

As I grieved the losses in my life and our daughter's life because of CFIDS, I was able to accept that CFIDS would influence our lives for many years, perhaps forever. That acceptance prepared me to take the next step: to redefine our lives. I determined that if we were to have meaningful lives within the limitations of a debilitating illness, we needed to make many changes: in our physical lives, in our emotional responses, in our relationships, and in our spiritual lives.

The next two sections will explore those changes. Part 2 will reveal how people with CFIDS have made positive changes in their physical surroundings, emotional perceptions, and relationships with family and friends. Part 3 will focus on how people with CFIDS not only have redefined their perceptions of who God is but also have found spiritual balance and strength.

Part **2**

Redefine Life

Now, although patients generally submit voluntarily to technical prescriptions and agree to take medicine or a rest-cure, they are, on the contrary, quite reticent when it comes to changing something in their way of living.

PAUL TOURNIER, *FATIGUE IN MODERN SOCIETY*

- Make physical changes
- Find emotional balance
- Accept changing relationships

Chapter **4**

Make Physical Changes

I went through a death of what I thought was a good life. The future is still uncertain, but little glimpses indicate that it will not be a life form that resembles anything from my past. Which is not to say that it's bad, just different. And I know that the power source of that new life will be something I will not even be aware of. I accept that life will be different, and life will not be as I make it. It may be a different life form, but I know God is in it.

BRIAN VANDER PLOEG, BUSINESSPERSON WITH CFIDS

Once we begin to face the losses and move toward acceptance, we begin to ask new questions. The questions move from *Why?* to *What can God do with my life now?* They move from *When will I be well?* to *How can I live a meaningful life now, even when I am debilitated?* They change from *Will this ever end?* to *How can I move through this day of pain with grace and joy?* These new questions prepare us to redefine our physical, emotional, relational, and spiritual lives as we try to manage life with CFIDS for months or years or decades.

Change

As we launch into the process of adapting to our limitations, we need to remember several things about change. Any change is hard. By nature we resist change. We like what our lives were like before we became ill, and we see change as giving in, as weakness.

Change comes slowly. People who study psychosocial behavior tell us that it takes at least thirty days to change a habit, any habit. Because people with CFIDS need to make major changes in lifelong patterns of thinking and behaving, the process of change will take a long time.

Change takes energy. We underestimate the energy that it takes not only to think about what needs to be changed and to research the options for change but also to make the change and assimilate it into our lives. People with CFIDS need so much emotional energy just to survive the illness that we often have nothing left over to deal with change. Because the changes necessitated by CFIDS run so counter to the temperament of the people who have the illness, the process of change can seem monumental. But if we make the changes one step at a time, they become manageable.

What helps me see those changes as less threatening is a firm belief in God's sovereignty, his overarching control of all of life. I know that my life is not out of control but rests securely in his hands. He knows what he is doing with me, and I can trust him to be good. That belief helps me embrace change as an effective tool in helping us manage life with CFIDS.

Accept Limitations

Most of us who have CFIDS are "Type-A" people: high achievers, creative, goal-oriented, heavily involved, energetic, active, "superpeople." Suddenly this illness imposes limitations on our activity and involvements. We can no longer work long hours and cut corners on our sleep. We can no longer serve on numerous committees. We can no longer push beyond our limits. We can no longer "do it all." In fact, we can no longer do even a little.

At first we resist that. We want the old life back; nothing less will do. Then we realize that we need to accept our limitations rather than fight them. Our job becomes one of forging out a new life *within* our limitations. CFIDS doesn't end our lives; it only changes them.

During a consultation with CFIDS researcher David Bell, our daughter, Alisa, asked many questions about what her future might look like with CFIDS. Would she be able to go to high school? Could she even consider college? Dr. Bell said to her, "Alisa, you are a sick young woman, especially in this time of relapse. As you look at your future, I want you to remember that you can do anything you want to do as long as you remember that you will achieve those goals in ways that are very different from how your peers are achieving them. You will take a different path to reach the same destination. It may take you six years to finish high school, but you can do it. If you follow your dreams to become a veterinarian, it may take you twice as long, but if that is important to you, persevere. Remember that no one will ever understand what it will take you to achieve those goals, but you will know and you will be stronger for it. Use your common sense. Do what you can, when you can. Do things in moderation and don't overdo."

Four aspects of Dr. Bell's comments are important to examine. First, limitations need not limit us. We can have a full life, but a "full" life with CFIDS will be different from our "full" life before CFIDS. The rules and rewards will change. Second, living with the limitations of CFIDS takes perseverance. Achieving our goals, whether they are long-term or short-term goals, will cost us a great deal as we face discouragement, loneliness, and setbacks. Third, living with limitations will produce inner strength. As we exercise patience, endurance, and courage in dealing with CFIDS, we develop deep character strengths that will serve us in all of life. Fourth, living effectively within limitations forces us to set limits. We can no longer live by the old patterns. Instead, we must set new boundaries in all areas of our lives so that we can live well within our limitations.

Limitations are not all bad. In his book *You Gotta Keep Dancin'*, Tim Hansel explores the paradoxes of limitations. "What we have traditionally perceived as limitations are sometimes the lens that can bring our life into deeper and finer focus. . . . Our limitations can become the very invitation to discover fully the dimensions of grace, the improbable path to God's otherwise hidden blessing. God does his good work within us and wants to continue to expand it, not because of who we are, but because of who he is. That which appears to us to be limitation can actually become our unexpected advantage and asset. As we're forced to our knees once again, we discover the holy and wonder-full gift of life."[1]

Change Expectations

Most of the people I interviewed for this book had always lived with high expectations—of themselves, of other people, and of God. Before CFIDS hit us, many of us were able to live up to our high expectations of ourselves. We were used to soaring. As the illness has diminished our lives, we limp along and find we can't meet some of our minimal expectations of who we would like to be as students, spouses, parents, employees, church members, athletes, or whatever.

We can deal with our disappointments in one of two ways: We can continue to hold our high expectations and be disappointed; or we can change our expectations and live more contentedly. Instead of expecting to soar, we can learn to be contented with limping or resting. In her book *Riches Stored in Secret Places* Verdell Davis comments on a Scripture passage in Isaiah 40. "Little do we know that the greater miracle in the midst of our most grievous storm is when God gives us what we need simply to 'walk and not faint.' At first glance this hardly seems like a miracle at all. But then we realize that soaring is out of the question, and there is no more running to be done. There is left only the helplessness of a reality that has forever changed the shape of life as we have known it and loved it."[2] Our expectations must change. We may not be able to soar or run, but God gives us what we need to walk and not faint. And that, as Davis says, is perhaps the greater miracle.

Living with CFIDS also forces us to change our expectations of other people. Most of us came into our illnesses with high expectations of the support we would receive from medical professionals, family members, friends, and our churches. But in some cases our expectations have been dashed, and we've had to make major changes in what we expect from our relationships. Chapter 6 will explore those changes.

Several people I interviewed felt CFIDS changed their expectations of how God would act. Mark Fuller, a counselor with CFIDS, reflects, "I never envisioned I would feel some of the things I have felt with this illness. That has been hard on me because I expected God to use the things I have studied for my doctoral degree to help me get better. But I've found many of the principles don't work for me as I thought they would. When I see the people I'm counseling get better and I don't, I get angry with God. I ask, 'But, Lord, what about me?' In the last week or two I have turned a corner. I finally have released my expectations and can say, 'Lord, I trust you with my life, even if I don't recover.'"

As we explore ways to make changes that will help us cope with a debilitating illness, three principles will help us focus our efforts:

1. Although CFIDS is incurable, it is manageable.
2. Accept what you can't change, and change what you can.
3. Know what drains your energy, what conserves your energy, and what gives you energy.

Make External Changes

Because CFIDS reduces our ability to function, we need to make many external changes—in our physical surroundings, in how we do things, and in taking care of our bodies.

Change Your Physical Environment

When CFIDS hits, our physical environment changes. Instead of spending our days traveling in cars, working in offices, going to school, moving in and out of buildings, participating in a wide spectrum of activities, we may need to spend much of our time at home—in bed, in a recliner, or on a couch. That is a major transition for most of us.

"Before I got sick," Dick Fritz reflects, "I never wanted an easy chair in the house. I didn't even like the *idea* of an easy chair: Life was too full to take it easy. Now a recliner is a necessity for me."

Create a Healing Spot

For the first few years after I became ill with CFIDS, I was bedridden, except that I chose not to stay in bed. Psychologically I perceived myself as less sick if I spent my day on the couch rather than in bed. I moved to a couch in our living room and created an environment that both conserved my energy and lifted my spirits. Terri Mosely Wood calls such a place a "healing spot."[3]

I assessed what drained my energy: walking from one room to another, standing, needing to get up for things, needing to hold up my head. Then I changed what I could. By moving the end of the couch to a wall and by banking pillows, I could recline comfortably. A rolled-up hand towel placed at the base of my skull gave my head support and reduced the head pain a bit. I kept a table in front of the couch to store everything I would need for a few hours: books, paper, pens, tissues, phone numbers, and office supplies. Once I dressed in the morning and moved to the couch, I would cuddle under a quilt and could be there for several hours without moving. The term *couch potato* took on new meaning for me.

I also assessed what would *give* me energy: soothing music, flowers, fragrance, color, harmony, light, a warm beverage, occasional conversation with a friend, continued involvement with my profession. I added to the table the remote control for the stereo, a small vase of flowers, a piece of fruit, and a thermos of tea. We placed the couch in front of a window so that I could have a view of the outside world while reclining, and I hung in the window a stained-glass Celtic cross. By adding extension cords, we moved a phone to the windowsill next to the couch so that I could make or receive calls without moving. To continue to edit a few hours a day, I set up a laptop computer that I could use while I reclined. When close friends stopped by to see us, they rang the doorbell and let themselves in, grabbing an empty cup from the kitchen so they could sip some tea while they sat at the end of my couch.

Our daughter's healing spot, on the other couch in the living room, included her special quilt, stuffed animals, books and a reading light, a tape recorder to play books on tape when she was too sick to read, and lap desk for doing homework.

Change Your Surroundings

In the third year of our illness, after we had regained some strength, Alisa and I planted what we call our "health garden." Before we got sick, she and I had planned to design and plant a perennial garden near our back door. Because we were too sick to do anything about it, the area filled up with weeds and was a constant visual reminder of what we felt inside: two lives on hold, gathering weeds. We decided we would take the summer and change the visual image. For five or ten minutes a day, we sat on mats in the garden and dug up as many weeds as our strength would allow. Slowly, week by week, we replaced the weeds with ferns, violets, bluebells, columbine, hostas, sedum, and other flowering plants. An old stone bench and several clay rabbits became the focal points of the garden. Now, every time we come in the back door, we see the new visual image and think, *Once we were so sick that we couldn't move from the couch. Then we were well enough to plant this beautiful garden, five minutes at a time. Now it blooms every year on its own and reminds us that life can be full of growth, beauty, color, fragrance, new life, and hope, even though we are still debilitated.* That simple change in our physical environment gives us a continual image of what God is doing in our lives.

We made other changes in our house to accommodate our limitations. Alisa rarely had enough energy to stand up for a shower, so we put a plastic chair in the shower stall and attached a hand shower so that she could wash her long hair while she sat down. We reduced visual clutter so that things appeared to be under control. In addition to adding a phone near my couch, we used extension cords and adapters to place several other phones near recliners and beds. One CFIDS sufferer says, "I sleep with the phone at my bedside, its stretchy umbilical cord connecting me to a world I'm not able to participate in."[4]

Change the Way You Do Things

Not only can we change our surroundings, but we also can save energy by changing the way we do things. Most people would laugh, for instance, if they could have seen how we conducted the seventy hours of interviews for this book. I reclined on pillows and used a speakerphone so that I didn't need to hold the receiver for hours at a time, and the person whom I was interviewing was reclining or lying in a similar position in his or her home. Sometimes we would have to cut short our interview because one of us lost brain power or became too tired. I taped each interview so that I wouldn't need to take notes while I listened. Then I hired someone to type the transcripts of the tapes onto a computer disk.

You may find, as I did, that changing the way I did things was a difficult process. The way I had done things before I became ill was based on a well-developed system of values. For example, because of our family's concern for the poor, we had chosen to live simply so that we could use our money to help others. That often meant we did things ourselves. We prepared our food from scratch, using no mixes or packaged food. When guests were in town, we invited them to stay in our home and served them homemade meals. We did our own yard work, car maintenance, home repairs, vegetable and fruit gardening. However, CFIDS forced us to change the way we live. What seemed like unnecessary luxuries to us before have become essential tools to help us cope with our new limitations. While we are happy for the new options, we still feel as if we have compromised some values that took us decades to put into place.

Simplify

We needed to redefine what it meant to simplify. Whereas before CFIDS a simple life to us had meant not buying services or ready-made products, a simple life now means using paper plates, buying dinner at the grocery-store salad bar, getting our car serviced at the garage, and putting away things that need frequent dusting.

Conserve Physical Energy

Let your fingers do the walking, or at least let the delivery services do the walking. Order goods by phone or mail. I have become so grateful for postal and delivery services. Many years they have picked up and delivered my communication and gifts to family members and friends, my editing work, and the goods I've ordered.

When I was the most sick, I lived by several rules. Never stand when you can sit; that included standing for singing in church. If you have to stand, lean against a wall or on a chair. Always call ahead before shopping; if I needed items advertised in the newspaper, I called the store to have the items at the cashier's desk when someone came in the store to pick them up. Always park closest to the front door of the building you need to enter; many people with CFIDS use handicapped-parking permits. Take elevators whenever possible. Use motorized carts provided in grocery and department stores.

Let Other People Help

After decades spent helping other people, I had to learn how to let other people help me. Not only was that a hard transition emotionally, but it also was difficult practically. I was so used to doing everything myself and doing it my way. It took me a while to determine what other people could do for me and what only I could do. Other people couldn't be our children's mother, but they could pick up library books that Alisa needed for a project or take Matt to an evening concert. Other people couldn't be Bas's wife, but they could bring in meals so that I would have energy to spend time with him. After seven years of living with CFIDS, I still do not do a good job of letting other people help. I still am too quick to refuse help. But I'm learning.

What are the things other people can do for you? Some of you may be thinking, *If only I had that problem. If only people would offer to help!* While that may be true in some cases, all too often *we* are the reason we don't get help. Our pride prevents us from asking. Sometimes we hesitate to ask for help because people have said no in the past and we don't want to risk rejection. Or when people do ask, we don't know what to say. Make a list of what other people can do for you. You may find ideas in this list compiled from my interviews with people with CFIDS. Customize your list. Post it in a prominent place like a bulletin board or the refrigerator so that any member of your family can see it, any friend coming into your house can see it. Photocopy it and give it to friends who want to help.

Ways You Can Help Me
While I Cope with CFIDS

1. As you read this list, remember that I want to do all of these things by myself. But I can't. I need to save my energy for those things that only I can do. Thanks for considering anything on this list.
2. When you cook a meal, make a double recipe and share it with us. I'll keep it in the freezer so I have a meal to heat up when I'm too sick to cook. Or if I'm too sick to eat, the other family members still need food. Be sensitive to ask about special diets.
3. When you go out for an errand to the post office, the cleaners, the library, or the mall, call and ask if I need anything done while you're out.
4. Offer to spend an hour cleaning my house or apartment, even if that means cleaning only one room or only vacuuming.
5. Offer to help me balance my checkbook and pay my bills. My mind can't handle the math.
6. Bring a flower from your garden if I'm too sick to get out.
7. Some days just come by and wash my dishes or take out the garbage or wash my pet or get my mail.
8. Make me laugh. Send me cartoons or jokes. Bring a funny video and sit and watch it with me.
9. If you are a family member or colleague, carry your own responsibilities so that I don't have to do your work and mine.
10. Offer to lend me books, tapes, CDs, or books on tape.
11. Call after a snowstorm and offer to help with snow removal.
12. Offer to take my healthy children with you to a movie or an outing.
13. Offer to drive me to medical appointments.
14. Offer to help with car maintenance like winterizing the car or getting a tune-up.
15. Offer to spend an hour on a yard project I can't do.

Buy Energy

Sometimes we will opt to buy services rather than have others do them for us. "At various times Mary 'bought help' and used a cleaning service. Sometimes it worked. Finally she found what helped her the most: a woman who would buy the groceries and then prepare dinner and deliver it four nights a week. This saved all kinds of decisions, energy, and stress."[5] For the past seven years I have hired a student from nearby Wheaton College to clean the house, do the laundry in the basement laundry room, run errands, and shop for groceries when Bas is out of the country. Some people with CFIDS order prepared foods, use shopping services provided by some grocery stores in larger cities, pay for lawn services, hire people to help with child care, or buy whatever service they can to help them manage their load.

Bring the World into Your Home

Many of us with CFIDS miss not being able to go out to concerts, museums, sports events, movies, restaurants, activities, church. Just because our bodies don't function well, it doesn't mean we can't feed our minds and senses. We just need to do it differently. The public television station serving our area has lived up to its name: WTTW, "Your Window To The World." During the past seven years I have "attended" some extraordinary concerts, "visited" many foreign countries, "participated" in fascinating lectures—all from the comfort of the couch. When Alisa was too sick to attend her school's drama performance of *Anne of Green Gables*, she was crushed. Several days later she lay on the floor, under a quilt, propped up with pillows, while she watched the video the drama instructor had made of the performance. Several people stay involved with their churches through audio tapes of the worship service. Many of us have used cable television and rented videos to provide hours of medicinal laughter.

Do Normal Things, Even When That Means Doing Abnormal Things

Jim Hekman's family likes him to go shopping with them or to be in the town's Tulip Time parade with them, so he has bought an electric wheelchair. Now he feels he can do some of the normal things with his family, even though he has to do it in an abnormal way. With the help of the wheelchair, he can accompany his son's class on a field trip, and his son's classmates like getting a ride on the electric wheelchair.

Our family has always enjoyed visiting special exhibits at Chicago's Art Institute, so when a Monet exhibit came to Chicago, the four of us went: Bas and Matt dropped off Alisa and me at the door and then got two wheelchairs for us. For two hours the guys pushed us through the galleries as we reveled in the blues and greens of Monet's impressionistic masterpieces. Four years later I don't remember how wiped out we were for a week afterward, but I do remember that we went to the Art Institute for a family outing.

Set Reasonable Physical Limits
Know Your Limits

As you live with CFIDS, learn to know your physical limits. Cynthia Moench, who has had CFIDS for several years, says, "I like to picture my energy as liquid in a one-cup glass measuring cup. The hardest thing is trying to guess *how much* liquid is in the cup each day and how much I will choose to dole out for each project I assign myself. Some days I get up and the cup is about three-fourths full, and I can dole it out about one-fourth cup at a time. Those are my 'good days.' Then there are the days when I get up and there's only about one-fourth cup of liquid in the entire measuring cup, and I must make difficult decisions about what to do and what to let go."[6]

For people who live in families with more than one person with CFIDS, the job is overwhelming. Cyndi Volkers, whose CFIDS allows her only a few good hours in a day, is also the mother of five children with CFIDS. "When I wake up in the morning, my first words are, 'Lord, which sick kid needs my energy today?'" Even though this mother is well-organized and clearly sees the priorities, she has very little control over what will sap her energy each day.

When Alisa and I first became ill with CFIDS, things were much more clear-cut. I had to say no to everything. As I gained strength, the decisions and the balance changed. I could afford to say yes to some things, but which ones? What are the priority activities on which I would expend energy? Walking with my husband at night? Attending one of Matt's concerts? Going to church? Attending a church function during the week but then not being able to go to church on Sunday?

Most of us can do only a fraction of what we were once able to do. When you decide whether or not to be involved in an activity, ask yourself several questions: Can I afford this activity? What will I gain and what will I lose? Will it send me into a crash? Can I afford a crash at this time? What will I gain emotionally and spiritually by this activity? Will the energy I spend on this activity endanger my priority relationships?

Find balance. This is much easier to say than do because CFIDS does not yield to formulas. What works one week will not work the next. The same activity your body handled yesterday may send it into a crash today. I would have thought that after seven years of practice, I would be an expert at knowing my limits. But I'm not. I make lots of mistakes. Each day, each week the balance points change because the factors change: my symptom level changes; Alisa's symptoms change; her need for my involvement in her illness changes; the lives of the people around me change; the external demands on my energy change.

Your limits and your decisions will be different from mine. For instance, I choose to use energy each day to get dressed and fix my hair, even if I'm headed for the couch for the day. I decided it is worth the exhaustion to gain the psychological health I achieve by not looking as sick as I feel. When I catch my reflection in a mirror, I don't want to think, *You look awful,* even though I feel awful. It's not that I want to deny the illness or make people think I'm well; I just want to feel as good about life as I can. My friends and family also benefit from my choice to use my energy in that way.

Sometimes we choose to be involved in certain activities even though we know we will pay a high price. Occasionally Bas and I allow Alisa to attend a sleepover with her teenage friends, even though we know it will take her several days to recover. We judge that what she will gain in feeling somewhat normal, in giggling with her friends, in feeling a part of a social network is more important than what she will lose. Obviously we can't make these decisions too often, but we also can't put our lives on hold.

Take Care of Your Body

Do what you can to keep your body healthy. Eat a healthy diet, drink plenty of fluids, and exercise when you can. Again this is easier to say than do. Winona Offray, a single mother with grown children says, "Living alone with CFIDS is hard. I don't eat right because I feel too sick to get up and fix anything. I grab what I can grab. Just going to the store is a chore."

Knowing whether to exercise is also not easy. Many of us find that any exercise leads to a crash. However, we also know that exercise stimulates the production of endorphins, the body's natural painkillers. Exercise whatever parts of your body can tolerate it. If you can walk around the block once a day, do it. If you can exercise in a swimming pool, do it. If you can only lift your arms and legs several times a day, make it a discipline. Easy stretching exercises help tone the body without requiring lots of energy. Whenever you can, increase your exercise.

Learn to Say No

Even though it is hard for us as nurturers and achievement-oriented people to say no, we need to practice saying it. While saying no may be a sign of our physical weakness, it is not a sign of character weakness. Learning to say no to certain involvements may be the only way for us to say yes to relationships. One couple has decided that in order to maintain a healthy marriage with CFIDS, they needed to limit their involvements in outside activities like serving on several church committees, singing in the choir, working with refugees, playing tennis once a week. Although those things were hard to give up, the change allowed the couple needed time to keep their family and marriage on track.

Learn to say no without feeling guilty. Learning to say no leads to saying yes to health, yes to balance, yes to survival through CFIDS.

Set Guidelines

"The primary lifestyle change that my husband, Dave, and I have had to make is to slow down our lives," says Carla Crosby. "After

seven years of living with CFIDS, I know that I function best when
I've had adequate sleep and limit my involvements. So with the Lord's
guidance we have set some guidelines that will help me sustain a level
of functioning. The guidelines include things like these:

- We schedule only one night activity per week.
- If we are out at night, we need to be home by nine o'clock.
- I need at least one of the weekend days to sleep in.
- When our toddler sleeps in the afternoon, I sleep too.
- We focus on only one ministry area in the church.

"These guidelines have had incredible impact on us. Every time
anyone asks us to do anything in the evening, we run the option
through the grid of our guidelines. If we already have one evening
activity planned, we say, 'No, it's not healthy for us to do that right
now.' We have reduced the stress of needing to deliberate about every
option, and by having objective guidelines, we have reduced some of
my guilt in needing to say no. So when our church asked me to be the
missions chairperson or Dave to become an elder or vice-president of
the congregation, we could say no with freedom because we know our
one area of focus this year is on the worship committee. Other people
might look at our guidelines as cramping our lifestyle, but we feel that
the Lord has used them to enrich our lives.

"Sometimes we have no control over our lives, and the guidelines
get swept away. When that happens, we see a domino effect in our whole
family. By the end of that week, we are all crashed-out dominos."

You will not set the same guidelines that Carla and Dave Crosby
have set, but you may find that setting some broad guidelines that the
whole family agrees to will help your family function more effectively
while you all deal with the impact of CFIDS.

Compensate for the Losses

Through the years we have learned to compensate for the losses
CFIDS has brought into our lives. For the first five years of her illness, our daughter, Alisa, was unable to be involved in social gatherings with her friends, a critical part of her development as an early

adolescent. One of the ways we compensated for that loss was putting a phone in her room so that she could relate to friends in private while she rested on her bed.

I have used books to compensate for some of my relational losses.[7] A well-written novel or biography allowed me to become involved with another person without the physical stress or emotional drain of interacting with people in a group or at a social function. I enjoyed the company of the people in the book, but they didn't drain me. If I wearied after ten minutes of reading, I could close the book and rest. The people in the books demanded nothing from me; I didn't even need to respond to them.

In his book *Taken on Trust*, former hostage Terry Waite tells of finding a similar solace in books. "Reading in captivity is sheer delight. I have time to enter into the mind of the writer, and to be caught up in the flow of her thoughts without interruption is a great pleasure. . . . Part of the secret, I think, is to make a companion of the experience. . . . If I ever leave captivity, I will take this precious gift with me."[8]

Sharon Postma's family learned to compensate for Sharon's inability to sit at the table by eating their meals in the living room, where Sharon could be in a recliner. "For over a year we had picnics in the living room. The kids and my husband would spread out beach towels on the floor and bring me a plate of food. We decided that it was more important to be together than to be at a table."

Having reviewed changes we can make in our physical environment and our way of doing things, let's explore some emotional changes that will help us manage our lives with CFIDS.

Chapter 5

Find Emotional Balance

> *Coping with CFIDS is by far the most trying experience
> I've had to deal with in my life. It was hard when my
> mother died, but that was before I had CFIDS, and at
> least I had the physical and emotional energy to deal
> with stress then. Now I have very little emotional energy
> to cope with an illness and the rest of my life.*
>
> JORGE ESTRADA, BUSINESSPERSON WITH CFIDS

Terri Mosely Wood, author of *Life in the Slow Lane: Coping with Chronic Fatigue Syndrome*, shares Estrada's perspective. "I had cancer and, believe it or not, I think that in some ways the cancer was easier because I got sympathy. People wanted to do things for me. But now, with CFS, I look fine, but I don't feel fine. I have to deal with a lot more psychologically."[1]

Most people with CFIDS agree with Estrada and Wood: The psychological aspects of coping with CFIDS are intensely challenging, in some ways more challenging than the physical aspects of coping. "The hidden symptoms—the grieving process, the emotional impact—are just as real as the swollen glands and the aches and the fever," says Tara Allen, editor of *Shadow & Light: The Voice of CFIDS*.

What makes CFIDS such a difficult illness to handle emotionally are the characteristics we examined in chapter 2: CFIDS is difficult to diagnose, incurable, invisible, and misunderstood. When we add to that list the frustration of dealing with relapses, with symptoms that wax and wane from week to week, and with the major losses we experience, we can understand why some people with CFIDS give in to despair.

Although it would be easy and understandable for us to stay in the anger and bitterness we feel about CFIDS and although it may feel good to blame others or complain or wallow in self-pity, getting stuck in these responses will not help us work toward wholeness and health in this illness. Other people facing difficult experiences agree. Former hostage Terry Waite said of his survival during years of captivity, "If I keep my mind alive and my soul free from bitterness, I'll survive. Perhaps even discover what it means to be transformed. God, please help me."[2]

Just as redefining our physical life will help us cope with CFIDS, allowing the Lord to transform our emotional responses will help us carve out a meaningful life in the midst of the limitations of CFIDS. Let's explore ways we can redefine not only who we are but also how we can maintain emotional health and how we find the "good life" while living with CFIDS.

Redefine Your Identity

CFIDS seems to strip us not only of physical health but also of our identity. One person with CFIDS said, "CFIDS violates my temperament, my personality, and my soul—the core of who I am. I feel this illness has betrayed me on all levels."

Brian Vander Ploeg expressed the changes this way: "The process of recovery from CFIDS is one of learning to *be* somebody else. That was a challenge because I didn't see a whole lot wrong with who I was. But I had to, in effect, die to self. I don't think I consciously thought of myself as lord of my own life, but now I'm *sure* I am no longer lord of my life. I am being raised anew—passive—*being* raised, not raising myself. The Lord slowly is shaping me into a new person."

In exploring her identity while debilitated with CFIDS, Helen Gruelle says, "We find much of our identity in the work we do, in providing for our family, in providing for ourselves and not being dependent on the state or anybody else, in being able to volunteer and help people, in the relationships built through working together, in having a job to go to where we are needed, or even in our ministry to God and others."[3] When those activities are no longer options for us, how do we rebuild our identity?

Redefine Your Sense of Self-Worth

"I definitely lost my sense of self-worth because I can't support my family of five children," says Jim Hekman. "That's what a man is supposed to do, and I can't. But I now have a new value in our family. My wife, Lynn, has had to return to the workforce, but I am now home. I have essentially raised our younger son. Now two of our children have major illnesses: Our youngest child has a heart defect and will need valve replacement, and one of our daughters was diagnosed with lupus two years ago. As the kids adjust to the implications of their illnesses in their lives, I am here to be a sounding board for them. I can take our daughter out for coffee just to let her talk through her anger or sadness or whatever stage she is going through at the time." Hekman's wife feels he has been an effective model for both of their ill children.

In his book *When the Night Is Too Long*, Robert Wise says, "We mistake activity for life, business for vitality, and sensation for soul."[4] Our thinking needs to change. The truth is that our self-worth rests not in what we do but in who we *are*. We are more than our activity or achievements.

Just as we need to acknowledge our losses because of CFIDS, we need to recognize the deep changes in our lives. What character qualities are growing in you during your battle with CFIDS? What qualities have developed only because you have been ill? Has your illness been of value to any person in your experience? Make a list, however short, of these growing changes.

Redefine Your Sense of Calling

Most of us are somewhat willing to allow our identities and our self-worth to change, but we get confused when those changes touch areas to which we felt God had called us, areas for which we felt he had shaped and given us desires and abilities. The year I became ill with CFIDS, for example, I was involved in designing and implementing a project to educate North American church women about the needs of Third World women who live in poverty, famine, and refugee situations. I felt energized and passionate about the project. I felt that God had given me unique experiences and abilities to carry it out. But when CFIDS hit, I had to give up that project, along with many others. I was confused. My journal records some of my conversations with God: "Lord, I don't understand. I was so sure you were preparing me to reach out to needy women. Now I can barely move from room to room. I know you care for those women, and I know you care for me, but I'm confused. Where do I go from here? Now that I'm confined to a couch, who do I *be* from here?"

Many of you have had similar experiences. Before we became ill, we were the active ones, the ones who not only served on committees but also led them. We had been useful—to our families, our friends, our community, our church, and to the Lord. Suddenly the very things that have fueled our lives and given us identity are gone. We are forced to become someone else. I think that change is very, very hard. We ask, *Of what use are we now?* We know somewhere deep down that it doesn't matter to God that we are no longer able to be what we were and that it shouldn't matter to us, but accepting that reality is not easy.

A letter from a friend helped me gain some perspective about how God may be redefining my life through this illness. "As I studied the New Testament book of Ephesians recently, I thought about your situation. I was struck that in the final chapter, as Paul asks his friends to pray for him while he is imprisoned, he doesn't ask them to pray for his release. Instead, he asks them to pray that whenever he opens his mouth, he will have the appropriate words to explain the mysteries of the gospel. He sees himself as an 'ambassador in chains.' Could it be that your situation with CFIDS is like Paul's chains? Could it be that my prayers for you ought not to be so much for your release from CFIDS as for you to have the words to explain the mysteries of the gospel? Could it be that you and your family are 'ambassadors in illness'? Pursuing such lines of thought leads to some interesting things: My preoccupation moves away from you as a semi-invalid to you as an ambassador of the gospel. My intercession for you takes on a more positive note. I ask God to work powerfully through you and your family, and I allow him to determine the physical condition in which you can be most useful to him."

My friend's insights affirm a foundational truth: God can use ill bodies as effectively as he can use healthy ones to reveal his purposes and character. As you think about her comments, consider ways in which CFIDS has redefined what your calling is, what your ministry is.

Tame Your Temperament

As I interviewed people for this book, I discovered that most of the people with CFIDS are "Type-A" people: driven, goal oriented, well-organized, in control, independent. In many areas of our lives, those qualities have served as virtues. People liked us to be on their committees because we would organize the project, make sure everyone was on target, motivate others to act, and get the job done. Teachers liked us as students because we did the project well or worked beyond the assignment. People applauded our abilities, and we saw those characteristics as strengths.

However, when CFIDS hits, those same characteristics—the drive, the need to achieve—become our enemies. The virtues become vices. The strengths become weaknesses. The changes necessary for us to live with CFIDS run counter to how we are wired, how we are geared to function. Our patterns of thinking and behaving need major restructuring.

From Goals to Giggles

Many people with CFIDS know only one method of living: to push forward until you reach the goal, no matter what. One professor who had CFIDS for several years said, "I was happiest when I burned the candle at both ends. I would go real hard. I used to be able to get up at two or three o'clock in the morning and go all day. I exercised hard, running three miles a day. I fasted and prayed three days at a time. But when I became ill, all that changed. I began to get depressed because I couldn't push hard. I like to be very busy, but I couldn't. I had to go half-speed. After teaching one class I would go to my office, put my head down on my desk, and pray that I could go again for another hour. In between classes, I would sleep for an hour or two."

Jody Hurst comments, "The work ethic in which I was raised said, 'Just do what you have to do and work through it. Push through it.' Those thinking patterns are incompatible with CFIDS."

A journal entry expresses some of my turmoil as I tried to tame my need to achieve goals. "Because I'm so sick, I need to pull the plugs on most of my activity. And I need to evaluate my energy on an hour-by-hour basis, not by whether or not I reached the goal I set when I woke up this morning. I need to be *free* from my own goals, not *driven* by them as I have been in the past." My new goal, my work, my achievement was to rest, to stay well, to stay emotionally as balanced as I could be.

My ability to reach my goals has been frustrated so often that the results border on the absurd. I've decided that rather than cry about the failures, I would laugh at my mistakes and move my expectations down a peg or two. What surprises me is that several people have said to me, "I like you more now. You may have reached lots of goals before, but I like you better when you can giggle at yourself and have less need to be on top of things."

From Control to Contentment

Another part of our temperament that needs to change is our need to be in control. Bob Scrudato found that CFIDS forced him into new patterns of thinking. "After I became ill, I realized that I had been too focused on getting ahead, on having control of my life. Two things have changed. First, I have given up the drive to control. I am learning to depend on the Lord to provide instead of relying on my ability to do everything. Second, I am learning to appreciate what I have. I really have so much to be thankful for. The good has outweighed the bad in my case."

Robin Ralston has had a similar experience. "I needed to be in control of my environment and my life. I grew up with competent parents who told me I could be anything I wanted to be. And until I got CFIDS, I was able to do that. Now I feel as if I can't even come close to being what I want to be. The illness also forced me to deal with my control and perfectionism in relationships. I lived most of my life needing to please people. Now I'm too sick to keep anybody happy. But do you know what? I've also discovered that people love me just as I am, even if my whole world seems out of control."

From Independence to Interdependence

Before we became ill with CFIDS, we took pride in our independence, in our ability to give to other people. If you are like me, you didn't know how to be needy, how to be dependent, how to be on the receiving end. In the beginning I was very clumsy about responding to offers for help. First, I was too independent even to recognize that I could use help. Second, I was too proud to let someone do something for me; I put people off, saying, "Oh, we'll manage," when I knew we were not managing well at all. Third, I somehow felt that if I let people do things for me, then I would be accountable to them for how I used my energy; I didn't want people looking over my shoulder, second-guessing or judging what I do and when.

But people saw through me and persisted in their attempts. Gradually I learned the joy of saying, "Yes, we would love to have help with meals this week. How thoughtful of you to offer."

The givers also graciously helped me learn to receive. When Kathy arrived at my doorstep with a warm pan of lasagna one day, she said, "Lynn, thanks for letting me do this for you. I know your family is carrying a lot right now, and it helps me feel part of your struggle when you let me do things for you." Her comments reminded me that all my stammering and refusing of previous offers for help had been an insult to the givers, an obstacle to their opportunity to share in our struggle. Slowly I have moved from independence to interdependence.

Set Reasonable Emotional Limits

Just as setting physical limits will help us deal with CFIDS, setting emotional limits will help us find balance. By suggesting that we set emotional limits, I do not mean to say that we should not allow ourselves to feel all the emotions associated with CFIDS. I hope I've made that clear. But we need to remember that "Limitations are not necessarily negative. In fact, I'm beginning to believe that they can give life definition and *freedom.* . . . Unrestricted water is a swamp—because it lacks restriction, it also lacks depth."[5]

First, we need to assess our emotional energy and decide how we will expend it. Let's go back to the image of the measuring cup. How much emotional energy is in your cup? Is it half full? How are you going to use that emotional energy today? Remember that it takes a great deal of emotional energy just to live with a body that feels lousy. What emotional energy do you have left for the rest of what you will face today?

Is your cup only one-eighth full? Then go into the day knowing that you're nearly running on empty. Avoid situations that will sap that energy. Say no to things that will drain your emotional reserve. Many days we will not have the luxury of choosing to save or use emotional energy; circumstances beyond our control may completely drain us in the first hour of the day. But when you can, think about your emotional energy and set limits that will help you have enough to survive the day.

Assess What You Can Give to Others

Because our emotional energy is limited, we need to set limits on what we can give to others. For some of us, like Helen Gruelle, this is a major change. "I just don't have the energy to deal with people. I never knew how much energy it took to be with most people because it was usually such a positive experience. Then CFS hit, and just a five-minute phone conversation would leave me shaky, and I'd have to lie down, sometimes taking an hour or more before the trembling feeling would stop. This happened regardless of whom I talked to or what we talked about.

"Attending meetings or gatherings of people was difficult. A church service was one of the hardest times for me. After a few months I started back to church but could handle attending only one service. We would sit in the balcony, where fewer people sat, which lessened my opportunities to talk, but I'd still come home wiped out. . . . I had to avoid being around people. I'd leave church early so I wouldn't have to talk to anyone . . . because it cost me energy.

"Slowly I *graduated* to being downstairs at church and was back to attending church and Sunday school. . . . Even now, after dealing with chronic fatigue syndrome for seven years, my energy still fluctuates, and on a 'bad day' sometimes I'm tired before I *get* to church and feel overwhelmed with the idea of talking to *one* person, let alone *ten!*. . . On days like this, I sit with my eyes closed through most of the service. I can't keep them open; it's just too much work."[6]

Shawn and Gregg Fisher, who both have CFIDS, have also needed to assess what they can give to others. "We have learned that if we push beyond our limits, we feel worse and we have nothing to give to each other. One time during my most debilitated years, I had a short conversation with a neighbor when I went to the mailbox. Afterward I was completely exhausted, in pain, and crying. Gregg was very upset with me because I had no strength left to give or receive love from him. He helped me realize that many times I was using my strength in places I couldn't afford to give it. It wasn't healthy for our marriage for me to give strangers all my smiles and Gregg all my tears."

Live in the Present

Before I became ill with CFIDS, I spent lots of emotional energy living in the future. Because of my goal orientation, I was a planner. I lived three months ahead, emotionally preparing for this event or anticipating that project. I can't afford to do that anymore because I can't predict how I'm going to feel. When I have made plans for the future, I have had to cancel most of them. I finally realized that I was wasting my energy, not only planning things that may never happen but also fighting the disappointment when I had to cancel out. I decided it's not worth it.

I also needed to put limits on living in the past. If I spend my emotional energy on regretting that I can't be the person I was eight years ago, I use up the very emotional energy I need to face today's physical and emotional challenges.

Sharon Gray, who was seventeen when she became ill with CFIDS, agrees: "Tomorrow hasn't started, and today is not over with; now is all we have. That's my whole philosophy, living in the now. It's all that's important. I think that if we live in the past or in the future, we kill the now."

When I look back on how I lived before CFIDS, I realize that the present was incidental to me, a stepping-stone toward the future and the things that I needed to do. Now I realize that the present is the only real moment I have. Yes, I still have a future, but I don't plan for it much anymore. I still have a past, but I don't feel self-pity for what I have lost. I have had to learn to say, "This is the day that I have. How can I best use my emotional energy in this day?"

It all begins to sound biblical, doesn't it? "Do not worry [or be afraid or be depressed] about tomorrow. . . . Each day has enough trouble of its own."[7] And, "This is the day the Lord has made; let us rejoice and be glad in it."[8] It doesn't say, "This is the day the Lord has made, let's spend it in anxiety and anger and regret and self-pity." Let's live fully in the present, enjoying every moment for what it has to offer.

Recognize Chronic Emotions

In her book *Mainstay: For the Well Spouse of the Chronically Ill*, Maggie Strong reminds us that along with chronic illness come *chronic emotions*: sadness, guilt, loneliness, jealousy, annoyance, anger, isolation, boredom, humiliation, depression, anxiety, and feeling overwhelmed.[9] Those of us living with CFIDS or with family members who have CFIDS also need to remember that just as the chronic physical symptoms wax and wane, the chronic emotions will also wax and wane. Knowing that the emotions will come and go helps us not to panic when feelings we thought we had dealt with return in full force. We may feel that our sadness or our hurt is a feeling of the past, only to have it surface with overwhelming power.

Mark Fuller, a clinical therapist who has CFIDS, says, "It's important to keep our emotions up to date. We are in touch with the hurt, but we often deny the anger. My wife bought me a punching bag. I don't use it that often, but just walking by it reminds me to deal with the anger I feel because of CFIDS. Today I may feel anger, tomorrow it may be loneliness or hurt or discouragement or lack of hope. I need to expect that these emotions will arise somewhat regularly."

Find a person who can help you process these chronic emotions as they keep popping up. If a close friend or your spouse can be that person, fine. But be aware that sometimes the people closest to you may also be dealing with their chronic emotions about your illness. Several people I interviewed found that meeting regularly with a therapist helped them have a safe place to take out the tangle of emotions that continues to swirl through their lives. "In the first eight years of our CFIDS, Gregg and I were too sick to go for counseling," says Shawn Fisher, "but during the last five years, we have found occasional counseling to be very helpful and healing. I think that dealing with the continual onslaught of raw emotions at a time when I have no emotional reserve to cope with them has been as painful and challenging as the physical pain of CFIDS. When I feel very ill, I can be incredibly irritable. A typical example is one day I was trying to floss my teeth and the floss broke. It was a very minor thing, but I had no emotional strength to handle even the tiny things. I sat down on the floor and cried, and I lashed out at Gregg. He knew I didn't mean to take out my anger on him, but it still hurt. This type of irritability is very difficult to live with. It has been helpful that Gregg can go to his counselor and have an outlet for his frustration with my illness as well as his illness. It helps us both that I can feel my emotions, put them into words, and let them go with my counselor. It is important to have support and help in learning healthy ways to express these powerful emotions."

Or you may find that writing out your feelings in a journal will help you process the emotions that sometimes threaten to overwhelm you. Debi McAdoo, a marriage and family counselor with CFIDS, says, "My journal has been an invaluable tool in coping with the intense feelings that have surfaced during my illness. I tend to intellectualize my feelings, but when I write them in my journal, they just pour out. Journaling for me has been the avenue that I can feel."

In her book *Write Now: Maintaining a Creative Spirit While Homebound and Ill,* CFIDS sufferer Susan Dion suggests the therapeutic value of keeping a journal. "Journals ... offer opportunities for journeying through our interiors. They are often considered a place for reflection, commentary, soul-searching, and private wanderings." Dr. Dion's book suggests various ways to begin and keep diaries and journals.

Resist Destructive Emotions

Another set of emotions we need to limit is those emotions that can destroy us. I've already listed several potentially destructive emotions at the beginning of the chapter: anger, bitterness, blame, and self-pity. In a consultation with Dave and Barbara Masoner about their daughter Nancy's CFIDS, Dr. David Bell told the Masoners: "Bitterness, anger, and self-pity lead only to self-destruction."

Setting limits means resolving not to let destructive emotions have power over us. Former hostage Terry Waite recognized the importance of setting such limits when he began what would become years of captivity. "I made three resolutions to support me through whatever was to come: no regrets, no sentimentality, no self-pity."[10] By deciding not to give in to three emotions he knew would sap his emotional energy, Terry Waite conserved his energy so that he could survive his fight with isolation, loneliness, uncertainty, illness, and fear.

Learn to Disengage Emotionally

In a study done for her doctoral dissertation in psychology, Susan Schmall, a person with CFIDS, studied what factors helped people cope successfully with CFIDS. Of the factors she listed, two struck a chord with me: positive reappraisal and distancing.[11] The distancing, or what I prefer to call emotional disengagement, was a new thought to me in the context of the illness. I am, as are most of you, an intense person. Emotional engagement is my instinct. When people hurt, I'm empathetic and caring; I listen and try to help. When family members or friends are in trouble, I feel their pain. Until I became sick with CFIDS, this emotional engagement had been a virtue, a strength. It helped me in my relationships with friends, in my role as a teacher, in my work with the poor. Now that very quality has become an enemy.

I had to set emotional limits by practicing emotional disengagement. At first I felt that disengaging emotionally was betraying who I am. It felt dishonest. Then I realized I don't have to shut down my emotions completely, but I had to back off from where I normally went. I had to take a more laid-back approach. I could reduce my number of deep emotional involvements. For instance, I chose to reduce my relationships to only a few close friends with whom I experienced a balance of give and take, of need and independence. Emotional disengagement means recognizing when I am becoming entangled in a situation that would cost me health if I continued to stay engaged. That's a major change for a Type-A personality.

Sometimes we have no options. Crises don't stop while we deal with one chronic illness. During the years I have been ill, my husband has been hospitalized with life-threatening malaria, our son has had injuries, and our daughter has had a serious relapse in her CFIDS. While Helen Gruelle copes with her CFIDS, her husband has had a kidney transplant. Steve and Cyndi Volkers have no options to disengage as they have watched each of their five children become ill with CFIDS.

People with CFIDS sometimes feel threatened when their spouses disengage emotionally. That's understandable. But we who have CFIDS must also understand that our spouses don't intend to cut themselves off emotionally. It's what they must do to survive. It's often a positive coping mechanism for them.

Stay Emotionally Healthy
Avoid Negative Ways of Coping

As we try to stay emotionally balanced and healthy while living with CFIDS, we need to avoid several negative patterns of coping. As we have mentioned before, denial, avoiding the problem, glossing over the pain, and refusing to grieve lead only to delayed pain. Manipulating the illness for personal gain and becoming demanding cut us off from the people whose support and understanding we need. Talking self-centeredly about CFIDS traps us into believing we *are* the illness.

One other negative pattern deserves mention: comparing ourselves to who we were before CFIDS and comparing ourselves to healthy people. "Whenever I fall into the trap of comparing my present situation to what my life was like before I got sick with CFIDS, I begin a fast-moving downward spiral," says Robin Ralston. "Nothing that I am now is anything of what I thought I would be. I am sick, but sometimes I still try to live out my dreams of what I wanted to be: the perfect wife, mother, teacher of English and drama, graduate student. Whenever I compare the present to the past, I feel as if I am a failure at everything. I end up wondering if my husband is sorry he married me. It becomes a nightmare. When I find myself slipping into this negative thinking, I need to stop comparing myself to my past."

Practice Positive Ways of Coping

In addition to the positive coping skills we have already mentioned—understanding CFIDS, admitting the pain, grieving the losses, accepting your illness, making physical changes, setting emotional limits—four other skills deserve attention: communication, humor, positive reappraisal, and compensation.

Communication

"Communication has become a very important tool in maintaining emotional balance for Gregg and me," says Shawn Fisher. "First, we try to tell each other when we're having a difficult time. I have to remember to say, 'The pain is unbearable today. I'm sorry I'm in such a bad mood.' Second, we have learned to identify what we call 'illness fights.' When we snap at each other, we sometimes have to stop, look at each other, and say, 'This is an illness fight.' We can stop the fight because the fight wasn't about what we were fighting about. And it was just that we were both exhausted and felt so sick."

Humor

Most people I interviewed said they never would have survived CFIDS without laughter therapy. They have learned to laugh at situations they did not think were funny at the time. Diane Lamont recalls, "During one hospitalization, I put up on my hospital room wall a large sign that said, 'THERE IS HOPE.' One day a woman came in to 'comfort' me and said to me with a glum look on her face,

'Well, you're going to get sicker and sicker, and then you'll die.' Obviously she hadn't read my sign. At that point I wanted to throw my bedpan at her. Now I can revisit that scene in my mind and laugh hysterically about it."

During the second year of my illness, my friend Chris came to sit on the other end of my couch and pray with me once a week. We would start each week by describing what our week had been like. Often our weeks had been such disasters that we would end up laughing at the absurdity of it all. We would laugh so hard that tears rolled down our cheeks as we deteriorated into coughing spasms. When my children would walk through the room, they would scold us, "Mom, Chris, I thought you two were supposed to be praying." Well, we did eventually pray. But we also found great release in the rollicking laughter. We came to refer to our Wednesday-night prayer and laughter sessions as our healing meetings.

Dr. Katrina Berne's prescription for CFIDS includes her book *CFIDS Lite: Chronic Fatigue Immune Dysfunction Syndrome with 1/3 the Seriousness.* CFIDS jokes, riddles, and cartoons are guaranteed to make CFIDS sufferers laugh—or at least groan.

Positive Reappraisal

In an earlier paragraph I mentioned Susan Schmall's observations that people who cope successfully with CFIDS practiced two skills: positive reappraisal and distancing. We've already discussed the importance of distancing, or what I prefer to call emotional disengagement. Let's look at her idea of positive reappraisal. Positive reappraisal is the ability to take a negative circumstance and reappraise it in a positive light. Positive reappraisal is not putting our heads in the sand and ignoring the painful parts of our lives. Positive reappraisal is not merely positive thinking or seeing the difficulties of life through rose-tinted glasses. Rather it is a realistic, conscious choice to find meaning in pain, stress, uncertainty, and debilitation.

"At one point in my struggle with a sense of worthlessness as a pastor's wife because of CFIDS, another pastor's wife helped me positively reappraise my situation," recounts Sue Hedlund. "She had just read a biography of William and Catherine Booth, the founders of the Salvation Army. She said, 'They both fought with frail health throughout their lives, but they believed God used their frailty to shape them into effective and compassionate communicators of the gospel to the frail people of society. They believed that God used them more in their frailty than he could have used them in strength.' Her comments helped me see that the Lord can use me more in my illness than in my capability. Before I became ill with CFIDS, a lot of my identity came from my capabilities. I'm learning to enjoy times of resting in the Lord and allowing him to use my illness and my weakness."

I was astounded at the way several of the teenagers with CFIDS have been able to practice positive reappraisal in their lives. Ann McErleane says, "Living with CFIDS has been one of the hardest things I've ever had to do, but I am thankful for it. I feel as if I've just mastered one of life's experiences. It's not an experience I was expecting at this stage in my life, but it has shaped me in positive ways. Not that I don't have times of turmoil and depression. But overall, it is as if God closed one door in my life—like doing the normal activities my friends are doing—but he has opened a window in my emotional and spiritual growth. I feel that so many insecurities and fears I had earlier in my life no longer can touch me. I am much more at peace with myself through this whole experience, and I'm not afraid to be myself anymore. I find I'm much more accepting of others too. I can honestly say CFIDS has been a blessing."

Compensation

Closely tied to the idea of positive reappraisal is the idea of *compensation,* of making up for a loss with a gain, of counterbalancing a negative experience with a positive one, or, in the case of living with CFIDS, of turning a disability into an ability. Compensation helps us redefine the "good life." Many people I interviewed have mastered the skill of compensation.

Janet Bohanon, along with five other family members, has battled with CFIDS for twenty years. In addition to that, Bohanon's husband has been disabled by a heart attack he suffered ten years ago. As a result, they lost their grocery business and all their savings. If anyone has reason to give in to discouragement and despair, Bohanon does. However, she has resolutely chosen to turn her disability into an ability. In 1985 Bohanon began one of the early support groups in the Midwest. Later, in 1989, Bohanon, along with Orvalene Prewitt, founded the National CFS Association, which is still in operation today. For many years Bohanon directed these organizations from her house, which was often strewn with articles, papers, and boxes. Most recently, Bohanon has begun the International Share and Prayer Chain, which helps people around the globe face the emotional and spiritual dilemmas caused by the constant stress of coping with CFIDS and related illnesses. A newsletter that shares personal stories, inspirational verses, book reviews, and prayer requests keeps readers informed and connected. See the "Find the Help You Need" section of this book for more information about the International Share and Prayer Chain and the National Chronic Fatigue Syndrome and Fibromyalgia Association.

Sharon Walk, a teenager with CFIDS, has had a similar experience. "Worse than anything else, CFIDS made me feel alone. I didn't understand why this was happening to me. I didn't think anyone understood what I was going through. But I was wrong. I just wasn't looking for support in the right place. I found support from a group that matches up people with similar illnesses as pen pals. I got in touch with people who knew what it was like to be sick. I now have friends all over the world, people who have CFIDS, lupus, or other chronic illnesses. This circle of friends has become my lifeline; I know that there is always someone who will listen and understand. I don't know if I could cope without them." In 1992 Sharon Walk began CFS Youth Outreach (CYO), a network of young people with CFIDS. A bimonthly newsletter includes poems and stories about life with CFIDS, profiles of CYO members, advice and suggestions for coping, and a column for parents. CYO also offers a pen pal club. See the "Find the Help You Need" section for more details about CYO.

Stung by some disappointments with insensitive people, Candy Feathers has turned her difficult experience into a positive one for dozens of CFIDS sufferers. "I didn't want other people with CFIDS to experience the loneliness I felt in the beginning because of people who couldn't or wouldn't understand. I began writing letters to people suffering from CFIDS, and I've met some wonderful people through that process. Their letters have blessed me immeasurably, and from what I read, my letters have helped other people with CFIDS to feel connected and cared for. We pray for each other and encourage each other. I consider it to be a support group by mail." See the "Find the Help You Need" section for more details about Feathers' support group by mail: CFS Adult Uplift.

Disappointed that CFIDS forced her to leave her position as her church's music director, Sharon Postma felt a deep loss. But Postma has turned her hours in her recliner into times of deep spiritual reflection and planning as she has created litanies for her church's worship services. "Even though I couldn't attend most of the special services, planning the litanies—writing the dramatic readings, creating responsive readings, and coordinating music—gave me great joy. I had a part in the body of Christ, even though I was off life's merry-go-round. God gave me a unique sensitivity because of my illness, and he used that to express his character in the worship services."

"Sometimes I get really frustrated and think, What purpose does this illness serve?" reflects Karen Lang. "I'm sick with CFIDS; I can't do anything. Our son Calen is sick with CFIDS; he can't do anything. But beyond these questions is my underlying belief that God has a purpose for me and for Calen. Maybe we can express something that will be of benefit to someone else with this illness." Lang has indeed expressed many things that benefit others. Frustrated by the lack of educational resources available to Calen as he struggles with CFIDS and some associated learning disabilities, Lang has used her frustration to fuel her determination to effect legislative change that will benefit children suffering from CFIDS, not only for her son but also for any CFIDS child in California. In her recent appointment to The CFIDS Association of America's Public Policy Advisory Committee, Lang is working with the U.S. Department of Education to ensure educational rights for the country's children with CFIDS. Parents of children with CFIDS will benefit from Lang's suggestions outlined in the "Education and CFIDS" section of chapter 12.

Deal with Depression and Despair

Depression and CFIDS

While CFIDS is not the same as depression and while depression does not cause CFIDS, CFIDS can be accompanied by depression, either because of additional chemical imbalances or because of the overwhelming stresses that CFIDS sufferers face. Do not ignore signs of true depression, feeling that you have to tough it out. Get medical and counseling help.

Mark Fuller, a clinical therapist with CFIDS, reports, "The chemical depression is as bad as any part of CFIDS for me. One hour I feel fine; the next hour my emotions are a mess. I know from my education that it is not a personality disorder problem because the changes happen too quickly. Overexertion, stress, bad diet can bring on depression for me. Sometimes it just happens with no apparent cause. I have to be careful not to blame myself for the depression. I am aware of what's physical and what's not physical, what's thinking or what's not thinking. The depression is unpredictable. It can come and go without warning. I have come to the point now that when the depression hits, I refrain from trying to understand it and just go through it. I will come out of it just as mysteriously as I went into it. I have found it essential to have professional help with my depression."

Fuller is wise not to blame himself for the depression. After experiencing deep satisfaction and joy in putting together his *New Testament in Modern English* along with several other books, J. B. Phillips fell into a deep depression. He shares some of his thoughts about his depression in his autobiography, *The Price of Success*: "There are diseases of the body which produce depression of mind, a phenomenon which many of us have experienced after recovering from influenza or some other virus infection. The colour, the meaning and the point of life simply disappear for a time. We pray apparently to an empty heaven, and in our misery we torture ourselves by brutal self-condemnation."[12]

Phillips recognizes the comfort in knowing that others have walked the same path. "It may help simply to know that one whom the world would regard as successful and whose worldly needs are comfortably met can still enter this particular hell, and have to endure it for quite a long time. . . . I can only testify to the fact that it would have been of inestimable comfort and encouragement to me in some of my darkest hours if I could have come across even one book written by someone who had experienced and survived the hellish torments of mind which can be produced."[13]

Several people with CFIDS voiced their fears that they have lost their ability to feel any passion. What particularly disturbs them is losing their ability to feel close to God. They feel numb, totally unresponsive, even though they know God has not deserted them. J. B. Phillips echoes these thoughts, "The heart of the matter was that the very faith which I had striven to impart to others had now deserted me emotionally. I say emotionally deliberately, for never in the dark days that were to follow did I ever doubt the reality of God."[14]

Suicide and CFIDS

People who have studied CFIDS believe that the only fatal aspect of the illness is suicide. After facing misdiagnosis, misunderstanding, and mistreatment, some people with CFIDS become so despondent that suicide appears to be the only way out. When I asked the men, women, and children whom I interviewed if they had ever contemplated ending their lives, most of them said they had.

One month before she was to marry, one woman who had already struggled with CFIDS for three years expressed these very real feelings in a letter to her fiancé: "I have to be honest. I woke up this morning saying to myself, 'I wish I were dead. If I were dead, it wouldn't matter that I was sick and in love with a wonderful person. It wouldn't matter that I desperately want to be alive and happy and full of energy.' I know those are horrible thoughts, but I awoke so tired and in pain that I just didn't care. I tried to care, but I had no energy to care, no will. I simply want to give up the fight because it seems hopeless and useless. Please don't get upset with me. I'm telling you exactly how I feel. Nothing seems to be working to heal me—not vitamins, not God, not exercise. And what good am I if all I can do is be in bed and take hot baths three times a day? I look at the wedding gifts we've received already, and I wonder if we are making a mistake in getting married. Will this illness ruin us?"

A few of the people I interviewed have attempted suicide. Obviously they did not succeed. But their times of deep despair have been very difficult for their families to manage. One attempted suicide carries with it a sharp irony. The fifty-two-year-old mother of a friend has CFIDS. Stripped of all will to continue fighting CFIDS, the woman prepared for her death and then called to say good-bye to each of her children. She did not tell them where she was. For sixteen hours her children frantically searched for their mother, hoping to talk her out of suicide. As each hour ticked by, they lost hope of finding her. Then my friend received a phone call. Thinking it was the police informing him that his mother's body was in the morgue, he was shocked to hear his mother's voice on the other end of the phone. She was giggling hysterically. Relieved to hear his mother's voice but sure that she had lost her mind, my friend asked his mother to calm down and tell him what was happening. "You won't believe this. When I lay on the bed to kill myself, I fell asleep and didn't awaken until sixteen hours later. CFIDS has robbed me of so much throughout the years; now it has even robbed me of the energy to kill myself. What a joke. I'm better now, Son. You need not worry about me."

On a more serious note, if you have contact with a CFIDS sufferer who expresses the wish to die, take the advice of a counselor who struggles with CFIDS: "Don't try to talk the person out of being so pessimistic. Listen and ask questions. Be supportive but not overly optimistic. Ask what you can do to help. Keep the person on the phone or stay with him or her until you are certain that any danger has passed. Suggest resources such as counseling, group therapy, a meeting with a pastoral counselor, or suicide hot lines. Get help when you know you are in over your head."

Cling to Hope

These words from a CFIDS sufferer demonstrate the power of hope: "What keeps me going is hope. I have to cling to hope. If I didn't have the hope that I might get better in this life—and I might—or if I didn't have the hope that God might choose to heal me or if I didn't believe that God is in complete control, I could not handle this illness."

> Yet this I call to mind and therefore I have hope: Because of the Lord's great love we are not consumed, for his compassions never fail. They are new every morning; great is your faithfulness. I say to myself, "The Lord is my portion; therefore, I will wait for him." The Lord is good to those whose hope is in him, to the one who seeks him.[15]

Chapter 6

Accept Changing Relationships

> *CFIDS changes us. We need to understand our changes in order to cope productively with changes in our relationships. We need the cooperation of others in order to adapt and cope with our relationships.*
>
> KATRINA BERNE, *RUNNING ON EMPTY*

CFIDS forces changes not only in our physical and emotional lives but also in our major relationships. If we are going to live a meaningful life in the midst of debilitation, we must redefine how we will relate to people. This chapter will discuss the impact of CFIDS on three major areas of relationships: family, friends, and the church.

CFIDS and the Family

CFIDS alters family life. Parents with CFIDS find they can no longer be the parents they wish to be; children with CFIDS, even adult children with CFIDS, often are homebound and need ongoing care from their parents. Healthy parents and healthy children carry more responsibility as they try to pick up the slack left by sick family members. Families with more than one CFIDS sufferer sometimes teeter out of balance as they try to adjust to the changes necessitated by two or more debilitated people.

In her book *What Is a Family?* Edith Schaeffer compares the family to a mobile whose various parts form a delicately balanced piece of art. However, when the winds of stress or illness blow against the mobile, the individual pieces flail about, hitting each other and destroying the sensitive balance. CFIDS blows a fierce wind across the family mobile. How can we avoid damage to our family mobile and restore a sense of balance in the midst of CFIDS? Let's examine some of the unique stresses CFIDS places on our families. Because chapter 10 will examine the impact of CFIDS on the marriage relationship, this chapter will limit its focus to the parent-child and sibling relationships.

CFIDS Stresses the Family

As you read through the following list of stresses, identify what stresses most affect your family situation. Your stresses may be similar to the ones listed; they may be different. As you begin to formulate a list of the unique pressures your family faces, ask yourself several questions:

- How does this stress affect our family?
- Who is most affected?
- What can we as a family do to counterbalance this stress?

1. *The family can no longer function as it did.* Candy Feathers, a mother with CFIDS, laments, "I miss not being able to be involved in activities with my family. I think that's the worst thing. I can't go out shopping with my daughters. I'm not able to attend church with my family. We've lost a whole avenue of bonding."

2. *When CFIDS hits a family, roles change.* Feathers continues, "Our daughters have had to take on so much responsibility that I almost feel as if there's been a role reversal of the normal parent-child relationship. I feel our daughters are sometimes taking my role, and I'm taking theirs."

Sue Hedlund, a mother with CFIDS, says, "I'm very grateful that my husband helps with the housework and the laundry, but sometimes I feel as if I'm robbed of my identity. It is very hard for me to give up all my roles."

Lynn Hekman, whose husband has had CFIDS for twelve years, comments, "I have gone from being a full-time mom for our five children to baby-sitting part-time to becoming the sole support for a family of seven. While I went back to school, we had two years with virtually no income, and we ended up with a lot of debt. By the time I have taught all week and managed a household and cared for a sick husband, sometimes I feel as if I have two forty-hour jobs a week. It's hard to feed and clothe seven people on a teacher's salary, let alone help provide tuition for our three children in college. I feel the constant stress."

3. Parents of children with CFIDS take on a more active caregiving role. For the past seven years our sixteen-year-old daughter, Alisa, has needed more than normal amounts of parental involvement. When she is sickest, she needs help with washing her hair, changing her clothes, and moving from room to room. Even when she feels at her CFIDS best, she needs lots of emotional support as well as physical support like transportation to and from school for the few hours she can be there. For parents whose teenagers are completely homebound, the adjustments are many. Several mothers of CFIDS teenagers talked about the adjustments they and their children needed to make as they learned to be together all the time, an unnatural circumstance for both the parents and the teenagers.

Several of the children with CFIDS were off at college or involved in full-time jobs or in their own apartments when CFIDS forced them back into a dependent role with their parents. Thirty-year-old Diane Lamont says, "I know my illness puts pressure on my parents. They have been helping with my medical expenses because I am unable to work. But I know they are digging deeply into their retirement savings. That hurts me."

4. Parents with CFIDS struggle with feelings of inadequacy. One mother reflects, "I often get stuck feeling inadequate as a mother. How will I ever manage to help our four daughters plan their weddings? Will I be able to function as a grandmother in the future? What do our daughters really think about me as a mother? That worries me. I've been able to play such a limited role in their lives for five years now."

Jody Hurst, mother of two young children, finds that her CFIDS deeply affects her ability to be an effective mother. "Several times I have been extremely despondent because I am unable to be the kind of mother I want to be. I worry because when I first got sick, our seven-year-old daughter needed to get up by herself in the morning and get her own breakfast. She had to do many things that I felt a child her age shouldn't need to do for herself. She managed it well. But I always felt that it was a terrible thing for her."

Helen Gruelle reminds us that "Our kids will ... remember a mom or dad who modeled, imperfectly, acceptance of new, unwanted glitches in their lives because they chose to trust God *in the midst* of all that was going on. We want to build that ... into our kids, too, and God often allows it to be demonstrated for them, not just talked about.... Often, though, the best memory we can give our children is that of a mom or dad who trusted God in the good times as well as the hard ones, and maybe even laughed a little as the hard times came along."[1]

5. *Children whose parents or siblings have CFIDS sometimes feel angry or afraid.* "One of our sons is very angry about his father's CFIDS," reports one mother. "He feels that because my husband is not working to support his family, that he doesn't deserve respect."

"In the early years, when I was so sick, our young children were afraid that I was going to die and that they would need to grow up without me," recounts Sue Hedlund. "But they are doing better now. They can see me wiped out on the couch for two days and not be stressed out over that. They do what they can to take care of themselves during those days, and they know I'll eventually bounce back a bit."

For a while, thirteen-year-old Brooke Volkers was the only well child in a family of CFIDS sufferers. Her mother and four siblings all are battling CFIDS. "I'm a worrier. When somebody in my family goes to the hospital, it's really hard on me. I don't say much about it at school. I'll tell my teachers when someone in the family is in the hospital. One of the hard things is going to church, when people ask me, 'Where's your mom?' or 'Where's the rest of your family?' Those people go to church every Sunday, and we can't do that. They ask tons of questions about the illness and my mother. And I feel like crying because it makes me think about what's going on. I like to ignore it, but it's really hard to ignore when everybody asks me about it all the time. I would like it all to go away. But it won't.

6. Siblings of children with CFIDS often feel neglected. "While our son, Eddie, has responded to Beth's CFIDS with fear and worry, regularly reporting to his teachers what is happening with her," reflects Linda Waysek, "our other daughter, Rebecca, felt neglected. She felt as if Beth was getting all the attention, and she was getting none. And in a way she was right. The first few months of Beth's illness were so intense as we tried to find out what was wrong with her and as we tried to discover what this illness meant for her and for us as a family. None of us knew how to handle this thing. After getting an accurate diagnosis and adjusting to the reality of the illness, I think we all have settled down a bit, and Eddie and Rebecca are starting to feel less neglected."

7. Some parents with CFIDS feel as if they have lost their identity. "When I got sick over eleven years ago," says Sharon Postma, "our children were five, ten, and twelve years old. I feel they don't even know the real me. Sometimes we'll be talking, and I'll mention something from the past, and one of our children will say, 'Mom, you used to do *that?*'"

8. Some parents with CFIDS find themselves getting paranoid when their children get sick. Jody Hurst, a former nurse, admits, "Whenever our daughter would tell me that her throat hurt, I was afraid that she was getting CFIDS too. One day her kindergarten teacher called me and said Olivia was so tired she couldn't do her work. I panicked. Later on we discovered she had allergies that were making her fatigued, but I was afraid she was getting CFIDS. I find that I've had to release my fears to the Lord and not give in to my fears when one of our children gets sick. I feel that if our children are going to get it, there's nothing I can do. And I've just got to try to make things as good as they can be for us right now."

CFIDS sufferers who already have at least one child with CFIDS wonder if their other children are ticking time bombs. Our twenty-one-year-old son, Matt, teases me whenever I inquire about his health and his sleep patterns. "Mom, I'm okay. Hold down the paranoia, please."

Whenever I feel that the weight of having CFIDS and being the parent of a child with CFIDS gets unbearable, I think about Steve and

Cyndi Volkers. With Cyndi and all five children fighting CFIDS, their family mobile has gone wild. Multiply any of the stresses listed above by seven, and we have a glimpse of the stresses their family faces on a daily basis. "Some days when I am barely hanging on," says Cyndi Volkers, "I look back and am speechless to realize that the Lord has helped us get through *every day* in the past nine years. It is truly a miracle, not only that we are all still surviving but also that we haven't all gone crazy. Sometimes we look at each other and wonder, but then we just have to laugh."

CFIDS Strengthens the Family

The Volkers have not only survived through their nine-year nightmare with CFIDS, but in many ways they have *thrived*. Steve and Cyndi are still married. The children are all still on target in their education. And they all like each other a lot. In fact, when I interviewed the Volkers' children—I talked to each of them separately—each said a variation of the same thing: "Our family has really gotten close through CFIDS. We are each other's best friends. We can't afford to be mean to each other. We have to pull together." Those were not rehearsed comments. These children mean it. Several of them pointed to a brother or sister as the person who most helped them endure the agony of CFIDS. Nearly all of them pointed to their mom as the person responsible for helping them have the courage to face another day. Christina Volkers, the first person in the Volkers family to be ill with CFIDS, said, "My mother has given me so much through these nine years. I can talk to her about anything and know she understands. When I'm discouraged, she'll rub my back and pray with me. I see her strong faith in God as she faces CFIDS in her own body." Not bad for a mother who feels as if she's running on empty most of her day. Not bad for a dad who comes home from work every day to a house full of six CFIDS sufferers.

The Volkers family demonstrates the paradox that difficult, crushing experiences often strengthen us rather than destroy us. Threatening situations like living with CFIDS give us the opportunity to rally around each other and become closer. With the Lord's help, we can find strength in the midst of the stresses of CFIDS.

Accept Changing Relationships

While those of us who are parents with CFIDS often feel that the illness cheats our children, we must remember that each day CFIDS gives us an opportunity to model to our children things we will never be able to quantify or express: courage, faith, trust in God's goodness, perseverance, sacrificial love, optimism, hope, loyalty, to name a few. As I listened to parents with CFIDS express the pain they felt at not being able to be an adequate parent, I found myself saying, "Every day your children watch you model how to handle adversity and suffering and pain. Every day your children see two parents who are committed to each other, to the Lord, and to surviving this illness. They see you refuse to crumble, to allow CFIDS to become an obstacle in your relationship. They see you persevere and love each other selflessly. Those are lessons they can't learn in school. That's a model you may not have been able to give them if you were well."

CFIDS Causes Misunderstanding

One hostile breeze that has threatened the family mobile of several families coping with CFIDS has been the lack of understanding and support they have received from their extended family. I was surprised at the amount of pain I heard as people described the rejection and indifference they have suffered from their extended family.

One older woman with CFIDS laments, "I don't think my grown children really understand what I'm going through. They have not taken my debilitation seriously. And when I explained to my sisters recently about my hassles with finding a doctor who could help me, they told me the only doctor they think I need is a psychiatrist. That just cut me to the core. People just do not understand. Even my own sisters. That was devastating for me."

Another mother of grown children echoes this woman's frustration. "My children don't have a clue what it's like to live with CFIDS. They can't understand why I can't baby-sit for their children. 'After all,' they say, 'you're home all the time.'"

Don Jolan, who along with two of his children suffers from CFIDS, has experienced deep pain from his parents and from two siblings who are medical professionals. The siblings do not believe in

CFIDS as a diagnosis and have persuaded Jolan's parents that CFIDS doesn't exist. What is particularly sad about this story is that the parents are in public ministry, where they extend understanding and comfort to many suffering people. But they are unable to extend that same compassion to their own child and grandchildren. They believe their grandchildren are faking the illness and using it to get out of school. It doesn't matter to them that the grandchildren have been hospitalized several times. Finally Jolan and his wife had to separate emotionally from Jolan's parents. They said, "We have tried to help you understand what is going on in our family. We have explained the illness to you. We have sent you videotapes and books. We can't do any more. Right now we need you to be our allies, not our enemies. Trying to live with your hostility and disbelief is too hard on us, and it takes too much energy. We have decided that we need to spend our emotional energy on helping our sick family members, not on trying to fight your insensitivity."

CFIDS and Friendships

A second area of relationship that changes drastically when CFIDS strikes is our friendships. CFIDS pulls us out of the flow of life. While initially I was too sick to be involved with people at all, as the months and years wore on, I began to suffer from the loss of friendships. As in every other area, I had to redefine what my friendships could be. I had to carve out a new relational life. Not only did I lose many friends, but I also had to redefine the remaining relationships and build new ones.

Accept Losses

As I listened to people talk about their relational losses, I heard several themes. CFIDS causes us to lose friendships for several reasons:

1. CFIDS keeps us from activities that build friendships. Your experience may be similar to mine. When I first became sick, I was bedridden and housebound for over a year. That meant I had to pull the plugs on nearly all the avenues that had provided friendships: involvement on committees, in prayer groups, and in Bible study groups;

attendance at school, church, and social functions; having guests in our home; and the list goes on.

2. *Our friends don't understand or can't accept CFIDS.* How do you explain to people that you are ill? "Do you tell the truth? Do you keep explaining over and over about your illness in an effort to communicate? Or is there a time when you're tired of being preoccupied with your illness, and you bluff your way through? Sometimes *you're even cheered for pulling off the masquerade successfully.* It would be easier having to wear a brace or some outward symbol so people would know we are exhausted and that we aren't coping."[2]

Most of us share the frustration this woman with CFIDS expresses: "When friends see me doing something I don't usually do, they think I'm better and ready to go back to work. What they don't understand is that it may have taken me several days to conserve enough energy to do that particular thing. Then, when I overdo, I spend from a few days to a week in bed. At this point just getting up, getting dressed, and eating breakfast wipes me out. After an hour or two, my mind fogs over. Many days it is foggy and numb all day long. They don't understand."

A husband of a CFIDS sufferer recounts, "I am sad to report that I don't have anyone who believes the seriousness of the situation. I have tried to share some with my pastor, and though he appears sympathetic, he seldom remembers what we discuss. I have found the same response from most of my other friends. I have finally decided that it is better for me to not mention anything about my wife's illness than to get into a losing conversation."

3. *CFIDS keeps us from maintaining our side of the relationship.* Jorge Estrada effectively articulates his situation. "I am not able to be consistent with people. I feel that my personality requires a certain level of energy, and it isn't there. What my friends see of me is dramatically affected by CFIDS. I am much less expressive, much more self-centered because I don't have the energy to care for other people. I basically do what is necessary to survive. Sometimes that means I will not talk to people or I will have to leave a social gathering or I will appear to reject people or I will just stay home. That behavior can be

perceived as rude or selfish. I don't like the inconsistency of it. My behavior varies from hour to hour, literally. As a result I haven't really been able to develop that many personal relationships and have lost a lot of my previous personal relationships."

4. *CFIDS makes our lives unpredictable.* "The frustrating part is we never know how Mark is going to feel each day," says Nancy Fuller. "We can't plan. When we have made tentative plans with other married friends, we often have had to cancel. Most of them have stopped inviting us. Even if I make plans to see one of my friends so that I can have some sort of social life, I often need to back out because Mark becomes too ill to be alone. Our need to cancel out of plans at the last minute leaves lots of room for misunderstanding in our friendships."

Redefine Friendships

CFIDS forces us to redefine our expectations of our friendships as well as the quality of our relationships. While it would be wonderful if all our friends understood CFIDS and knew exactly how to respond each day, we all know that is unrealistic. Even *we* don't know how to respond to ourselves from day to day. We can ease the pain if we keep in mind the following two things:

Expect That Many People Won't Understand

When Dr. David Bell talked with our daughter, Alisa, about her CFIDS, he said to her, "Don't ever expect anyone to understand what you're going through. I recommend that you not even waste your time on it. Choose your goals, then make sure you reach those goals, but don't let the lack of understanding be an obstacle for you. Don't hold it against people if they don't understand. Part of my job as a CFIDS researcher is to help find the cause of CFIDS so that people will begin to understand and accept it." His words were helpful not only to Alisa but also to me. I have always felt that it is important to help people understand our illness. I felt I needed to bring everybody on board so that we could work together. And over the years I have spent a great deal of energy on that. Dr. Bell's comment has freed me from needing to make others understand. If people don't understand, I have to let it go and move on.

We've all had to deal with people's "helpful" comments:

- You *look* fine.
- CFIDS is all "in your head."
- Chronic tired syndrome? We all get tired.
- CFIDS is a fad disease; it's really nothing.
- Are you sure you're not just depressed?
- Do you have AIDS?
- Your husband isn't sick; he's mentally ill.
- If you would just get out and get busy, you would be fine.
- Have you tried vitamins? I use pep pills, and I feel fine.

Although we may often be tempted to strangle the people who offer such suggestions, we need to remember that they say these things more out of ignorance and misguided goodwill than out of malice.

Value a Few Close Friends

In redefining my friendships, I have had to reevaluate how many friends I could have as well as the quality of these friendships. I credit four or five friends—many of them single women—as the people who have helped me survive battling CFIDS and helping our daughter battle CFIDS during the past seven years. As I look back on our relationships, I see several characteristics that made them valuable friends:

- They were not afraid of CFIDS and the changes it caused.
- They were interested to know what I was experiencing, and they believed me.
- They allowed our relationship to be two-sided; they shared their joys and pains with me and needed me.
- They offered help, especially when my husband was traveling overseas: They shoveled snow, cooked us meals, brought gifts for Alisa or helped plan a birthday party for her, ran errands for us, took us out for wheelchair rides.

- They allowed me to be sick; they did not place unreasonable demands on me.
- They were effective comforters; they sat at the end of my couch to talk, listen, and pray with me. They allowed me to cry or be angry without judging my emotions or spiritual health. They sometimes cried with me.
- They were not afraid to confront me.
- They helped me laugh.
- Because they chose to walk the journey with me, they could encourage me by looking back and recounting good things that were emerging because of CFIDS.
- They committed themselves to go the distance with me.

The Lord has graced me with one exceptional friend whom he truly has used to help me cope. Sue and I were friends before CFIDS hit, but our love for each other has only increased during these long years. Sue came to my house within an hour of my returning home with a diagnosis of CFIDS, and without knowing what the diagnosis would be, she gave me the first article I ever read about CFIDS. From that moment on, she has played a key role in my slow recovery. I never kept track, but I think she must have come over to our house once a day for the first few years of our illness, especially when Bas was out of the country. She would let herself in the back door and tiptoe into the living room. If I was asleep, she would leave a note or a book or an article. If I was awake, she would sit at the end of my couch and find out how I was doing. Before she would leave, she would tell me what she was going to do for the rest of the day and ask what she could do for me while she was out.

Sue has seen me at all stages of collapse—physical, emotional, and spiritual. Although she is my friend, she has always been as interested in Alisa's situation as she is in mine. As one of her gifts to Alisa, she has recorded over one hundred twenty episodes of *Little House on the Prairie* on videocassettes. When Alisa was too sick to read or have friends over, Laura, Mary, and the other children of Walnut Grove became her friends. Sue became a second mother to our son, Matt, transporting him to school events, attending his concerts, encouraging him.

Sue never tried to be what she is not. She has always felt embarrassed that she has not brought us meals while we were sick—she's not a meal person. She's an encourager, a detail person, a good listener, a loyal friend. She gave me what she had. She has always expressed such joy at being part of our lives during this illness that I never felt uncomfortable receiving so much from her. If I could clone her, I would. And I would send a clone to every person with CFIDS. Instead, I pray that God will send such a friend into your life.

Make New Friends

Although CFIDS forces us to lose many friends, it also introduces us to new friends, often people who have suffered or who understand chronic illness. Support groups play an important role in establishing friendships with people who understand CFIDS. For some people the support group represents the first time they feel understood at all. "As the people [in the group] spoke, I was stunned. The words could have all been coming out of my mouth. Everyone felt just as I did, except the others had been sick much longer. We all had the same odd group of symptoms. We had severe fatigue, memory disturbance, depression, sore lymph nodes, muscle weakness, and on down the list. There were some who identified with my sore skin. They understood what I was talking about! This illness was real, not just imagined by my stressed-out mind. Other people had it, too."[3]

Sharon Walk, Becky More, Ann McErleane, Sharon Gray, and Beth Waysek—whose voices you will hear in chapter 11—have become friends since they became ill with CFIDS as teenagers. They are a few of the many members of CFS Youth Outreach, a network of teenagers with CFIDS. Each of the girls pointed to the others as the key friends who have helped her adjust to the loss of her other friends and adjust to the debilitation of CFIDS. "We have been an incredible blessing to each other."[4]

Even if you are not in a support group, finding one other person with CFIDS can help you persevere. Carla Crosby reflects about the CFIDS person who helped her cope. "I never got to a support group, but I had one friend who had the illness, and that gave me great comfort. God spoke to me through my friend as she shared medical information with me, walked the path in front of me, and gave me hope. I think that because God gave me this friend, I have never really felt that fear of isolation. In a lot of ways God used my friend to answer fears before I even had them. When I wondered if I could make it another day, I could look at my friend and see that even though her symptoms were more severe than mine, God had helped her through another day. That relationship was crucial to my ability to cope."

CFIDS and the Church

CFIDS has an impact not only on our relationship to our family and friends but also on our relationship to our churches. Most of us have found that when we became ill with CFIDS, we had high expectations of the help and understanding we would receive from our churches. Some of us found that our churches met those expectations; others of us experienced great disappointment.

Help from the Church

CFIDS introduced our family to the warm ministry of the deacons in our church. When our church learned that Alisa and I were sick, the deacon in charge of ministry to homebound people called us and asked how the church could help. At first I was unsure how to respond. Not ruffled by my stammering, Sally continued, "Let me tell you what we can offer your family, and let me recommend some things." She proceeded to tell me that the deacons were prepared to help us with transportation, meals, finances, or whatever special needs we had. She recommended that we consider allowing people to bring in meals when Bas was out of the country. "What weeks will he be gone this month? How many meals would you like each week? On what days would you like them? What special food needs does your family have?" When I hesitated, she said, "Lynn, people *want* to do this. I have a long list of people who have offered to prepare meals for families who need them. I don't think you should say no to them." I agreed to let people bring meals to our house three times a week while Bas was gone. The meals were often so generous that we had enough leftovers for the next day or two.

Sally called each week Bas was gone to find out what we needed. Much to the joy of our kids, she also asked what foods we were tired of having. We like chicken and rice, but if we had it three or more times a week, I was afraid the kids would mutiny. Sally also then called me back each week to tell me who would bring meals on which days. I never had to make one call. I did not have to ask people for meals; people in the church didn't have to ask me if we needed meals. We all knew the deacons were organizing whatever we needed. The deacons also offered money at various times they knew our expenses were high, and several times a year they sent a floral arrangement or a gift of books and tapes to encourage Alisa.

Lest you think this wonderful response was the result of some superchurch with an incredible staff, you need to know that our church was a very ordinary 150-member church at the time. But somehow the people chosen for the board of deacons demonstrated true compassion and love for our church family. They also had devised a system that we found to be very user-friendly. Although most people didn't understand our illness, they surrounded us with love and care.

Jim and Lynn Hekman have also found their church to be of great help and encouragement. "I remember the one year that Jim was incredibly sick, and we didn't know what we were going to do. One night we heard a knock on the door. A church couple whom we didn't know that well walked in and said, 'We were praying about your family, and the Lord told us to do this.' They brought in several bags of groceries. And it wasn't all just basic food. They pulled out a bag of walnuts and chocolate chips and said, 'We want you to be able to make Christmas cookies for your kids.' It was just wonderful.

"The boys' program in our church has been a valuable source of male role models for our sons. One of our sons was quite young when Jim first got sick, and Jim hasn't been able to go out hiking or camping with him—all the dad things. But at church our sons have had men who will do those things with them. If we didn't have that, they would see only what it's like to have a sick dad and not what it's like to be a man in a normal role. It's been very healthy for them.

"Our church's youth leaders have set up a mentor program that provides mentors and prayer partners for the young people throughout their high school years. One of the youth leaders takes our daughters out for coffee just to talk with them and catch up on their lives."

One of the significant ways the church has helped people with CFIDS is through prayer. "I don't think I could have survived," adds Carla Crosby, "if people had not been praying for me. It makes all the difference."

Our family has been surrounded by the prayers of the church, both our local church and the church in other places. Several people in our church have prayed for us every week for the past seven years. Our pastor and elders have been in our home several times to pray with Alisa and me. And we know that our parents pray daily for our family as we struggle with CFIDS.

Even more touching have been the prayers of people I have never met. One year when Bas was visiting Vietnam, he met a pastor who was in his seventies, bedridden himself. The staff person who was traveling with Bas told the pastor that Alisa and I were struggling with a chronic illness. When the pastor heard that, he told Bas that he would pray regularly for us, asking God to do a deep work in us. We receive occasional word that he is still praying. Then we learned of a woman in Malawi, in southern Africa. She prays for us regularly and sends us notes of encouragement. This woman lives a very hard life, marked by poverty and the death of a child to AIDS. But she also has a heart touched by the Lord's love and compassion, and that love has moved her to pray for a woman and young girl whom she will never meet this side of heaven. The body of Christ truly has touched us during our years of illness.

Disappointment with the Church

I am sad to report that most people I interviewed for this book experienced pain and disappointment from their churches. One woman with CFIDS said, "Before I got sick, I had been very active in our church. I felt it was a joy to serve on committees, attend every function, be as helpful as I could. However, when I got sick, nobody ever brought us a meal or offered any help. That was hard for me to accept. I always assumed that if we needed help, our church would be there, eager to help. Instead of offering help, the people speculated about what was *really* wrong with me: 'Oh, she's emotionally disturbed,' or 'Sometimes we all have to make ourselves do things anyway, even if we don't feel like it."

Another woman who had devoted her life to her church found a similar response: "Our church as a whole does not understand my illness. Most of the people in our church are over age sixty, so they *all* feel really tired and unable to do things, but some of them push themselves anyway. They don't understand why I can't. When someone in Sunday school asked me how I was one day and I responded that I was really tired and hardly able to function, the teacher commented, 'Well, we all feel that way, don't we?' They think I am trying to escape from responsibility. A few will not even speak to me cordially anymore."

When I hear the pain expressed about the church, I think of the words from one of David's psalms, which I've paraphrased here to speak to our experiences with CFIDS: "If an enemy were insulting and ignoring me, I could endure it; if a foe were trivializing my pain, I could understand. But it is you, my own church members, my companions, my close friends with whom I have worked on committees, with whom I have studied the Bible and prayed, for whom I have made meals, with whom I have enjoyed sweet fellowship as we have worshipped and served God together."[5]

What accounts for the difference in how these churches respond? That remains a mystery. It's not that some people tried harder than others. One person who has experienced pain from her church says, "We've continued to try to educate the church about CFIDS and how they can minister to us. My husband has worked with the church. If I didn't know that the same situation would exist probably no matter where we were, I would have left our church. I love our pastor, I love his preaching, but there is no real depth of compassion. Our child, who also has CFIDS, has been almost totally ignored, even after loving confrontation with the couple that were the youth ministers before. For a while my husband also was calling our pastor every two weeks to remind him to call our child. And that has stopped too."

It's not that some people are more worthy of help than others. It's not that some churches intend to hurt people. But somehow we in the church need to learn how to be compassionate people.

CFIDS sufferer Karen Lang reminds us that "Illness brings out the best, and it also brings out the worst. And with our churches, we expect nothing but the best." Lang's point is important. We have such high expectations of our churches that when they can't meet those expectations, we are crushed.

Answering Job's Friends

Most of us have encountered people like Job's comforters, people who try to help but fail to understand some of the larger issues involved in our illness or fail to understand God's purposes in and through our illness. What do we say to comforters who ask if our illness is the result of some deficiency in our faith? Let's explore some responses to several statements made by these comforters.

"Your Illness Is the Result of Unconfessed Sin"

"We who have been ill with CFIDS for over a decade are a threat to people's theology because we don't get better despite daily prayers and everything else," says Shawn Fisher. "In order to explain our illness to themselves, and I guess to us, people tell us that we are not well because we have some sin that we have not confessed, as if that had never occurred to us. When Gregg and I became ill, one of the first things we did was confess every sin we knew as well as any that we didn't recognize. We totally opened ourselves to God, asking him to do with us what he needed to do. It was a time of real surrender and openness to his will. We have continued to confess our sin and listen to him. Having done all that, I must conclude that God is not punishing us with CFIDS."

A pastor's wife with CFIDS recalls, "Yes, I did have somebody say that if my sins were confessed and my life was in order, I would feel better. And there's some truth to that. Unresolved anger and bitterness, self-pity and resentment do affect us. But I don't believe unconfessed sin is causing my CFIDS or preventing me from recovering. I believe God has other plans for this illness in my body."

While we all need to wrestle with our sin and confess it to the Lord, the conviction for that sin will come from God, not from finger-pointing people. We must also recognize the truth expressed in a New Testament story. When Christ's disciples saw a man who had been born blind, they asked their teacher, "Who sinned, this man or his parents, that he was born blind?"

Christ answered definitively, "Neither this man or his parents, but this happened so that the work of God might be displayed in his life."[6] The man's blindness and our CFIDS did not happen because of someone's sin but so that God's work may be displayed in our lives.

"You Are Sick Because You Don't Have Enough Faith"

Most people I interviewed have prayed to be healed of CFIDS. They have asked others—pastors, elders, prayer groups, Bible study groups, family, and friends—to pray for them. Nearly all of these people are still sick. Does that mean their prayers are inadequate or that they don't have enough faith?

"We have gone through some real disappointment with the whole issue of healing," says one man with CFIDS. "I believe God chooses to heal some people miraculously. I've seen it happen. And my wife and I were very open to God's power to heal me. We went to the elders of our church, and they anointed me with oil and prayed over me, according to the New Testament instructions outlined in James 5:14–16. This happened several times. But I have not recovered. I can live with that. I have a peace about my situation and trust that God's purposes for me do not include a miraculous healing at this point. But the people who prayed for me could not accept that I remained ill. They told me I wasn't 'stepping into my healing.' They told me, 'God wants you well. God does not want this illness. It is the illness of the Devil. Maybe you need to do this; maybe you should do that. Maybe you need to fast.' I consider myself a mature and grounded Christian, but I found this a devastating experience. I've wrestled with all these issues, and I continue to believe that God could heal me if he chooses, but he has not chosen to heal me for the moment. I do not believe I am still sick with CFIDS because my faith is inadequate."

127

"You Are Still Sick Because You Haven't Done Enough"

Some of Job's comforters come to us and blame us for not try-ing hard enough to become well. "I find it wearing to respond to all the people who think they know what is best for our daughter," says Linda Waysek, mother of a child with CFIDS. "Some people chide us because they think we're not doing enough. Others tell us they think we're doing the wrong thing. Everybody seems to know what we should do. We've tried nearly everything. We've had Beth to some of the best medical professionals in New York City."

Other comforters force on us treatments we don't feel are appro-priate. "If only you would try this medication or that supplement or this combination of twenty-four pills, you would be better." We some-times found it exhausting to fend off well-meaning people who had a miracle cure for CFIDS. Each of them assumed we had not explored a myriad of options ourselves or assumed we would respond "just the way Aunt Jane did. Once she started taking those pills and using the green oil, she perked right up. Why haven't you tried her remedy? Don't you want to get well?"

We've had to remember that our comforters want the best for us. We try to take each suggestion seriously. We explore each option, talk to people who have used the therapy, and pray about each opportunity. Often we decide against the treatment. We want not to seem ungrate-ful or rigid or stubborn, but we don't always feel a certain remedy is appropriate. People need to give us the space to make our choices.

When people suggest remedies, don't feel pressure to try them. You know your body. You know what works and what doesn't. Don't feel pressured to do something you don't believe in. Use your common sense. Do what you can afford.

As we respond to the comforters in our lives, remember that they do not intend the malice we perceive in their responses to us. Most of them are genuinely trying to help. Their responses are their misguided ways of coping with their own disappointment with God or their sadness or their feelings of helplessness.

Verses from the end of Job's story help us deal with our com-forters. When everyone is finished speaking, God addresses Job's three comforters. He says, "I am angry with you . . . because you have not spoken of me what is right." He chides them for presuming to know what his intentions were for Job's suffering, for misrepresenting him to Job. He tells them they were out of line to blame Job or to blame him. Then he instructs them to offer a sacrifice in Job's presence in repentance for their actions. God also instructs Job to pray for his misguided friends. When each of the four men does what God has asked of them, God forgives the comforters and restores Job.

As we deal with people who have hurt or disappointed us, whether they are family members, friends, or church members, let's release the pain of misunderstandings and forgive those who have hurt us, using as a model these words from Scripture: "To this you were called, because Christ suffered for you, leaving you an example, that you should follow in his steps . . . When they hurled their insults at him, he did not retaliate; when he suffered, he made no threats. Instead, he entrusted himself to him who judges justly."[7]

Open Letter to the Church

In an attempt to help the church become a more effective reflection of Christ's compassion and love, I have included an open letter to the church from those of us suffering from CFIDS. Please photocopy this letter or write one of your own and give it to your pastor or deacon board. Or you may wish to send it to your church's newsletter or your denomination's official periodical.

Dear brothers and sisters in the body of Christ,

Along with perhaps as many as two million other Americans, we suffer from a debilitating illness known as chronic fatigue and immune dysfunction syndrome (CFIDS, pronounced *see-fids*), also known as chronic fatigue syndrome (CFS). While the causes of CFIDS are not known at this point, several researchers believe this immune-system illness is caused by an insidious virus that merges itself with the DNA of the human cell and uses the cell as a shield. As the immune system tries to fight this virus, it dumps into our bodies chemicals that cause neurological dysfunction, debilitating fatigue, and a whole host of other crippling symptoms. While the media and much of society have trivialized this illness, it is very real. It wreaks havoc on men, women, and children, on families and marriages.

The people who fight CFIDS are not malingerers or hypochondriacs. We are courageous, intense people; most of us are high achievers, leaders. We were busily involved in satisfying work and ministry when we were struck down by a crippling illness that left us bedridden and unable to function for years, and for some of us, for decades. We have lost more than our health and our ability to function; we have also lost a sense of who we are and where we fit into God's plan.

Many of us have faced misunderstanding and rejection from the medical community because the illness does not show up on normal diagnostic tests. We are sad to report that many of us also face misunderstanding and rejection from our churches. Unable to deal with the ambiguities of CFIDS, many churches have been unwilling to reach out in support and compassion to us, even though many of us have served the Lord through our churches for decades. The hurt resulting from this response has only compounded the pain we feel in this illness.

We know you do not intend to hurt us or ignore us. We believe you wish to be the compassionate arm of Christ. Let us help you understand how you can minister to us:

1. Trust us. Believe that what we are experiencing is real. Although we may look normal, our immune systems are fighting a fierce battle that often leaves us bedridden after attending a church service or activity.
2. Understand that when we are too sick to come to church or too sick to be on committees as we had done before CFIDS, we are not shirking our spiritual responsibilities.
3. Don't blame us when we don't get better, assuming that we harbor secret sins. Trust that we have confessed our sins and received forgiveness.
4. Pray *for* us and *with* us. We need you to stop by our homes and pray with us. If you are uncomfortable with us, we'll help you get over it. Remember to pray for us in the church's prayer groups. *Keep* praying for us, even if we stay sick. Pray not only for us to be restored physically but also for us to

have the strength to survive the struggle if God chooses to use us *in* our illness rather than heal us.

5. Help us keep perspective. Help us endure with patience the path we have been called to walk. The battle we fight is not only physical but also emotional and spiritual.

6. Go the distance with us. Many of us have already been sick for years, and our illness may last for many more years.

7. When you wonder how to help us, think of the basics: clean a room; drive us to appointments; do an errand; bring books for us to read; loan us videos to watch when we are too sick to read; offer to help with medical expenses.

8. Help with our family responsibilities. Offer help with child care if we have young children. Take our kids with you on an outing or take our spouses out for coffee. Dealing with CFIDS is hard on them too.

9. Send us notes and cards. Some days that's our only contact with the outside world. Share meaningful verses from Scripture or a funny story; both have healing value.

10. If we're too sick to answer the phone or have visits, leave a message on our answering machines or a note on our back door. Read us a Scripture verse or leave a prayer on the answering machine.

11. As this illness robs us of life as we knew it, we grieve. Allow us to grieve, and come alongside us as true comforters.

12. Help us to find a place in the body of Christ during these years. Help us find ways to be "wounded healers."

Words from Walter Wangerin's book *Mourning into Dancing* describe an effective comforter. "The comforter is not a teacher, a moralizer, a quoter of helpful Bible verses, a preacher of timely sermons—just a servant, serving. The comforter is not a prophet, pointing out the errors of the bereaved, interpreting sorrow as a visitation of an angry God, but a servant, serving. . . . The comforter is, simply, a servant of God so healthy in the holy relationship that though he is no lover of grief, he will live beside it for love of the griever; so happy in the divine relationship that grief shall not impair him; so empowered by his relationship with Jesus that he expects absolutely nothing from his relationship with the griever: he is Jesus come near unto her, and his presence in every sense is Grace."[8]

Thank you for reading this, and thank you for caring.

Your wounded brothers and sisters who suffer with CFIDS.

To summarize, we have discussed several steps in the journey to find wholeness and meaning in the midst of a painful, debilitating illness:

- understand the illness
- grieve the losses
- make physical changes
- find emotional balance
- accept changing relationships

Part 3 will focus on what is perhaps the most important step in the journey—finding God's strength in the midst of our weakness. Chapter 7 will explore the importance of choosing to trust God in the midst of difficult circumstances. Chapter 8 will discuss various ways we can maintain spiritual health while struggling with CFIDS. Chapter 9 records various voices in the CFIDS valley—voices of reflection, hope, direction, acceptance, and encouragement.

Part **3**

Find Strength in Weakness

My grace is sufficient for you, for My strength is made perfect in weakness.

2 CORINTHIANS 12:9 NKJV

- Choose to trust God
- Maintain spiritual health
- Voices from the valley

Chapter 7

Choose to Trust God

Every circumstance that is a part of our lives can be used by God to teach us things that strengthen our character and change us on the inside. We have a choice whether or not we choose to learn them.

HELEN GRUELLE, *HORIZONTAL IN A VERTICAL WORLD*

Within the first months of my becoming ill with CFIDS, my husband, Bas, said to me, "This illness has the power to destroy us, our family, our marriage, and our faith. If we're not spiritually vigilant and if we don't do everything we can to help you maintain spiritual health, you'll go under, and the rest of the family will follow."

I knew he was right. Several weeks before I became ill, I had said in a women's prayer group, "What would really shake our marriage is if I would have a long-term, nondescript illness. That could destroy our marriage." My statement arose from experiences Bas and I had shared in our nearly twenty years of marriage. Rarely sick with even as much as a headache or cold, Bas would become impatient with people who had nondescript illnesses. If someone had a broken bone or clear, objective symptoms, that was different. However, people who looked fine but said they were sick frustrated him. He had seen too many people use inconclusive illnesses in manipulative ways. I harbored a fear that if I were ever sick with a hard-to-diagnose illness, he would lose patience with me.

Several months after I made that comment in the prayer group, we were in the middle of the very situation I had said would threaten

our marriage. Not only was I sick with a long-term, nondescript illness, but our daughter, Alisa, was sick as well. Bas's words were right.
This illness did have the power to destroy us. It could undermine our
relationships, crush us with emotional pressure, plunge us into despair,
and cause us to doubt the very essence of our faith.

Choices in the Difficult Times

We realized we needed to make several foundational choices at
that point. We had to choose whether or not we would allow CFIDS
to destroy our family, our faith, and our marriage. We had to choose
what price we were willing to pay to fight this illness. We had to
choose to cooperate as a family and as a couple. We had to choose to
make our spiritual and emotional wholeness a priority.

In most of my life, I hadn't been aware that I had choices. I took
life as it came, not really thinking about how I was going to respond.
I just reacted, especially when life was going along smoothly. But
when CFIDS hit our family, choices became important. I remembered Paul Tournier's words: "Perhaps the most powerful and unused
gift from God is choice." It was time to use that gift.

What would we use for guidelines to help us make the right
choices? Words from the Old Testament gave us direction: "Now
what I am commanding you today is not too difficult for you or
beyond your reach. . . . See, I set before you today life . . . and death . . .
Now *choose life*, so that you and your children may live and that you
may love the Lord your God, listen to his voice, and hold fast to him.
For the Lord is your life."[1]

Choose life. What does it mean to choose life in the midst of the
pain, debilitation, and uncertainties of battling with CFIDS? What
would happen if I didn't choose life?

Resist Destructive Choices

During the past seven years, I have faced many temptations to
choose things that were not life-giving. It was very tempting to choose
to be bitter. It was tempting to become angry. At times it was tempting
to demand that God explain his actions, that he tell me why, or at least

give me an explanation. I have faced the daily temptation to be discouraged. Many days I have felt at the edge of despair, thinking, *I can't possibly do this one more day.* I was tempted to choose to believe lies—lies about my situation, lies about what was real, and lies about God. These lies came from the thief, the robber who "comes only to steal and kill and destroy."[2] In contrast to the robber, Christ tells us he has come to give us life, to the full.[3] Here again is the choice: life or death.

As much as God offers us life and ability to choose life-giving things, we must also reckon with the thief who would like nothing better than to see us make the destructive choices, to choose the things that kill, that destroy.

Lies

The New Testament describes the thief, Satan, as a liar: "He was a murderer from the beginning, not holding to the truth, for there is no truth in him. When he lies, he speaks his native language, for he is a liar and the father of lies."[4] When I look back, I realize I was tempted to believe many lies.

Lie 1: My life is over. Certainly life as I knew it *is* over, for now and maybe forever. I don't know. It's a real temptation for me to feel, "This is it. I *am* this illness. I will never be healthy again."

Lie 2: God is good only if he heals us. I never doubted that God could heal us. I have seen him miraculously cure several friends. But what if he doesn't heal us? Do I still believe he is good?

Lie 3: Difficulty, hardship, trials, and suffering are bad and should be avoided at all costs. We humans spend lots of energy trying to avoid hard times. We feel blessed if we manage to live a trouble-free life. Because we incorrectly equate an easy life with blessing, we see difficulties and trials as a curse.

Lie 4: I'm worth something only if I can be active. This lie haunted me a lot in the first few months, when I was struggling most intensely with the losses and changes. When I became sick, I could no longer be active. Instead, I spent my days on a couch, barely able to walk from room to room, too sick even to read or to watch a video on some days.

I deeply questioned my value. Was I worth anything? Was I as valuable to God and others while I lay on the couch as I was when I had been free to be involved in many activities?

Lie 5: I can't possibly cope with this another day. This lie badgered me often, especially when Alisa was sickest. I was often an inch away from throwing in the towel, from giving up the fight, from giving in to the discouragement and despair that was breathing down my neck.

Lie 6: If only . . . If only I weren't sick, then . . . If only my daughter weren't sick, then . . . If only . . . If only . . . If only. . . And we can choose to live with the "if onlys," but they are crippling, incredibly crippling. And they are tempting.

Had I chosen to believe those lies, they would have led to destruction, a death of sorts—not physically perhaps, but certainly emotionally and spiritually.

Make Life-Giving Choices

Instead of choosing death, I have determined to choose life. What does it mean for me to choose life today—in internal attitudes, in behavior, in actions, in relationships? One of the essential dynamics in making life-giving choices is *choosing* to believe that God's Word is true. Although it would have been easy to listen to the thief, the liar, I have chosen instead to trust God and take him at his word.

Choose to Trust God for a Full Life

Trusting God means choosing to be content with what *is*—even though it's far from perfect. When I'm tempted to believe the lie that my life is over, I can choose to believe what Christ said in John 10, "I've come to give you life—full, abundant life." And that includes life on a couch. Life on a couch can still be full and abundant because of Christ.

Even though my life has been severely limited, I still have deep and satisfying friendships. I still experience pleasure in art and nature, even though I have to be pushed in a wheelchair at an art exhibit or in a forest preserve. I still enjoy musical performances, although I "attend" most of them through television or radio.

I think we often live under the illusion that we can be useful to God only when we are in top shape, when we are whole. I now know that he can use broken, weak bodies as effectively as he can well bodies.

I look at the rich relationships in my life right now, and I realize that most of them have come as the result of my illness. I spend a lot of time with women who live in pain or with an uncertain future or with unbearable heaviness. We have learned together to wait on the Lord, to trust him with a painful today and what probably will be a painful tomorrow. We have learned to say that nothing really matters except the assurance that whatever tomorrow holds, God will be there, and he has invited us to lean on him.

Choose to Trust That God Is Good

When I'm tempted to believe that God is good only if he heals us, I can choose to believe that God is good *even if* both Alisa and I are ill, *even if* Alisa and I remain ill. I remember one Sunday when our pastor preached about fear. At the end of the service, he asked us to recognize our fears, admit them, and offer them to the Lord. That week I had been wrestling with the implications of my illness on our children. I had been troubled with a growing sense of anxiety and inadequacy as a parent.

I had been sick for all but two months of our son's high school life, and I had been unable to attend his concerts, speech competitions, and other events parents want to share with a child. I was afraid that our children would feel they were getting shortchanged by CFIDS, that they would look back on their lives and see these as the "black hole" years, the nothing years. That was the fear I gave to the Lord that Sunday morning. I remember praying silently through tears, "Help me be the kind of mother our children need, even though I'm only a fraction of the mother I have been before this."

Then it occurred to me, with incredible force, that the thing that most prepares me to be a good mother to Alisa is carrying this illness in my body. The thought shocked me. I had to repeat it. I'm the best possible mother for Alisa because I know what it's like to live with CFIDS. I know the pain Alisa feels, the discouragement she faces, the effort it takes her just to keep up with her schoolwork. I know that what she's experiencing in her body is a real disease. If I didn't carry the same illness in my body, I would have had a hard time understanding her when she would report her unusual and sometimes erratic symptoms. Because I have the same illness, I understand her in ways no one else can. I can be a more effective advocate for her needs in the school system and in the medical community because I can speak for her with authority.

Because Alisa and I are both sick, we can work as a team. Some days we are both so discouraged that we just hold each other and cry. When Alisa is sickest, I can comfort her and help her get through the waiting. Some days she feels stronger than I do, and she is the comforter.

The very thing I had feared was the blessing. It's not a tragedy that both of us are ill; it's a blessing. God is good even if Alisa and I both are ill.

Trusting God's goodness has been the foundation of my ability to accept CFIDS in my life and in Alisa's. From the beginning of the illness, I knew acceptance was essential, but I wasn't sure how to accept CFIDS without allowing it to have power over me, without giving in to it, without giving up. Over time it became clear that acceptance meant I needed to give the whole matter to God. I needed intentionally, consciously, and completely to place myself (and Alisa) in his hands. My "self" included not only my physical body but also my gifts, abilities, time, desires, plans, relationships—everything. They were his to begin with, and they are his now, to do with as he pleases, even if that means we will be ill for the rest of our lives.

This paradox—that acceptance involves giving—was new to me. I couldn't find words to clarify it sufficiently, to unravel the mysteries of it. Though I couldn't explain it, I knew that the key lay in the character of God. I could give it all up—all the things I thought he had given me to fulfill his will, to answer his call—because he is so thoroughly good, so utterly dependable.

I felt a shadow of what the Old Testament patriarch Abraham must have felt when God asked him to give up his son, Isaac, on an altar.[5] I felt some of the same questions Abraham must have asked:

But God, wasn't this child your gift to me? Wasn't this gift your idea of how you were going to fulfill your plan of creating a great nation? Why, now, do you ask me to give up the gift you gave me?

But Abraham, trusting more fully in God's goodness and wisdom than in his own human understanding, gave his gift back to God. Similarly, trusting in God's goodness and wisdom, I gave him myself and my daughter. It was not an offering made into an unknown expanse, into the dark silence. It was an offering made willingly to the hands and heart of love, to the one who had made us, to the one whose love had claimed and named us, to the one who could be thoroughly trusted.

Then came the ram, God's gift back to us. Just as God had provided a ram to take Isaac's place on the altar, he has given us a ram. The ram for us has not been restored health, but it has been God's tender mercies to give us a glimpse of his purposes with our broken bodies. I'm continually aware that God doesn't owe us a glimpse. I had given him a gift, and it is unconditionally his. But in his love, he has allowed us to catch sight of the ram.

Choose to Trust God in the Midst of Difficulties

When I'm tempted to believe that difficulties are to be avoided at all costs, I can choose to believe that difficulties, hardships, trials, and suffering can be good. Not that I ask for them or enjoy them in some masochistic way. But I have learned more clearly what James, the New Testament epistle writer, meant when he said, "When all kinds of difficulties and temptations crowd into your lives, don't resent them as intruders, but welcome them as friends! Realize that they come to test your faith and to produce in you the quality of endurance. But let the process go on [allow yourself to welcome more troubles] until that endurance is fully developed, and you will find you have become people of mature character."[6]

Choosing to trust God means choosing to believe that the difficulties I am experiencing now—difficulties I would like to avoid at all costs—can be good, that God's overall purposes in my life are good. God redeems my difficulties and uses them to produce endurance and maturity—good things—in my life. I can choose to believe that God is in control, that he knows what he's doing, even though life may seem chaotic, unbearable, painful, and out of control.

Choose to Trust God for Personal Value

When I'm tempted to believe that I have no value now that I'm ill, I can choose to see how God values his children. Even though my ability to do the kinds of things I did before I became ill with CFIDS is severely limited, I can choose to believe that I still have value—to God and to other people. For most of my adult life, I have been involved with helping ministries: teaching inner-city teenagers, working with homeless alcoholic men and women, teaching Bible studies for women whose husbands were hostile to their faith, advocating for the needs of the poor. But CFIDS changed most of that. For the first few years of illness, I spent most of my day on a couch. Of what value was that?

Several single women thought it was very valuable. They found their way to the end of my couch, where I was free to listen to their struggles and pray with them through difficult transitions. One friend had just come through a canceled wedding and was without confidence or hope. Another friend was in the process of leaving a secure teaching career in the States (against her parents' wishes) to teach in foreign countries where she would use her ministry skills to encourage the church. A third friend was leaving a lucrative, fast-paced executive job to move to California and work with Iranian believers; she would need to learn to live on one-tenth of what she was accustomed to earning.

My life on a couch was valuable to these women because I had time for them, time undisturbed by busy schedules and activities. But more than that, my life on a couch was valuable to them because they knew I understood suffering, uncertainty, waiting, and questions. Together we experienced life without our normal props. Together we learned what it meant to cling to God alone. Together we prayed and waited.

I came to believe that my value as a person lies not in what I do but in who I am. I came to believe that I am as valuable to God when I am on a couch as I am when I am leading a Bible study or traveling with my husband or cooking a meal for my family. What counts is not my accomplishments but my faithfulness to God's purposes in my life.

I could practice obedience as effectively from a couch as I could from behind a podium.

I learned the truth of the apostle Paul's words: "Praise be to ... the God of all comfort, who comforts us in all our troubles, so that we can comfort those in any trouble with the comfort we ourselves have received from God. For just as the sufferings of Christ flow over into our lives, so also through Christ our comfort overflows."[7] I could trust that God would use my suffering for the good of others. I could choose to see that he was giving back to me new gifts, even though the gifts did not come in packages that I recognized as gifts.

Choose to Trust God When You're Discouraged

As the days and months and years have gone by, I have been tempted to believe the lie that I can't possibly cope another day. As I have faced overwhelming discouragement, I have had to choose to trust God's words from Joshua 1:9, "Be strong and courageous. Do not be terrified; don't be discouraged, for the LORD your God is with you wherever you go."

Trusting God means choosing not to worry. Again the instructions are clear and strong: "Don't worry about anything. Pray about everything."[8] Again this is not an option; it's a command.

I need to choose to believe that God is in control—in spite of what I may be experiencing. I must choose to trust God's Word, which says, "I know the plans I have for you, ... plans to prosper you and not to harm you, plans to give you a hope and a future."[9] These words anchor me when I am tempted to fall apart.

Choose to Trust God When You Don't Understand

I wanted to demand that God give me an explanation of what was going on. What is this illness? How can we get better? And certainly, How long is this going to last? I really wanted an answer for that question. But God has chosen not to answer many of our questions. He hasn't explained why or how long. Whenever Alisa has a relapse, we face the open-ended questions again. Is this a short-term relapse? Or will she slip into a greater level of debilitation? We don't have answers to a lot of those questions.

Instead of giving me answers, God has said, "Lynn, are you willing to trust me? Are you willing to trust me even if you don't understand? Will you trust me to let you know day by day what you should be doing? Will you trust that I will give you grace to handle every fearful moment, every painful day, every difficult month, every long hard year?"

When I am tempted to be angry with God because I don't understand, I need to remember that it's not that God has forgotten me or that he's incapable of answering my questions. Perhaps he has other intentions. "And where is God in all of the confusion? My experience has been that most often absence is one of the ways he chooses to be present. Hiddenness seems to be one of his unique strategies. He uses the night like a craftsman wields his finest tool. So the absence of light is an invitation to us to keep on searching for where he has stored the candles."[10]

In all of this I have come to expect less of life and a great deal more of God. In the process I have become much more rooted, more stable, more contented.

Prism or Rock?

One week when I was helping Alisa with her homework, we studied light and refraction. As we worked with several cut-glass prisms that hang in our kitchen window, we watched the sun throw rainbows onto the wallpaper. As we observed what the prism did to the light, I began to understand some spiritual principles more clearly.

The function of a prism is to reveal what the light is made of. On one side of the prism, light is general and indistinct. But when that light passes through the prism, it separates into layers of distinct, recognizable, pure color, each with its own beauty and purpose. A prism allows us to see what our physical eyes cannot see by themselves: the colors of light.

Difficult experiences in our lives can be like that prism. Before difficulties happen to us, we know God is real, but he often is general and indistinct. But when his light passes through our difficult experiences, it separates into its distinct components. Through the prism of difficult experiences, we can see the different aspects of God's character. The prism throws on the wallpaper of my soul the various layers and colors of God's character. I now can see more clearly that he is good. I can see more clearly that he knows what he's doing. I can see more clearly that he is sovereign. I can see more clearly that he is merciful.

Alisa and I also studied various kinds of rock. As we worked with a piece of quartz, I thought about how it was different from a prism. Light also hits the piece of quartz. However, when it does, the light only bounces back; it doesn't go through the rock. On the other side of the rock we see no rainbows, no distinct layers, no clearer vision. The light remains indistinct, general.

I believe that we can choose to see the difficult experiences of our lives as prisms or as pieces of quartz. Will we choose to allow God's light to pass through us, revealing on the other side of our difficulties a God whose character is beautiful and diverse? Or will we choose to be like a piece of rock quartz, refusing his light and sending it back to him, never allowing it to touch another person or reveal the components that our physical eyes can never see?

When difficult experiences come our way, we can choose to trust God. We can choose to be a prism.

Chapter 8

Maintain Spiritual Health

God always answers us in the deeps, never in the shallows of our soul.

AMY CARMICHAEL

Living with CFIDS forces us to change not only our physical, emotional, and relational lives but also our spiritual lives. "I had to redefine what my faith was," says Jorge Estrada. "Before I became ill with CFIDS, my faith was tied to a certain level of service and action and Bible study; suddenly I couldn't do those things. I finally came to realize that my faith was not at all dependent on what I did. It didn't matter whether I was able to exercise the spiritual disciplines that had been important to me. It didn't matter whether I was able to attend church. It didn't matter whether I was a part of a Bible study group.

"What really mattered was that God had already paid the price for my sin, and he was waiting for me to come to him. I was able to interact with him within the limits of the illness. I realized that what pleased God was something much more basic than I ever assumed. Sometimes it pleased God for me to take from him, to sit in his hand, like Moses in the cleft of the rock, and just receive. I had nothing to give, but I could give him my emptiness. That was a new experience for me, and it redefined my faith in a major way. My faith is now dependent more on gaining an understanding of who God is and what he did rather than what I do."

Redefine Your Perception of God

Estrada's words aptly describe what many of us have experienced. CFIDS has redefined our faith and our perception of who God is. Most of us came into our illness with certain expectations of who God is and of how he will act.

Disappointment with God

One man whose wife has had CFIDS for over twelve years expected God to act a certain way in their situation. And when God failed to do certain things, he experienced deep disappointment with God. When the devastation hit and continued to pound us, I asked God to help me. But he hasn't helped me in a way that I feel is satisfactory. Now I have a hard time spending time with God, and I feel distant from him. I certainly don't get any comfort. I don't feel as if God took care of us. It's wrong for me to be bitter, but I've been hurt, and that turns into bitterness if it's not dealt with properly. I often feel as if I'm wandering in the wilderness. I don't know if God is punishing me or if I'm learning. I'm totally lost in that area of my life."

Expectations of Healing

"I experienced disappointment with God in the area of healing," says Keri Sanders. "Before I became ill with CFIDS ten years ago, I was a theologically grounded person. I had done years of biblical studies and had been actively involved in various forms of Christian ministry. However, during the first several years of CFIDS, I was too sick even to attend church, read the Bible, or pray. I had to depend on other Christians to pray for me. I encountered a group of Christians who felt strongly that God was going to heal me. They told me, 'God wants you well. Do this and that, and he will heal you.' These people had experienced miraculous healing, and they wanted me to be healed too. But God hasn't healed me. At first I was disappointed with God. Then I was disappointed with myself because I obviously wasn't doing the right thing. Then I became disappointed with the people who insisted that God wanted to heal me. I am now in the process of reevaluating what I expect of God, what I have been taught, and what other Christians say to me. I believe in the end it will be a healthy process."

Other people have experienced similar situations. One man who has struggled with CFIDS for over a decade recounts, "Several men were sure God was going to heal me. I remember one night when they prayed over me. One man cried out, 'God, heal him. God, heal him.' But God hasn't healed my body. The people who were praying for me could not live with that outcome. They felt that if God didn't heal me, then it was my fault: I have unconfessed sin or my faith isn't big enough or I'm not allowing God to help me. I am uncomfortable with those expectations of God. I don't believe we can order God around, telling him what to do and when to do it. I have learned to submit this situation to him and rest in his wisdom and love."

Gregg Fisher, who was a seminary student when he became ill with CFIDS, offers his thoughts about healing. "I'm the kind of person who needs to understand intellectually who God is and what my relationship is to him. During the first years of my illness, I was too debilitated to do any thinking about theological issues. In fact, I could barely pray. As I've begun to recover slightly, I've been wrestling with some of the questions about healing. If God wants me well, why am I still sick? If other people are healed of their illnesses, why am I not healed? At first these questions led me to blame myself, and I began to lose my sense of identity in Christ. But slowly God has rebuilt the foundation of my faith: He loves me, and I can trust him completely.

"I remember when I first became ill, I would pray, weeping and begging God to heal me. Occasionally I would feel as if I were in God's very presence, and I heard him say in a very gentle voice, 'It's okay, Gregg, not now.' In that moment, the desire to ask for healing vanished as I felt flooded with his total peace and love. Because of those experiences, I believe that I'm in the place God wants me to be. I am learning to relinquish my expectations of how God will act and just allow him to do what he needs to do in and through me."

Christ Understands Your Illness

"In the midst of CFIDS," one woman reports, "I have come to have different expectations of God. I value the fact that he truly understands what I am going through and that he is deeply involved in my pain and suffering. Along with the psalmist, I can say to God, 'You have seen me tossing and turning through the night. You have collected all my tears and preserved them in your bottle! You have recorded every one in your book.'¹ Knowing and feeling that presence gives me great strength.

"Shortly before I became ill, I had studied Christ's suffering. He was physically abused, mentally abused, spiritually abused (kicked out of his own church); the scribes and Pharisees told the people he was crazy; even his own family misunderstood him and denied his deity; people talked about him behind his back; and he was deserted at the time of his greatest need for encouragement. He died a terrible death. He did not have CFIDS, but I am sure he was bone-weary many times. When I feel as if no one understands what I am experiencing, I take comfort knowing that Christ understands. He knows what I endure, and he stands beside me to help me walk through this illness."

Those words have helped me. As a parent of a child with CFIDS, I take comfort in knowing that God understands the pain of watching a child suffer pain and misunderstanding. He knows how my parent-heart aches when I see Alisa too sick to be with friends, too sick to enjoy the life of a normal, growing young woman. But just as God had other, deeper purposes for his Son's life and suffering, I trust that he has deeper purposes for Alisa's life as well.

Know Your Enemy

Not only do we need to know who God is, but we also need to know our enemy. We need to know whom and what to fight. When I first became ill with CFIDS, I fought the illness. I fought the people who didn't understand. I fought the medical people who didn't seem to have answers. And then I realized that this illness wasn't going away, that the people who didn't understand maybe never were going to understand. I decided that my fight was somehow to stay whole in the midst of the debilitation, the limitations, and the stripping process. My fight was to remain faithful to God, to do what I could to be an effective parent and wife. My fight was to refuse to give in to the discouragement.

In clarifying the battleground, I also identified the enemy: Satan, the great discourager. I never felt that he gave me the illness, but I knew that he wanted very badly to use it to destroy me, our family, our marriage. That was clear. I had to choose: Would I allow CFIDS to achieve the goals of the enemy or would I allow the fires of pain and suffering and uncertainty and grief to purify me and allow God to shine through it? I decided I would draw a line in the sand and say to Satan, "You will not defeat me or my family in this battle. We know what you're capable of doing, and we will stand." Using the image from Ephesians 6, I said, "We have armed ourselves with the resources God has given us so that when you attack us, we will be able to stand our ground. And after we have done everything, we will stand. We will stand firm. We will stand against discouragement. We will stand against family pressures. We will stand against other crises you toss our way. We will stand in the midst of your onslaughts and experience joy and faith and peace and strength."

"I remember feeling so spiritually dead," reflects Linda Moore Driscoll. "Here I was, a seminary professor on the mission field, and I felt empty. It was scary. I remember questioning many basic tenets of my faith: Did God really love me? Was I safe in his arms? Had he abandoned me? Had he rejected me for something I had done? Looking back, I can see that Satan was using the extreme fatigue and exhaustion in my life to distort my view of God and my relationship to him. I realize now that my spiritual deadness was more a function of my illness than my true spiritual state. But I couldn't see that then, and I was frightened."

Set Limits on the Questions

Linda Moore Driscoll's insights are significant. As CFIDS leads us to ask many questions about who God is and what we believe, remember that some of our questions are merely a reflection of our exhaustion and emptiness on all levels: physical, emotional, and spiritual.

Just as CFIDS forces us to set physical, emotional, and relational limits, we also need to set spiritual limits. Don't misunderstand me.

151

I'm not suggesting that we put a lid on all our questions. The psalms are full of anguished questions with which we can identify.

But realizing that exhaustion is one of the greatest threats to our spiritual health, let's not expect to answer deep spiritual questions when we have barely enough energy to survive physically and emotionally. We make a healthy choice when we decide to live with unanswered questions. "In everyone's life there is a point where all reasons, answers, and suggestions are completely exhausted. Circumstances are of a magnitude that is beyond rationality. To continue to pursue explanations would be like a surgeon who continues to probe a gunshot wound weeks after the bullet was removed. All poking will do is prevent healing. Even without insight, we often have to trust that healing is going on both physically and emotionally."[2]

A second rationale for setting limits on our questions comes from the Old Testament story of Job. As Job suffers losses on every front, he and his friends question God, often with brutal honesty. And God allows the questions. But he doesn't answer them. When God finally speaks, he asks Job questions that help Job realize who he is: the creator and sustainer of every aspect of life, the keeper of the mysteries, the source of reality. When God stops speaking, Job is quiet. He says to God, "My ears had heard of you but now my eyes have seen you."[3] In other words he says, "I thought I knew who you were, and I was upset with how you were treating me. But now that you have revealed yourself to me in such magnificence and power, I have no more questions and am sorry that I was so brash and demanding. Through all of this I have learned who you truly are."

Instead of answering Job's questions, God gave Job himself. And that's what he does with us too. We can afford to live with unanswered questions because God has promised to stand with us, to give us himself. We can afford to let go of our questions and respond to God when he says to us, "Trust me. Trust me." And that is the true basis of faith: choosing to trust when we have no answers.

Integrate Your Illness into Your Life

In her book *Why Waste Your Illness? Let God Use It for Growth*, Mildred Tengbom says, "If illness is to play a meaningful role for us, our task will be to integrate it into the fabric of our lives. How we integrate it, the difficulty or ease with which we integrate it, and the extent of its influence on our lives is determined by a number of different factors: our backgrounds, ages, intelligence, emotional development, religious beliefs, personalities, and past experiences with illness, suffering, death, or adversity."[4] She goes on to say that the first important step in integrating our illness into our lives is acceptance: "Dr. Paul Tournier points out that 'Resignation is passive. Acceptance is active. Resignation abandons the struggle against suffering. Acceptance strives but without rebellion. . . . Still there is no attitude more impossible for people—without the miraculous intervention of Christ—than the acceptance of suffering of any kind.' Without acceptance, however, integration will be impossible."[5]

Accept Your Pain

Acceptance results not only from learning to live with unanswered questions but also from learning to accept our pain. Scripture reminds us that pain is part of life. "Dear friends, do not be surprised at the painful trial you are suffering."[6] Twentieth-century people expect life to be free of pain. When we do feel pain, we rush to alleviate it or fix it. And when we can't do that, we feel victimized, singled out, rejected. But we have choices. "Pain is a bridge that we have to cross in this world, but we have to decide whether we will park on the bridge or go across to the future."[7]

As we mentioned in the last chapter, pain, suffering, and hardship are not all bad. God can use them as effective tools to shape our lives. That's one of the paradoxes of the Christian faith. In her lecture series *Suffering Is Not for Nothing*, Elisabeth Elliot says, "The deepest lessons in my own life have come out of the deepest sufferings. Out of the deepest waters and the hottest fires have come the deepest things I know about God."[8] I have always valued Elisabeth Elliot's insights, and during the first several months of living with CFIDS, I looked again to her words and writings. I chose to see Elliot as a mentor, someone who has walked the path of pain and has chosen to remain utterly faithful to the God who allowed her first husband, Jim

Elliot, to be brutally killed by a group of people with whom he was hoping to share his Christian faith. Her faith has substance precisely because it has been tested by loss, disappointment, and suffering. Her obedience is a model because it is a hard obedience, a choice made in the midst of many unanswered questions and pain.

In a letter to a friend, CFIDS sufferer Deborah Lynn Jansen wrote, "Karen, at times I would rather *not* pass through the fire. It hurts so much. But God is using CFIDS to make and mold Timen and me to be more like him. And that makes the pain worth it. I would rather live in pain and be in the process of becoming more like Christ than to live without pain and be an ineffective child of God."

When we, like Elisabeth Elliot and Deborah Lynn Jansen, can embrace the paradox that out of our deepest sufferings come the deepest things we know about God and the richest changes in our lives, then we can begin to accept our pain. "Our dark nights can become the most important times of our life even though years may pass before we are fully aware of the meaning of these confusing times of transition. Without suffering, there would not be transformation. 'If it were not for our unique wounds, we would not have our unique gifts.' Pain has its place."

Offer Your Illness to God

Once we can accept our pain, we can offer it up to God. During the seven years of our battle with CFIDS, our family has drawn strength from a framed card that hangs on the wall of our sunroom. On the card are these words from John Henry Newman:

If I am in sickness,
   my sickness may serve Him;
If I am in sorrow,
   my sorrow may serve Him.
He does nothing in vain.
He knows what He is about.

The words are both a challenge and a reminder. We have chosen to give ourselves to the Lord, and that means we can also give him our

CFIDS. We can serve him by giving him our sickness. And we can do that only because of our unshakable confidence in his goodness and wisdom. He does know what he is about in our lives. He does know what he is doing with CFIDS in our lives. He does nothing in vain.

One October morning in 1972, Elisabeth Elliot scratched out some rough thoughts on a piece of paper: "How to deal with suffering of any kind: (1) recognize it; (2) accept it; (3) offer it to God as a sacrifice; (4) offer yourself with it." Little did she know that later that day she would enter another period of suffering that would test her ability to practice those steps. That afternoon Elisabeth Elliot and her husband, Addison, learned that he had cancer—a cancer that would eventually take his life. "The doctors were predicting hideous mutilations that would happen to Ad before he died, and I felt I *could not* stand it. I began to cry out to the Lord. It became clear to me one night that my anguish was something God had put in my hands. It was a gift, a gift I needed to offer back to him."[10] Elliot discovered that when she gave God her anguish, her questions, her fears, her nothingness, he took her gift, transformed it, and made it "bread for the world." He takes the broken crumbs of our lives and uses them to feed others. I have feasted on the crumbs of Elisabeth Elliot's suffering because she offered them to God as a sacrifice.

When we offer our pain and illness to the Lord, he—the Suffering One, the Misunderstood One, the Offered-Up One—transforms it and frees us not only to live beyond the pain but also to believe that he can use our illness for good. His strength is made perfect in our weakness.

Recognize the Purpose of Your Illness

"I could never have survived my illness if I had not believed that God had a purpose for my suffering," said Gregg Fisher. "For a long time I could not see any purpose in my illness. It seemed like such a waste. Then I remembered the Old Testament story of Job. If nothing else, Job's suffering glorified God in the heavenly realm, to angel and demon alike, because Job remained faithful; he refused to curse God. In the end God could say to Satan, 'You were wrong. Job's faith in me wasn't based on things going smoothly in his life. Even when he lost everything, Job continued to love me!' I began to realize that I could glorify God in the same way.

"When I think of the spiritual ramifications of loving God in the midst of suffering, that brings significance to my life. Just as he did in Job's life story, God can look Satan in the eye and say, 'After all you've done to rob Gregg of his faith in me, he is still in the palm of my hand. Yes, he is suffering, but look at the faith I've given him. He will never ever let go of me, and there's nothing you can do about it.' That gives my suffering a focus. It gives purpose to what I have gone through and what I will go through. When people say to me, 'This illness can't be God's will for your life,' they take away the purpose of my suffering and therefore the purpose of my existence. While I remain ill, my purpose is wrapped up in my suffering. They are intertwined. I cannot separate them. To deny spiritual meaning to my illness means denying spiritual meaning to my life. I like the way J. B. Phillips expresses this idea: 'Therefore, I have cheerfully made up my mind to be proud of my weaknesses because they mean a deeper experience of the power of Christ. I can even enjoy weaknesses, sufferings, . . . and difficulties for Christ's sake. For my very weakness makes me strong in him.'"[11]

Along with Gregg Fisher, we can look below the surface of things and find purpose in our illness. In his book *You Gotta Keep Dancin'* Tim Hansel says, "Pain forces you to look below the surface. The tragedy is that many of us never have the courage to choose to do that. Hence we waste much of our life in bitterness and complaint, always looking for something else, never realizing that perhaps God has already given us sufficient grace to discover all of what we are looking for in the midst of our own circumstances."[12] As you explore the various ways CFIDS has changed you or touched people's lives, consider the purpose CFIDS may serve in your life.

CFIDS Reveals the Invisible Truths

Martin Luther once claimed, "Were it not for tribulation, I could not understand Scripture." Many of us who suffer from CFIDS agree. Our experiences bring a new reality and vitality to Scripture. We end up saying with Job, "We thought we knew you before, but this illness has allowed us to see you in a new way." The power of the paradoxes has become more real to me. I believed them when life had been running smoothly, but from the bottom of the valley, the paradoxes become even more meaningful, less mysterious: Eternal life comes through Christ's death; true life comes through death to self; strength comes through weakness; freedom comes through sacrifice to God; joy comes through pain; wholeness comes through brokenness; growth comes through pruning; pure gold comes through intense fire. During the years of living with CFIDS, I would find myself reading the Bible and saying, "Yes. That's it. That's who God is. That's the truth."

Eugene Peterson probes this paradox in his paraphrase: "My grace is enough; it's all you need. My strength comes into its own in your weakness. Once I heard that, I was glad to let it happen. I quit focusing on the handicap and began appreciating the gift. It was a case of Christ's strength moving in on my weakness. Now I take limitations in stride, and with good cheer, these limitations that cut me down to size. . . . I just let Christ take over! And so the weaker I get, the stronger I become."[13]

CFIDS Reveals Who We Are

"It is important to know of pain. It destroys our self-pride, our arrogance, our indifference toward others. It makes us aware of how frail and tiny we are and of how much we must depend upon the Master of the Universe."[14] CFIDS reveals who we are. On the one hand it reveals our impatience, our helplessness, our anger, our selfishness, and our stubbornness. But it also shows us how frail and tiny and weak we are and how much we need to depend on God.

Becky Turner comments, "I thought my whole world was over when I got CFIDS. I thought it was the worst thing that anybody could ever have. But now I see that I definitely have grown. Living with CFIDS and all the pain it has caused has stretched me in remarkable ways. I've had to learn to depend on the Lord, which has been good. I'm so much closer to the Lord."

Turner has learned the truth of what Horatius Bonar said: "Sickness takes us aside and sets us alone with God and with all the props removed, we learn to lean on God alone. Often nothing but adversity will do this for us."

"Living with CFIDS has shown me how much I want to run from difficult circumstances," says Jerry Montague. "If I were left to my own instincts, I don't know where I would be. I would probably be a bum someplace, just eking out an existence without a care. But my commitment to the Lord and to my family keeps me from running. Christ is the model; he sacrificed everything for us. His example helps me keep going, helps me be willing to sacrifice to keep my family going. I don't want to run away so much anymore. I decided to stand up and fight rather than run away."

"Our family's struggle with CFIDS has revealed some remarkable qualities," says Dave Masoner, whose wife and daughter both have CFIDS. "When I look at my wife, Barbara, I see that the Lord has produced in her a courage and an unflinching commitment to please him. Sometimes she doesn't see that, and she feels that her life is not very useful. But the Lord continues to send people to her. She has had to minister in different ways now that she is sick, but I have to say that since she's had CFIDS, her impact on others' lives has increased, not decreased. I have seen in her such a desire to open herself up to the Holy Spirit and allow him to use her. That openness has convicted me. And I see in our daughter, Nancy, tremendous wisdom for her age. She has been able to accept her CFIDS and integrate it into her life with exceptional grace, despite many personal disappointments. This illness has revealed some extraordinary qualities that the Lord is developing in each of them."

In our weakness, God gives us strength.

CFIDS Reveals God's Character

In his book *No Wonder They Call Him Savior* Max Lucado reminds us: "The next time you are called to suffer, pay attention. It may be the closest you ever get to God. It could very well be that the hand that extends itself to lead you out of the fog is a pierced one." In many ways CFIDS allows us to see the character of God—his love, his comfort, his mercy, his wisdom, his faithfulness.

In the epilogue to her husband's book about his struggle with CFIDS, Hettie Kenny describes what she has learned about God's character through Tim's CFIDS: "I do not believe that God made Tim sick, nor do I believe that He is responsible for all the trials we have been through. Living as we do in the natural world, people sometimes get sick. But that was no reason for me to turn my back on my faith or to reject my belief in God. Friends, co-workers, family members, and doctors have all disappointed me during this time, but God never has. At times, He has been the only source of comfort I have had. I have had doubts about the future and have questioned Tim's lack of progress, but I have not questioned God. He has helped me through this period. He meets me at my level—all I need to do is ask, and His comfort is there."[15]

His strength is revealed through our weakness.

CFIDS Reveals God's Power

"When I normally think of God's power, I think of the supernatural works of God," says Dave McAdoo, whose wife, Debi, has had CFIDS for over a decade. "But I have also sensed God's power in some of the quiet things. For instance, my boss has said to me, 'I don't know how you and your wife can face this horrible illness. I could never do what you are doing.' I'm not always aware of God's power in our battle with CFIDS. I often think it's a battle just to survive. But apparently my boss sees in me a strength and a stability, even though I often feel that everything is chaotic and anything but stable. I guess the fact that Debi and I *have* survived, that we *have* stayed together, that I *am* still a functioning human being at work is a demonstration of God's power. Who knows? In the end our ability to put one foot in front of the other may exhibit God's power more effectively than if Debi were well and we were involved in some sort of public ministry."

God uses our weakness to display his power.

CFIDS Teaches Us Endurance

The blind poet John Milton said, "It is not miserable to be blind. It is miserable to be incapable of enduring blindness." Maybe we can say the same thing of CFIDS: It is not miserable to have CFIDS. It is miserable to be incapable of enduring CFIDS.

Dictionaries tell us that *endure* means "to carry on despite hardship" and "to suffer patiently without yielding." If anyone had told me seven years ago that I would be cut down by a debilitating illness for at least seven years and that I would be the parent of a debilitated child for at least seven years, I would have said, "You've got the wrong person. Not me. I could *never* do that." But as we look back, we realize that the Lord has given us the courage and the grace to walk into each new day, for seven long years. That's endurance.

The quality of endurance, or perseverance, is part of a chain reaction the apostle Paul describes in his letter to the Christians in Rome. He says that we can accept and rejoice in our sufferings because suffering produces endurance, which in turn produces character, which in turn produces hope.[16] Endurance is the stepping-stone to the shaping of character qualities that we could not buy or learn or develop in any way other than suffering.

When we are weak, then he is strong.

CFIDS Teaches Us Compassion

"One of the things that Kurt and I have learned from CFIDS and from having two people in our family ill is compassion," says Sue Hedlund. "As a pastoral family, we now can relate to families that become dysfunctional when stressful circumstances hit them. I don't think I ever would have understood that before. But since I've been ill, we've been under some extreme stress at times, and things get all messed up. We now have a level of understanding and love for people who are under great stress."

In his book, *The Wounded Healer*, Henri Nouwen reminds us that the "wounded healer is sometimes the best healer." People who have suffered are best able to comfort and understand other people's suffering. One woman with CFIDS has found that to be true as she has walked with her brother through his early days of CFIDS. "When my brother first got sick, he was terrified. He has seen what CFIDS has done in my life and body, and he wanted no part of it. He didn't want to talk with anyone about it, but he would call me and ask questions. When he's afraid, he knows he can cry with me and voice all his fears and doubts and losses. I can't fix his problem, but I can give him what no one else can: compassion. I can feel with him because I've been there, and I'm *still* there."

God uses our weakness to strengthen others.

Stay Spiritually Strong

Many of us have found that CFIDS has robbed us of the ability to do the things that had always helped us stay spiritually strong: We can no longer attend church, participate in Bible studies and prayer groups, and study the Bible on our own. Several people I interviewed were too sick even to read the Bible or to pray.

To maintain some level of spiritual health, we need to redefine our spiritual disciplines. But before we do that, we also need to adjust our expectations. Remember that "sometimes our inability to trust God and believe in his Word comes not so much from spiritual unbelief as from physical exhaustion."[17] Sometimes our lack of passion or spiritual vitality is not because we're not doing the right things but because we are sick and coping with cognitive dysfunction.

Church Attendance

One CFIDS sufferer says, "The hardest aspect of coping with CFIDS for me is not being able to go to church. The spatial disorientation I feel when I'm in a crowd makes me nauseous and unable to tolerate even an hour in church. I miss it so much. I can worship alone on my couch, but it's not the same. It's not that I miss the sermon; I can hear that on tape. I miss the thrill of congregational singing and the encouragement of hearing people share how God has been active in their lives during the week. My wife and children can come home and tell me all about it, but it's not the same."

Barbara and Nancy Masoner soak up the spiritual nurture on the Christian radio station in their area. "I don't know what we would have done without the radio. We have the Christian station on all day, and many times the Lord has used a teaching or music to encourage and strengthen us."

Bible Study

Sue Hedlund laments, "My ability to study the Bible has drastically changed. I can't focus for more than five or ten minutes. That's a hard adjustment for me because I used to study large passages of Scripture for an hour at a time. At one point I could hardly read at all. I bought a large-print Bible, which I read for a few minutes several times a day, and that has made a big difference in my spiritual life."

Several people have found certain translations and paraphrases of the Bible easier to handle since they've become ill with CFIDS. One woman reports that *The New Century Bible,* which is written on a third-grade level, has helped her. "Although I am a college graduate, this version is the only one I read now because of the shorter sentences. I find it easier to comprehend." Other people find *The Living Bible* more manageable because it simplifies the concepts, even though the sentence structure is not simplified. The publishers of *The Living Bible* also publish a *Bible for Students,* whose text is the Simplified Living Bible, written on a grade-school level. A third option is *Today's English Version,* also known as *The Good News Bible.* The TEV simplifies the sentence structure as well as the concepts.

Like Sue Hedlund, I found I needed to change the way I studied the Bible. Unable to focus on large passages, I had to break down my study into very manageable pieces. I limited myself to one verse or one short passage a week and to only one line of a verse each day. Then I studied that one line word by word. This is how it worked. I kept a journal because I found I could concentrate better if I wrote down my thoughts. For instance, one week I selected Psalm 16:5–6 from the *Today's English Version, GNB.* In my journal, I wrote the verse:

You, Lord, are all I have,
and you give me all I need;
my future is in your hands.
How wonderful are your gifts to me;
how good they are.

Each day I focused on only one line and wrote about each word. I addressed all of my comments to God, so that each day's study was an interaction with God about his Word. I didn't try to interpret the verse so much as concentrate on each single word and what it communicated to me. This is what two days from my journal look like:

Day 1—*You, Lord, are all I have.*

You—*You,* Lord, are all I have. Lord, you allow me to address you so familiarly, even though you are the Lord of the universe. You desire for me to have an intimate relationship with you.

Lord—You, *Lord,* are all I have. You are my Lord, my master, boss, supervisor, leader, ruler. I am your slave, employee, follower, subject. I take my orders, direction, assignments from you.

Are—You, Lord, *are* all I have. Present tense, right now. Your relationship to me is not limited to one day in the past, but you are my Lord, now.

All—You, Lord, are *all* I have. My life has been reduced. But you fill up all the empty space. You are sufficient, more than I need. You are complete. You fill me. You are all-powerful, all-sufficient, all-knowing, all-seeing, all-wise, all-caring, and all-loving.

I—You, Lord, are all *I* have. You relate to me personally, not as one dot in a large mass of people but as an individual person, your creature, your child.

Have—You, Lord, are all I *have.* You are dependable. Other people come and go or prove to be untrustworthy, but you are the one I can have today and tomorrow and every tomorrow after that. You possess me, but you also allow me to "possess" you, have you. Praise your name!

Day 2—and you give me all I need.

And—*And* you give me all I need. In addition to being all-sufficient, all-loving, all-caring, you do more. You do immeasurably more than all I could ask or imagine.

You—And *you* give me all I need. It is you who give me all I need, not other people, not family, not friends: you. Help me to look only to you as the source of all I need. You personally give it to me. I don't have to order it out of a catalog and wait four to six weeks for it to be delivered.

Give—And you *give* me all I need. You don't sell me what I need at some exorbitant price. You don't say to me, "Well, if you're good enough, I'll give it to you." No. You *give* it to me, freely, generously, even when I don't ask for it.

Me—And you give *me* all I need. You don't give what I need to my church and hope I get a smidgen. You personally give it to me. And what you give me is uniquely suited to my life circumstances at the moment. You made me; you know what I need.

All—And you give me *all* I need. Here's that *all* again. You don't give me just a taste of what I need, just a crumb of what I need. You give me all of it. That *all* is beyond my comprehension.

I—And you give me all *I* need. What you give me is uniquely suited to how you have made me, what you have allowed in my life, and what your purposes are for me.

Need—And you give me all I *need*. You don't give me all I want; you give me all I need. All I need for what? You give me all I need to do your will, in the middle of CFIDS, in the middle of other stresses. When I think I need something, I must learn to ask, Do I need that to do your will?

I found this method of Bible study helpful for several reasons. First, I was able to focus on the small bits. Second, as I wrote my responses, I felt as if I was truly interacting with God. Third, as I wrote the line at the beginning of each response, I was able to memorize that day's line. Fourth, later on that day or during sleepless nights later that week when I felt as if I was slipping away from God,

I could recall these small bits of Scripture and reconnect with the reality of who God is and what he was teaching me. Even though I first studied this passage five years ago, I still go back to it and many of the other verses in my journal because they have anchored themselves to a place deep in my heart and soul. They keep me grounded when I lose my moorings.

Robin Ralston has used a similar method to help her focus on Scripture. "I've written on note cards special verses that help me focus on God's goodness and his purposes in my life. When I am feeling very sick, my faith ebbs, and I start believing lies and negative stuff. I have learned to cling to the promises I've written on the cards. I keep them by my bed. Some of the cards have Scripture verses; others have meaningful quotations from books I've read. Still others are statements that I need to tell myself because I know it's a problem area. I've had these cards for over four years now, but I still use them. When I am severely sick, I read them over and over, every hour of every single day. Some of the verses and quotations on Ralston's faith-talk cards include the following:

> *Let the beloved of the LORD rest secure in him, for he shields him all day long, and the one the LORD loves rests between his shoulders.*
>
> DEUTERONOMY 33:12

> *The LORD will fight for you; you need only to be still.*
>
> EXODUS 14:14

> *Even when we are too weak to have any faith left, he remains faithful to us and will help us, for he cannot disown us who are part of himself, and he will always carry out his promises to us.*
>
> 2 TIMOTHY 2:13 TLB

I have also found that personalizing or paraphrasing Scripture passages helps me experience the reality of God's promises. For instance, words from Romans 8 come alive in new ways when I per-

165

sonalize them. "Will our family's experiences with CFIDS separate us from the love of Christ? No, in all our illness and limitations and seeming defeats, we are more than conquerors through Jesus Christ, who loves us. For we are convinced that neither the possibility that we will never recover nor the possibility that the rest of our family may become ill with CFIDS; neither misunderstanding from medical professionals nor disbelief from school officials; neither additional family stresses nor mounting medical bills; neither discouragement nor relapses—nothing will be able to separate us from God's love as he expresses it to us in Christ Jesus, our Lord."

During periods when Alisa is so sick that she loses perspective, I try to help her find spiritual balance. In response to a recent time of despair, I bought her a blank journal with a picture of a garden on the cover. Inside the cover I wrote this inscription: "This book is your secret garden. In it God has hidden treasures for you to discover. He says to you in Isaiah 45:3, 'I will give you the treasures of darkness, riches stored in secret places.' In the midst of your dark experiences, God has hidden special treasures."

Then on the pages of the blank book I wrote, "To find the treasure I have hidden for you, read [2 Corinthians 4:7–11 or Romans 5:3–5 or Isaiah 51:1–3 or others]." Then at the bottom of each page, I wrote a question: "What treasure did you find in your illness today?"

Meditation

Another helpful tool to maintaining spiritual health is meditation, which can take a variety of forms: meditation on Scripture, meditation with the help of devotional books, meditation on the person of Christ. Jan Markell, who has suffered from CFIDS since 1979, provides us a helpful resource in her book *Waiting for a Miracle: Devotions for Those Who Are Physically Weak*. Markell includes in each chapter a few quotations, a short reflection, a poem/prayer, and several Bible passages for further meditation. Topics include loneliness, laughter, waiting, fear, peace, and guilt. Candy Feathers has found in Oswald Chambers' devotional book *My Utmost for His Highest* a source of encouragement and strength, especially after she learned that Chambers suffered from debilitating illness for much of his life.

Like many of you, I struggle with long sleepless nights. In an attempt to hold at bay the anxiety and fear that so often threaten us in the silence and darkness of the night, I have practiced two forms of meditation that I can do while I lie in bed. First, I meditate on the Scripture verse from my Bible study journal, again walking through each line word by word.

Second, I visit a "sanctuary." I have always been intrigued by our use of the word *sanctuary* to describe a place of worship. The word denotes two things to me: This place is both sacred and safe. As I lay in bed, with both my body and my mind tossing and turning, I realized that I needed to visit a sanctuary, a place where I could meet with Christ in safety. Unhindered by the fact that I was in a bed in a dark room, I visualized meeting with Christ. My favorite sanctuary is the throne room of the Neuschwanstein castle in southern Germany. Several years before I got sick, Bas and I toured this fairy-tale castle that is featured on many German travel posters. Getting into the castle was not an easy thing. After buying our admission tickets, we walked up a steep hill for forty minutes, then stood in line for another hour outside the castle before we were funneled into an English-language tour line, where we waited yet another half hour. Finally we were herded along with dozens of other people through the various rooms of the castle. The room I remember most clearly is the throne room. The vaulted room is several stories high, with massive lapis pillars and detailed Wagnerian murals on the walls. The raised platform that would have held the throne is empty; King Ludwig, who ordered the opulent castle built, died before he could move in.

Whenever I visit this sanctuary in my mind, I have no trouble getting into the castle. There are no lines, no interpreters, no jostle of bodies. As I walk down the hall to the throne room, the light from the room pervades the dark hall. When I enter the room, the throne is there, majestic and grand. And on the throne sits Christ, the King. He is breathtakingly brilliant, and he is alone. When he sees me peer in the doorway, he gets up from his throne and bounces down the steps, his arms open in welcome. "Lynn! I'm so glad to see you. How *are* you? I have so much to tell you!" He leads me up the steps and lets me sit at his feet as we continue to talk. Again, he listens, encourages me, and gives direction.

I have learned to take other people with me into this throne room. On nights when I am particularly anxious about something in Alisa's life, I take her with me. When Christ sees her, he puts his arm around her and leads her up the steps. Most often I leave the room at that point, confident that Alisa is in good hands. Most often I also fall asleep at that point, knowing that Christ is with us and all is safe.

If you have had a hard time connecting with God, especially if you have been unable to attend church, ask the Lord to provide an appropriate sanctuary for you to meet with Christ. Visualize him as your comforter, counselor, healer, teacher, guide. Meet with him anytime. Entrust to him your cares and your family. Rest in his love.

Prayer

"When I became ill, I was in desperate need of prayer," says Shawn Fisher. "I couldn't pray for myself anymore. It was beyond me. I couldn't do it. That's when I learned what intercessory prayer is, that other people interceded and prayed my prayers for me. I really needed that, and it humbled me.

"Now that Gregg and I have recovered enough to go out occasionally, we attend a prayer group. The people in that group pray for us even when we are too weak to pray for ourselves. Unless people have been that sick, they can't understand what that means. The support and the power of the prayers were incredibly healing. Sometimes we would use all our strength just to go to that meeting, so when we got there, we were too sick to participate. When the people saw how sick we were, they would come over and pray for us right then. We felt as if we were bathed in prayer. We needed it every week. We needed people to pray *with* us, not just for us. Sometimes they had no words to pray. They would just lay their hands on us and say nothing. Sometimes they cried with us. Many times we could sense God touching us, releasing us from anger, delivering us from oppression, and freeing our hearts and minds to respond to him. The mysteries of prayer are so deep, but God has shown us that he does answer prayer."

Like Shawn and other people with CFIDS, my prayers are often mere cries for help. When I wake up in the morning, I face what I call "the wall"—a crush of pain, weightiness, stiff and painful joints, nausea, aching lungs, a sense that I can't move my body. I feel more exhausted and sick than when I crawled into bed eight or ten or twelve hours earlier. If I didn't know that these symptoms will pass, I would not get up. My first flash of consciousness is the pain and ache. The second is an instinctive cry to the Lord, "Help! Help!" Then the words take on a Jacob-like plea, "Unless you promise to be with me today, I cannot get out of bed and face the day." Then I repeat the phrases I learned as a child in catechism class: "My only comfort in life and in death is that I am not my own but belong—body and soul—to my faithful Savior Jesus Christ."[18] That is my grounding point: This body and this soul, weak and falling apart, belong to Christ and are his to do with as he pleases. That gives me the strength and the comfort and perspective to be able to go into another day.

Tapes

Although CFIDS may deprive us of the joys of meeting with other Christians, many CFIDS sufferers have compensated for this loss by listening to audio tapes or watching videotapes of their church's service and tapes of conference speakers. As I mentioned earlier, the tapes of Elisabeth Elliot's series *Suffering Is Not for Nothing* helped me turn the corner to acceptance.[19] I could lie on my couch, with my eyes closed, and listen to her authoritative voice reminding me that even though we fear the world may cave in on us, God walks through our pain with us and uses our pain for his good purposes. Helen Gruelle recommends June Hunt's tape, "Chronic Illness: Power Through Daily Pain."[20]

Books on tape can provide another source of spiritual nurture. Several people I interviewed use the Bible on tape. Books on tape are available in increasing number in bookstores and libraries. A large church in our town has stocked its library with hundreds of current audio and videotapes, which can be rented for a nominal fee. A talking-books service, offered by the Library of Congress and individual state libraries, is available to people with CFIDS. Most public libraries have a brochure, "Library Services for the Blind and Physically Handicapped," and application forms for this free service. If you are unable to find on tape a book you are interested in hearing, you can request that the service put that book on tape. See the "Find the Help You Need" section for more information.

Music

"I can't emphasize enough how important music was to my spiritual health during my most debilitated years," says Shawn Fisher. "I couldn't read books or listen to books on tape because my brain wouldn't process the words. But somehow music, especially praise music, penetrated the barrier and reached my soul. I didn't have any energy to sing along. I would just lie and listen, almost passively. Then suddenly one song would touch me deep inside, and my heart would whisper, 'Yes. I agree with that. Praise you, God.' The music was so healing, and it helped me worship in my heart when I couldn't worship any other way."

Robin Ralston also found solace and nurture in music. "I made a tape of songs that were special to me. One side of the tape included songs about suffering or pain or growing; the other side included soothing orchestral music. The music encouraged me and helped when I was too sick to read. I could just lie there, listen to the music, and focus my mind in the right direction. During a six-month relapse I listened to that tape sometimes five times a day. The lyrics were helpful because they were my personal songs. Music continues to be one of my major sources of strength because it takes my mind away from my body somehow."

If your spiritual health has been threatened because of your CFIDS, don't give up. Continue to search for ways that God can touch your life and help you to grow.

Chapter **9**

Voices from the Valley

God never leaves us in the valley alone, and this is our comfort. No matter how dark it becomes, how fearful it seems, or how intense the pain, God is with us.

CHARLES STANLEY, "THE BELIEVER'S VALLEY EXPERIENCES"

When CFIDS hit our family, it plunged me into a valley. I didn't want to be in the valley. I preferred the mountaintops, where I could see what was ahead as well as where I had come from, where I felt on top of things, where I felt secure. I had spent most of my life trying to avoid the valley, the place of wandering, shadow, fear, darkness, and suffering. Suffering. That's what I most wanted to avoid. I wanted to understand suffering, but from a distance, please.

When I first landed on the floor of the valley, I wanted to scramble back up the sides, to get to the ridges, to get *out* of the valley. But the sides were too steep, and I had no strength. I had to rest. I grumbled about being in the valley. I wanted to get back to the mountaintops, where *real* life existed. But I couldn't move. I couldn't go anywhere.

If I couldn't get out of the valley, then at least I wanted to find a shortcut through the valley or a path around the top of the valley. But I found none. Words from John Baille gave me direction: "When Thou callest me to go through the dark valley, let me not persuade myself that I know a way around." I had to accept that the only way to the other side of the valley was to walk through it.

Forced to rest, made to lie down, I began to look around. To my surprise I found the valley restful, lush, verdant. The quiet richness soothed me and helped me catch my breath. As I lay there, I could hear voices of people scurrying around the top edges of the valley, laughing, talking, staying busy, busy, busy.

But then I heard other voices, voices in the valley. As I looked around, I saw dozens, no, hundreds of people. Some of them lay in pain. Others rested in groups. Still others talked and laughed. As my eyes adjusted to the shadows in the valley, I noticed that some of the people had fallen into the valley from steep cliffs and were cut and badly bruised. Some descended somewhat gradually into the valley. Others, I could tell, had been in the valley for decades.

From the conversations, I could discern that some of the people, like me, had been pushed into the valley by CFIDS, others by various other physical, emotional, or spiritual crises. As I listened, I could hear them share their fears and pain or share words of encouragement and comfort.

As the weeks and months wore on, I discovered that the valley is a place of healing. The shadows that initially frightened me have become shade to protect me from the heat and storms. The quietness that initially made me feel alone has restored and revived my body and soul. I realized that the valley is not at all barren but full of wonderfully rich people from whom I have learned courage and faith and obedience and hope. I have found some of you in the valley.

And at the deepest and darkest part of the valley, I have found Christ, the Gentle Healer, the Comforter, the Encourager, the Faithful One. I was at first surprised because I thought he spent most of his time on the mountaintop. But he is here in the valley, every day, every hour to comfort us, feed us, fill us with joy, and help us find the way.

Some of us will move through the valley and come out the other end. Others of us will stay here to comfort the newcomers and introduce them to Christ, who will encourage and strengthen them and teach them the lessons of the valley.

Voices from the Valley

While we are in the valley, we can help each other. We can cry together, laugh together, pray together, and learn together. In an attempt to do that, this chapter shares several voices from the valley. Some voices are from people caught in frightening caverns. Others have just discovered a cool, refreshing river at the bottom of the valley. Others can see the beginnings of a path to a lush place. At other times we hear the voice of Christ as he speaks to people in the valley.

This chapter shares with you some of the voices I heard as I interviewed people for this book. Allow these voices from the valley to comfort you and give you hope.

Voices of Hope

"As I look back on the first eight years of illness," says Shawn Fisher, "I can't imagine how we got through them. I was so sick that all I did was hold on. I used all my energy just to move from one hour to the next, just to live through another day. Before we got sick, both Gregg and I were preparing for ministry, Gregg as a pastor, I as a counselor. When CFIDS hit our bodies, it stripped us of our ability to use any of the tools we needed to stay spiritually strong. We couldn't attend church. We couldn't study the Bible. We could barely talk to each other. We had no energy, no desire or ability to read. We did nothing to keep our faith alive.

"Only in the past few years have I been able to begin to process what has gone on in our life. And what amazes me is that through it all, the Lord hung on to us. He didn't let go. We had nothing to give, but he gave everything to us.

"When we look back, we can't imagine anything harder on a marriage. I remember feeling so sick that if Gregg asked me to repeat myself, I got angry. My throat hurt so much, and it was so much effort to say anything. How do you have a marriage when that's all the strength you have?

"We can only say again that God kept us together. Our marriage is a rock. We have a special bond that very few marriages have. On the one hand we have given up almost everything. We don't have a lot of the common and wonderful experiences that most married people have. But when we look at the love God has given us for each other, we realize how much we've been blessed. Even when we're so sick that

173

we can't move off the couch, we're blessed with a love and a friendship that is so deep.

"It is truly a measure of God's grace that our marriage is so solid. With two of us so sick and debilitated, what do we have to put into a marriage? Nothing. Nothing. Living with one spouse ill is hard enough, but at least the well spouse can be stronger physically, emotionally, and spiritually. With both of us ill, neither has anything to give. And we have been so needy.

"During the first six months of illness, I lived in excruciating pain. All I could do was to try to breathe and survive. A Bible verse I held on to in those months was from Ephesians 3:16. Part of it says, 'Out of his glorious riches, he may strengthen you with power through his Spirit in your inner being, so that Christ may dwell in your hearts through faith.' I thought, *This is a good promise. God will strengthen me with his power.*

"I believed and waited. I believed and waited some more. Then I got angry with God. I was believing his Word, but he wasn't giving me strength with his power. I felt he had let me down. Where was that strength? I was barely, barely surviving, and I didn't know how I was even going to go on. As I looked back and wondered how I had survived those six months, I realized that I had gotten through *every one of those days.* I realized that God *had* given me strength. I had thought 'strength with his power' meant that it would be easy, that he would lift me up, that I would be able to float through this. But I came to realize that he had given me a quiet strength, a strength to endure, a strength to sustain me. Looking back, I see his faithfulness. He brought strength for that day or that hour.

"When I first found meaning in this verse, I had concentrated only on the first phrase: 'strengthen you with power.' Only later did I see that the promise was, 'He may strengthen you with power through his Spirit in your inner being, so that Christ may dwell in your heart through faith.' That's what he was doing; he was strengthening me in my inner being so that Christ can dwell in my heart. The power was in my inner being. It wasn't in my body. I had been looking for the wrong kind of power in the wrong place. My inner being was truly strengthened by God; there's no other way I could have endured. God has been completely faithful to that promise. Christ does dwell in my heart through faith. That has never wavered. I don't always feel that faith, and I can't always act on it or relate to God the way I want, but that faith has been there, despite me, despite CFIDS. That is a powerful realization.

"I was troubled in those early years because I felt I couldn't 'seek' God. I have come to accept that God honors my inner desires, even if I can't act on that desire. If deep in my inner being I even only wish I could relate to God, then I think I will stay spiritually healthy. I have learned to accept my limitations. I believe God is still with me and that at some point I will be able to relate to him again in other ways. The verse in Deuteronomy 6:5 says, 'Love the LORD your God with all your heart and with all your soul and with all your strength.' Sometimes I'm too sick even to open my Bible for weeks, and yet I'm still loving God with all my strength. And he knows it. People have said to me, 'I don't see how you could ever be too sick to pray. Even people who are dying can pray.' Although people couldn't understand the type of debilitation I suffered, I knew that God understood, and I gave him whatever strength I had.

"The purpose of my life is for God to be glorified. And I feel that even if I'm lying in bed and no one ever sees me, even if God never uses my suffering to help others, God can still be glorified. I can fulfill what he wants me to do by being faithful to him, just by loving him and trusting him. When I was in college, I gave to the Lord by leading Bible studies and doing other acts of service. But all of that was nothing compared to this. I think that this is more pleasing to God because he knows it's like the widow's mite. I give him all I have to give. It may look like so little, but it's actually more than I've ever given him."

Voices of Direction

"Once I left school, I never heard from any of my 'friends,'" says Sharon Walk, who became ill with CFIDS while she was in high school. "Toward the end of the summer, I started to become depressed. All the kids in my class were getting ready for their senior year, thinking about what car they wanted, where to go to college, and I was going to miss another year of school. None of the treatments my doctor was trying were helping my symptoms, and that made me more depressed. I was so sick. I didn't think I could take it anymore. I didn't want to die; I wanted to live, really live, not have to fight to get through each day.

"Several months later I hit bottom. I was exhausted emotionally as well as physically. I wanted to give up. I prayed that God would tell me what I had to do so I would get better. I promised to help my mom more and to try harder in school. It didn't help. One day, when I was bored, I started to read *Comeback* by Dave Dravecky. Dave was a professional baseball player who got cancer in his arm. He talked a lot about God and that he didn't believe God punishes people with illnesses. He said that God has reasons for everything but that we aren't meant to understand the reasons. He said there is nothing we can do or could have done to change what happened in the past. Dave was able to put his trust in God and ask for strength to deal with whatever life had in store for him. While I was reading the book, I started to cry. It was the first time I truly believed in my heart that it wasn't my fault that I had gotten sick. I felt an overwhelming sense of peace. That changed my life forever.

"I realized that I didn't have to be miserable, that it was okay to be sick and happy. I asked God to help me to understand what his plan for my life was and to help me to get back on track. The answers didn't come all at once, but they did come. I've learned how precious life and health are. I've learned to appreciate all the little things in life and to treasure every moment. I also can find the good in almost anything."

Voices of Acceptance

"I've struggled with many questions during the thirteen years I've been ill," asserts Gregg Fisher. "But recently I've been trying to answer the most basic question: What does God expect of my life?

"I tend to think of myself as made up of a physical side, a mental side, an emotional side, and a spiritual side. The spiritual is most important, the mental is next, the emotional is third, and the physical is least important. Unfortunately, a chronic illness sometimes reverses those elements. The physical becomes the most important because we become so conscious of our pain and suffering. This causes us to lose emotional balance, which affects how we think, which in turn destroys our connection with God. All this happens because we've reversed the order of our relationship to God.

"The first verse of Romans 12 helps us restore our spiritual balance. 'In view of God's mercy, to offer your bodies as living sacrifices, holy and pleasing to God—this is your spiritual act of worship.' Anyone living with CFIDS can appreciate and really understand what it means to offer your body as a living sacrifice. It's saying to God, 'I trust that you know what's best for my life. Here is my body to do with as you will.' Chronic illness, lack of freedom, lack of money, whatever it entails, this is my act of worship. Worship is found not only in churches, singing hymns, but it's also found in saying, 'Lord, use my body.'

"Another Scripture passage that has helped is Ephesians 2:8–10. It reminds me, 'For it is by grace you have been saved, through faith—and this not from yourselves, it is the gift of God.' I think Christians tend to read that and believe that their salvation is a gift from God, but everything else is up to them. And that's not the way it is. Everything that I am spiritually is a gift from God. It's 'not by works, so that no one can boast.' But I am God's workmanship, created in Christ Jesus to do good works, which God has prepared from the beginning. Everything that I could possibly ever do for God has already been prepared in advance.

"Obviously faith is the key. But Hebrews 12:2 reminds us that Jesus is the 'author and perfecter of our faith.' I can't even have an ounce of faith if God didn't give it to me. The first part of that verse says, 'Let us fix our eyes on Jesus.' The time I mess up is when I start looking at myself and all my failures. That's my personality. I am very, very hard on myself. But if I can keep my focus on Jesus, I can believe that I'm where he wants me to be. Then I can know that what I'm going through and who I am is my spiritual act of worship to God."

Christ in the Valley

As I hear these various voices from the valley, I think of these words: "In the Book of Job it says that God will test us and try us until we 'come forth as gold' (Job 23:10). Someone once asked a goldsmith how long he kept the gold in the fire. His reply: 'Until I can see my face in it.'"[1] I see Christ in the faces of the people in the valley.

I see Christ in the valley not only in people with CFIDS but also in the thousands of other suffering people who cluster in the valley. Some of these people have endured suffering that is far beyond anything I could imagine.

I remember talking with a farmer in Senegal several years ago while traveling with my husband to famine areas in West Africa. It was November, the beginning of harvest. But the crops bore very little grain. The rains hadn't come at planting time, and when a few rains had come, they had washed away the seeds from the hard ground. Once again the farmers had to plant their crops, this time using their food grain for seeds. After several plantings, some of the millet had grown—a small crop, but at least a crop. Then three weeks before harvest, an infestation of locusts destroyed the rest of the crop. They had no food for the coming year.

As I listened to the farmer talk about his situation, I said, "This must be a very difficult time for you. How has this disaster affected your perspective of who God is?" I fully expected him to talk about his discouragement, his questions.

Instead, he said, "Oh, God is good! Just because we have no food doesn't change who God is."

I was stunned at his response. His words challenged and chastened me. And as we traveled that year from village to village in drought and famine areas, person after person said, "God is so good. He is faithful. He will care for us." These villagers, who had *nothing*, could affirm God's goodness in the midst of drought and famine.

Their voices in the valley have reminded me to affirm God's goodness in the midst of CFIDS and to affirm that our difficult circumstances do not change God's character.

Christ has also used other events to reveal himself to me in the valley. Before Alisa and I became ill, our family took very active vacations: We put our pup tents and a cooler in the car and hit the road to explore national parks, climb mountains, and probe caves together.

But for the last several years we've had to rent cabins with couches. Last year we bought a used camping trailer, thinking we were well enough to handle sedentary camping. We would still rest, but we could do it outdoors. We reserved a site on the shores of the Grand Traverse Bay in Michigan, a lovely spot from which we could watch the sun set, the schooners dance in the bay, the herons play on the shore, and the beam from the lighthouse rhythmically cut the dark sky. This would be a tranquil, restful time, right?

Wrong. A two-day storm of near-hurricane-force winds ripped apart the zipper of the tent on our trailer, so we not only had to move from our site to get out of the storm, but we also had to disassemble the trailer so that we could take the tent to be fixed. This was not restful. In addition, Alisa was very sick for most of the two weeks, unable to do much more than look longingly at the water. She couldn't eat; she couldn't even sit up.

One day it rained hard all day. Rather than feel like captives in our tent trailer, we opted to travel to a nearby coastal town to find dry refuge in a library situated on the waterfront. We had hoped a change of scenery and the lure of some books would lift Alisa's spirits. The library even had a couch on which she could lie. But instead of feeling any better, Alisa grew worse.

We finally packed up and returned to our dripping campsite. By this time the rain had cleared up, but our entire campsite was wet. My spirits were also damp.

Bas and I fixed ourselves cups of tea and took our chairs to sit at the waterfront to watch the sun set behind the lighthouse. I was losing it. Here we were on our vacation, trying to find a little rest, a respite from the stresses of life, and Alisa was too sick even to eat or to lie on a beach chair. It wasn't fair.

As my feelings tumbled out, I sobbed. "Bas, I can't take this anymore. I am so discouraged. Where is God in this illness? Can't this child have one break? Can't we have just one or two weeks that refresh us, that are not full of disappointment, that are not so hard?" I shook my fists at the sky. I wanted to scream out at the waves.

Then a rumble of thunder behind me caught my attention. As I turned around, I saw the dark clouds of the storm that had passed over us an hour or two earlier. And there in the midst of the dark, threatening storm clouds arched a magnificent rainbow. I gasped. It was as if the Lord was saying, "I know. I know your frustration. I know what you're going through. But I am here. I'm in the storm too."

That rainbow, and all that it represented of God's grace and mercy and faithfulness, gave me perspective that day to say, "Okay, we can go on. We will persevere, and we will not let this illness get us down. We will not crumble under it." The rainbow gave me that quieting sense that God would be with us forever, no matter what, no matter how sick Alisa gets, no matter how long she is sick, no matter how long I'm sick.

Through the rainbow I heard the voice of Christ say, "I am with you. And that's all that matters."

As we walk through the valley, may Christ speak to us in various ways: through other people who have CFIDS, through other people who have suffered, and through his creation.

Not only does CFIDS affect our physical, emotional, relational, and spiritual lives, but it also deeply touches our family relationships. The next section will explore ways to maintain healthy husband-wife and parent-child relationships. In chapter 10 spouses share ways they have worked to maintain a healthy marriage through the devastation of CFIDS. Chapter 11 helps us understand children with CFIDS as they share their struggles and insights. Chapter 12 looks at the unique challenges of parenting a child with CFIDS.

Part 4

Family Life with CFIDS

Chronic illness disrupts a family's usual patterns and dynamics. All families develop ways of coping with stress over time, but chronic illness ... lingers and causes continuing disruption. Families that are cohesive, flexible, resourceful, and adaptable will be more successful at coping with CFIDS.

KATRINA BERNE, *RUNNING ON EMPTY*

- Maintain a healthy marriage in spite of CFIDS
- Understand children with CFIDS
- Help and advocate for CFIDS children

Chapter *10*
Maintain a Healthy Marriage

CFIDS has threatened our marriage in many ways. I remember times when I wanted to walk away, thinking I couldn't take it anymore. But when I married Jim, I vowed to him and to the Lord that I would love him whether he was ill or well. I take that commitment very seriously, and the Lord has given me the strength to stay and do what needs to be done.

LYNN HEKMAN, WIFE OF A CFIDS SUFFERER

None of us would disagree with Lynn Hekman: CFIDS threatens the stability of our marriages. The losses, grief, changes, drain, and strain that are forced on our marriages seem overwhelming, endangering the very relationship that can most nurture us during the battle. Many marriages don't survive. One spouse interviewed for this book reports, "I was appalled to learn from one support group that twenty-three out of twenty-five of their members had lost spouses by divorce because of CFIDS."

I am happy to report that many marriages also survive CFIDS; some even thrive in the midst of the valley. This chapter will explore some of the ways husbands and wives are surviving the stresses of a debilitating illness. The marriages described in this chapter represent a broad spectrum: from young marriages to marriages of nearly forty years; from marriages that had a head start before CFIDS struck to marriages that have been marked by CFIDS before the couple spoke marriage vows; from marriages in which only one spouse is ill to marriages in which both spouses have been utterly debilitated. Some of the husbands and wives in this chapter are also parents; others weep because their battle with CFIDS prevents them from becoming parents.

Wherever you fall in this spectrum, your marriage faces unique stresses because of CFIDS. Any marriage takes adjustment and work as it moves through stages and faces various issues. But those issues are exaggerated and intensified by the illness. Husbands and wives who had trouble communicating before the illness struck often will have even more trouble when the illness adds further strain; couples who disagreed about finances before CFIDS will find those differences accentuated by the illness. Perhaps even more difficult are the dynamics faced by couples whose entire marriage has been marked by CFIDS in one or both spouses. These couples often do not have the objectivity to see what issues are related to the illness and what issues they would have faced even if one or both of them had not been sick.

Impact of CFIDS on Marriage

As you think about your marriage, remember that many of the CFIDS issues we've already discussed in this book are also true of marriage. Our marriages face unbearable losses: companionship, joint activities, joint social involvement, the ability to plan our lives together, the ability to care for each other the way we wish to, the ability to share in active ministry together, the ability to maintain a satisfying sexual life, and for some, the ability to raise a family together.

"CFIDS has wreaked havoc on our marriage," reflects Deborah Lynn Jansen. "When we were first married, we were such a happy couple, full of romance and love and care for each other. When we got afflicted with this disease, our lives were turned upside down. With both of us sick with CFIDS, it has been hard to earn money. We both have been too sick to have any quality time together. We are barely hanging on. Many problems have surfaced in our relationship, causing us to work very hard to maintain our marriage. It's a major struggle, but we are committed to each other, and we are trusting the Lord to give us the grace to persevere and love each other in new ways."

"Craig and I are on the journey to working out our marriage with this illness," says Robin Ralston. "When we got married, we dreamed of working together as a husband-wife ministry team. CFIDS shattered those dreams. At first we tried everything to get me better. Then we had to accept the fact that I wasn't getting better. At one point we were even separated for six months. Craig was finishing up his doctoral degree at the same time that I was in a relapse and needed constant care. We had no more money and couldn't pay our apartment rent. So we decided that I would move to my parents' home and Craig would move in with a single friend and finish his studies. That was a most difficult time in our marriage. Through all the ups and downs of our lives with this illness, the Lord is teaching us how to love each other."

Singer and songwriter Twila Paris describes the impact of CFIDS on her life. "For a long time I didn't talk about the extent of my husband, Jack's, struggles with chronic fatigue syndrome.... A few years ago we thought he had completely recovered, that his battles with CFS were behind us. But since then he has gone through some exceptionally rough times physically. I've realized that if we don't share what we are learning through a bad situation, part of the good God wants to bring out of it is lost.... The longer Jack's illness goes on, the more my heart is dredged.... I had all these dreams of what we would do together, like going out to dinner, visiting friends, simple things that we ended up not being able to do because Jack didn't have the energy. My dreams died hard. I felt like saying, 'Well, God, that's enough. That's all we can endure.' But God decides how much we can endure. And he knows we can endure more than we think we can. The Bible very clearly speaks about suffering being a critical part of the Christian life. Growth is almost always prefaced by suffering.... We can choose to believe not only in what God promises he will do, but also in who he is. I want to respond in a way that brings glory to God."[1]

As we recognize our losses and grieve them, we need to move on to redefine our marriage relationship, to carve out a new life that is meaningful within the limitations of the illness. Once again the irony is that coping with CFIDS drains us of so much energy that we often have no energy for the relational work that any marriage needs.

CFIDS demands from husbands and wives an uncommon love. It stretches and tests our commitment to each other, forcing us to face some hard questions. What can we expect from our marriage now that one or both of us are sick? How can we find meaning in our marriage even though one or both of us are incapacitated? What can we do to strengthen our marriage during the long siege of CFIDS? How can we maximize what we *do* have in our relationship? How can God develop an uncommon love in us so that we can love our spouses in the unique ways they need during a time of illness? How can God use this illness in our relationship for his good purposes? How can God use our marriage, broken though it is by illness and stress, to strengthen others?

As I listened to husbands and wives share their pain and hopes, I was struck by the miracles. It is a miracle that many of them are still together despite incomprehensible pressures. It is a miracle that they have been able to put one foot in front of the other, some of them for ten and twelve years. It is a miracle that some of them have learned to love in deep and tender ways. It is a miracle that many of these couples have maintained not only a balanced marriage through CFIDS but also a balanced family. These couples may not have seen miraculous healing of their bodies, but they have seen miraculous perseverance and grace to love and be faithful in the midst of debilitating disease.

CFIDS Stresses the Healthy Spouse

While this book focuses on the many stresses in the life of the CFIDS sufferer, it must not underestimate the pain, loss, and helplessness that the healthy spouse feels. "This illness has been devastating to my husband too," says one CFIDS sufferer. "He has lost his life too. When he wants me to go with him to social and church functions or to be able to hike and do the things we used to do, I have to say no. When I push to go or do things, it never is very satisfactory to either of us. He feels anger and frustration with my limitations, and I feel anger and frustration for causing him anger and frustration. I sometimes fear that he will leave me to get on with his life, and I would not blame him at all. CFIDS places on him stresses that are heavier than many he has faced so far in our several decades of marriage."

As I listened to healthy spouses talk about their experiences, I often felt that, in a sense, they "have CFIDS" too. Certainly not in the physical sense. But spouses of CFIDS sufferers face many of the same emotional, relational, and spiritual questions and challenges that their sick spouses face: the losses, frustration, helplessness, numbness, waiting, spiritual questions, anger, grief, changes, the chronic emotions. But very few people, including sometimes the husbands and wives themselves, recognize that. Few people recognize the burden that healthy spouses of CFIDS sufferers carry.

"Keeping a marriage going and keeping a family of seven going during Jim's long years of CFIDS is the hardest thing I've ever had to do in my life," says Lynn Hekman. "It helps me tremendously if people express genuine concern not only for Jim but also for me and for our children. Spouses of CFIDS sufferers carry a lot. They need someone to say, 'How are *you* doing?'"

"I need people to recognize the special needs that I have as a spouse of a CFIDS sufferer," says Dave McAdoo. "During the twelve years that Debi has been sick, people have assumed that because I am physically well, I am able to take care of everything Debi needs. But I am drained too. It's draining to come home to a sick spouse. It's draining to deal with all the sadness we both feel. It's draining to carry financial stress because of CFIDS. I need all the emotional energy I have just to be Debi's spouse, to do for her what only a spouse can do. When I become discouraged, I withdraw from people, and that's not healthy. I need a friend to call me to initiate conversations, to invite me to lunch. Similarly, I need people to make contact with Debi, to encourage her, to pray with her, to make her laugh."

Changes and Losses

Many spouses of CFIDS sufferers face profound changes and losses. "Brian's CFIDS abruptly changed both of our lives," says Jane Vander Ploeg. "I went directly from a graduate-school program in organization development to nursing my homebound husband, who was a shadow of his former energetic, conquer-the-world self. Although I fought the changes in the beginning, I had to learn to become free of my performance orientation and learn to be content with where God has placed me. God has brought us both to the point of nestling instead of wrestling with him.

"I found it difficult to accept having a private married life and a single public life. Brian and I are unable to go out much together or to have people in our home, so I have to make most social contacts alone. I keep telling people that I have this wonderful husband, but they rarely see him. I have had to take on the role of being the public relations person for our family, explaining Brian's illness to people, figuring out how to relate to people we want to stay close to as well as those we can't stay close to because of the illness."

Jeff McCullough expresses his pain and losses like this: "Donna got sick two or three months before we got married, but we didn't realize what she had at the time. We also didn't know that the illness would last so long. We felt that it was premarital jitters or a passing virus. But over ten years later, she is still sick. We had no chance to establish our marriage before Donna got sick.

"It's hard to connect. Donna's sleep disturbance means she doesn't fall asleep until late, so she sleeps in late. I tend to go to sleep earlier and get up earlier. When I'm ready to talk, she may be too drained or grouchy to talk. And when she's ready to share her feelings, sometimes I can't hear them because they seem too heavy to me. We can't participate in many activities together. We used to walk and take hikes, but obviously she's unable to do that most of the time. I feel lonely because I don't feel as if we're sharing our lives together.

"I found that there's no way to prepare for coping with CFIDS. No matter how much I thought I knew about the illness and no matter how much of a merciful, compassionate person I thought I was, CFIDS is a thousand times larger than I could possibly have imagined. I thought I could deal with it. I've been amazed at how much of a toll it's taken on me and how close I've come to taking my own life as a way of getting out of it."

Other spouses feel trapped by their spouses' CFIDS. One man said, "I am in a high-stress job, which I would like to leave. But I can't afford to consider that as long as my wife is ill. Neither of us can afford the stress of my searching for another job, not to mention relocating and starting over again with relationships and medical treatment. So I stay and tough it out. If my wife were not ill, she would work while I found another job, but obviously she can't do that. Besides, how do I find another organization that will understand why I need to come in late some days or go home early other days when my wife is crashing?"

One pastor whose wife has CFIDS wonders if several churches have decided not to hire him because of his wife's illness. "It seems that the interviews go well until we start to discuss our family situation and my wife's illness. Then the committee seems to back off. I don't think it's a case of conscious discrimination, but for some churches, the thought of hiring someone whose wife is debilitated, whose wife can't even attend church services, seems too overwhelming. I understand that, especially for smaller churches. But it's also frustrating. I hope someday a church will recognize that even though we are a family marked by a debilitating illness, we have a lot to offer. Much of the empathy, compassion, and mercy that the Lord has developed in us has come through our many years of battling CFIDS."

Pain of Helplessness

Other spouses comment on the pain of watching their sick spouses suffer. "Sometimes people say to me, 'Are you sure your husband's sickness is not his way of getting out of work?' I wish they could see the times he has crawled up the steps because his legs hurt so much or the times he never even made it up the steps to the bedroom because he was so exhausted. It's so hard for me to watch him be in pain."

"One of the things that gives me the most pain is watching Sheila get sicker and not being able to do anything about it," reflects Rob Wang. "Some days I will get a call at work and on the other end is this very small, scared, quiet voice. I know she's had another crash. Those are the times when my heart goes out to her the most. Sheila was one of these dynamos that could do the work of five people and juggle dozens of things. To watch her turn into a person who is some-times totally unable to function tears me apart."

Nearly all the healthy spouses I spoke with shared similar feelings of helplessness and pain. To cope with this pain, many of them have had to cork their emotions, withdraw, disengage emotionally. Unfortunately, what for them is a positive coping mechanism becomes a threat to the sick spouse, who interprets the distance as disinterest or insensitivity. Gregg Fisher offers some helpful insight here. "As a sufferer myself, I *know* what my wife feels like when she battles CFIDS. I understand. I'm not insensitive. Maybe it's that I'm too sensitive. It hurts to open up my heart to allow myself to experience her pain and suffering. It's not easy to see her unable to be the woman I know she wants to be, to see her struggling under this heavy load of debilitation. I know I am compro-mising my feelings by keeping emotional distance here—and I hate compromise—but I believe, at least at this point, that I must keep the distance in order to function at all as her husband. Maybe later on I will change my mind, but for now I feel some distance is essential."

Another spouse of a CFIDS sufferer expresses a similar deci-sion: "In some ways your illness is like another Vietnam to me. I am an unwilling participant in events over which I have no control. I did not vote for this illness and had not planned my life around being a caregiver. So I find myself falling back into the pattern of behaviors I had to learn for my survival in the war. I have withdrawn, become emotionally isolated and noncommunicative. I deal with activities rather than emotions. It is less painful to do than to feel."[2]

Energy Drain

"One of the greatest stresses on our marriage has been the energy drain for both of us," says Dave Crosby. "Even though Carla could work circles around me before she got sick, she now is often too sick to take care of the basics around the house. I have picked up the slack and do most of the household chores in addition to my full-time job. And that's fine. I'm willing to do that. But then I feel resentful when Carla feels strong enough to do something and chooses to use her energy on other people rather than on our relationship. Then I feel cheated. I guess I need to feel appreciated and affirmed for the extra load I have assumed in our household, but instead, I get what seem to be the leftovers. We are talking about this and working toward some balance. But despite our best intentions, it seems that the window of time and energy we have for each other shrinks."

My husband, Bas, describes a similar energy drain. "Dealing with CFIDS has sapped my energy. Before Lynn and Alisa got CFIDS, I considered myself to have a strong capacity for dealing with stress. But now, after doing my job with World Relief and helping Lynn and Alisa cope with their illnesses, I have very little left. I have no energy left to serve on a church board or participate in a small ministry group or deal with minor frustrations. I've had to become self-protective rather than self-sacrificing. I know I'm doing the right thing for the moment, but I haven't completely accepted these changes."

Loneliness

Spouses of people with CFIDS often suffer intense loneliness. "I often feel overcome by a large loneliness, a lack of companionship, a lack of understanding. I don't feel like a single person, but I don't feel like a married person either. I feel displaced. I'm disoriented because I don't know who I am or what my role is. Since my wife has been sick from the beginning of our marriage, I don't quite know what marriage is supposed to feel like. Many times I feel that we're two strangers living in the same house. And that saddens me a lot. I live with another person, and yet I feel so lonely. It's worse than being alone because this other person is physically with me, but we don't always connect."

"After sharing over thirty years of my life with my wife," says one man, "I have had to accept going to church and to some other functions alone. The almost complete loss of her company at church and inability to attend most other functions engulfs me at times with a sense of loneliness. I feel as if I am married to a memory more than to a real person. Part of my loneliness comes from knowing no one who has walked this road before. I am sad to report that I don't have anyone who believes the seriousness of our situation with my wife's

CFIDS. I have tried to share some with my friends, and though they appear sympathetic, they seldom remember what we discuss."

Keep Your Marriage Healthy

How can we maintain a healthy marriage through the stresses and limitations of CFIDS? How can we encourage each other to stay in the battle? How can we love each other in deeper ways? How can we allow the Lord to shape our marriage through CFIDS? Let's explore several paths to keeping our marriages strong in the midst of our struggle.

Accept Changes

Even though spouses feel alone and discouraged, many of them are doing exceptional jobs of adjusting to the limitations and of helping their spouses adjust. Because I was sick when Craig and I married," says Robin Ralston, "we have struggled to build a healthy marriage. Right now we are still adjusting our expectations of marriage, trying to integrate where we are and where we had hoped to be. Sometimes we feel empty and wonder how God can use us. That is our new journey, not one we expected, but one we have chosen to see as meaningful and purposeful."

"Because both Fred and I are medical professionals," says Jody Hurst, "it has been hard for us to adjust to some of the changes I've needed to make with CFIDS. I remember when I first began to use a cane, he was embarrassed. He wanted me to take his arm instead. It also was very painful for me to have to use a cane in public. I guess it's pride. Eventually I realized that the cane was a positive tool to assist me, and I need to use it. It's like needing to wear eyeglasses. When I decided to get a wheelchair so that I could go out, Fred again had a difficult time adjusting. Not that he minds pushing the wheelchair. It's just hard for him to see that. It has taken him some time to work through that."

"CFIDS forced many changes on our marriage," recalls Ruth Huizenga. "Tom had a hard time when his fellow counselors told him, 'Your wife really isn't sick. She just has emotional problems.' We had just gotten married, and Tom didn't know me well enough to know if that was true. So he came home doubting that I was sick, and we fought. I wondered during that first year whether I had married the wrong person. After hammering it all out, our marriage is stronger because of my illness. Tom learned that I was physically sick, not emotionally sick. He was forced to take control in the family and has learned to be a servant. Tom did all the chores when I was most sick. I mean he did *everything*. I could not have gotten through this without his understanding and love."

Develop a Life Outside CFIDS

"My doctor gave us a good suggestion for combating the limitations CFIDS has placed on our marriage," recounts Robin Ralston. "He encouraged us to establish one ritual that has nothing to do with the illness. Craig and I have decided to go out of the house to a nearby lake and sit. The other night we watched a sunset over the Rockies. It brought back the original feeling of closeness and care. It brought us out of ourselves and our difficulties. Taking time with each other aside from chores and the grind of living with an illness helps us remember we are first of all married. We happen to be a married couple that is living with a debilitating disease.

"We have tried to maintain our ritual, even when it would be easier to let it go. One time when I had a lot of pain and could hardly move, Craig insisted that we go to the lake. I objected, thinking it would make me feel even worse to use the energy to go out. But he persevered. 'You don't have to move. I'll carry you there. We'll take all the blankets you need to stay warm. You can just sit once we get there, but we need to do this.' I am so grateful that he saw beyond my pain to the closeness we would feel to change settings and honor our time at the lake together. After we returned from the lake that night, I felt twenty percent better than if Craig hadn't taken me out. It was so good just to be away with him, away from the house, away from our responsibilities, away from CFIDS."

David and Wendy Hill, who both have CFIDS, also have learned to separate themselves from their illness. "Before we became ill, we were both high-achieving, hard-working, hard-playing people.

David used to ski one hundred twenty days a year, and I skied fifty days. David used to bicycle over a hundred miles a day for fun. We both enjoyed outdoor activities, including hiking trips. When we faced the reality of our illness, we decided we would not wait in limbo for our old lives to return. We had to create a new life for ourselves. We have learned to separate our identities from the illness. We are both people first, people with an illness second."

Spouses of CFIDS sufferers also have had to work on building an identity that is separate from their sick spouses. Dave Masoner, whose wife and daughter have CFIDS, discovered that he needed to find some healthy separation. "Barbara and Nancy have convinced me that I need to have a life outside the illness. I really don't want to, you know. I really don't want to do stuff without them. So that's something I'm still trying to work through. I have been able to get involved in some legislative issues, and I am attending a small group, a couples' group, even though I'm the only 'single' person there. Barbara and Nancy feel I bring much more balance to our family if I stay active outside of the illness."

Give Each Other Support and Understanding

Another important ingredient of a healthy marriage during CFIDS is giving each other support and understanding. When that support is lacking, the marriage suffers. "During the first few years of my illness," says one woman with CFIDS, "my husband was oblivious to my situation and could give me no support. I still have to deal with my anger about that. At least he believed me. He wasn't critical, but he wasn't all that helpful. Through the years we have come to realize that much of his response was modeled on the dysfunctions in his family. Slowly, he has changed. Now he is supportive and much more emotionally expressive. We have both changed. We have learned to care outwardly for each other."

Lack of support and understanding can express itself even more destructively when people use the illness as a scapegoat and blame the illness or the sick spouse for everything that goes wrong. "The pressure is unbearable sometimes when my husband and I fight," reports one CFIDS sufferer. "He ends up saying that everything would be fine if only I would get better. Sometimes he even says to me: 'Just get better!' As if I have any control over CFIDS. As if I asked for CFIDS. As if I don't want to get better. He makes me feel so responsible for any unhappiness either of us feels. I *am* trying to get better. And I need to know we are on the same team."

How can we work on the same team? How can we help each other during the long years of CFIDS? What can the healthy spouse give to the sick spouse? And what can the sick spouse give to the healthy spouse?

What Can the Healthy Spouse Give?

"One of the greatest gifts Don has given to me during these past years," says Helen Gruelle, "is that he believed me: For a long time we didn't have a name for what was causing my fatigue, but he accepted that something was very wrong and worked with me to adjust to the new limitations."[3]

"Once my wife became so desperately sick," Dan Beecher reflects, "I determined I could give her several things to help her stay whole in the midst of a crushing illness. First, I could give her the assurance that I believe her illness is real. I must admit that in the beginning I had my doubts about my wife's mental health. I was given much advice by well-meaning but ignorant friends who suggested all kinds of causes for her sudden decline. I tried to keep an open mind and questioned her after each doctor's visit. Finally I realized my attitude was wrong. I decided to rest in the reality that I know my wife better than any other person does. I now believe that her struggle with CFIDS is very real.

"Second, I can give my wife the confidence that I will be faithful to her, as I pledged in my marriage vows. Again I admit that when I feel engulfed in the loneliness, I have been tempted to find other companionship. But I am committed to Evelyn, and that means I will honor my vow to 'forsake all others.' As I assure Evelyn of my love for her, she does not need to use any of her energy on feeling insecure.

"Third, I can give my wife the support of my prayers. When she is too discouraged or sick to be able to pray for herself, she knows that I pray for her continually.

"Fourth, I can understand my wife when she is too weak to help herself. I have had to choose to be more sensitive to my wife's unusual needs. She 'looks healthy' to me too! I think more carefully about her needs when we are out in public and try to protect her from criticism. I have had to learn how to give myself to my wife in her weakness. I believe that my spouse is learning the equally important gift of receiving. This can be very humbling. I believe our marriage is healthier. We both have faced the 'bear in the woods' and are learning to accept the new changes this brings. I actually find myself enjoying (don't get too excited) washing dishes. I look at ways to give to my wife as opportunities to minister rather than as obstacles to overcome."

"Kurt has made my ten years of living with CFIDS bearable," asserts Sue Hedlund. "He loves me for who I am, and he stays by me. He believes me. He is often aware before I am that I need to pull back and rest. He helps me set limits. Kurt is a hard worker and uses his energy to fill the gaps in our family. I don't think I could have survived without him. He's been such a gift."

Cyndi Volkers reflects, "Steve gives me a wonderful gift every day. No matter how sick I look or feel, he lets me know that he likes me as a person. He lets me know that whether or not I'm bedridden, he enjoys my company and he thinks I'm a valuable person. He tells me that he likes being with me, that he likes talking with me. Steve's decision to like me and love me has helped me maintain my self-esteem in the midst of CFIDS."

"I realized that one of the gifts I could give to Barbara was a spouse who tried to stay spiritually strong," recounts Dave Masoner. "After Barbara was debilitated by CFIDS, I realized that I had gained much of my sense of significance from her, from how she felt, from what she was able to do or not do. It has been a difficult thing for me to realize that I'm significant regardless of how she's feeling on a particular day, regardless of how attentive she is to me, or whatever. I have come to see that I am significant because I'm a child of God, not because I'm married to Barbara. I think this chronic illness forced me to question on whom or on what was I relying. I've come to see that in our marriage I had relied too much on how Barbara could fill my needs, and when she was no longer able to give that—decisions, leadership, or whatever—I felt empty. I began to see that I had been relying on her to do for me and in me things that only God could do. I think this new perspective brings me a greater sense of spiritual wholeness, which is a wonderful gift to give to my wife."

What Can the Sick Spouse Give?

What can we who are sick give to our healthy spouses? Although our first response may be, "We have *nothing* to give," we need to think again.

First, we can give to our healthy spouses our integrity. By that I mean that we will tell them the truth. We will neither manipulate the illness nor hide its reality, neither exaggerate it nor downplay it.

Second, we can give our healthy spouses our commitment to the growth of our marriage and family. That means we will not opt out of our responsibilities to grow emotionally and spiritually in the midst of our illness. That means we do not dump all our emotional and spiritual needs on our spouses. As Dave Masoner has pointed out, we must look first to the Lord for our sense of purpose and meaning. Then, when it is appropriate, we can look to others for nurture. When my husband travels overseas for weeks at a time, he needs to know that I am not going to wither and collapse because he is gone. He takes comfort in knowing that I will look to the Lord for strength and direction while he is gone and will depend on friends to help with various other needs.

Third, we can give our healthy spouses appreciation and understanding for what it costs them to live with us. We need to understand that our spouses are doing the best job they can, even if their coping mechanisms threaten us. We need to express our understanding that the emotional pain, physical drain, and loss our spouses feel are as important as our pain and loss.

My husband, Bas, reflects on several other gifts a sick spouse can give a healthy spouse. "Lynn has given me several gifts that have helped me cope with her CFIDS. First, even though she was very debilitated in the first several years, she stayed engaged in life within the limits allowed by the illness. She read, talked with friends on the phone, and stayed interested in the lives of our other family members. She did not 'become the illness.' I appreciated that. I needed to come home from work and know that she had done what she could to stay whole and healthy. One of the decisions Lynn made early on was to get out of bed, get dressed, and do her hair every day. I know she initially did that for her own sense of well-being and that it took a lot of energy to do that, but that decision became a gift to the rest of us too. When I came home from work, she was often lying down, but she was on the couch, dressed, in her 'healing spot,' with music on and a book at her side. She had already fed herself emotionally and spiritually and was ready to interact, even though she was far too sick to do most of the things she had done in our family before she got sick.

"Second, Lynn has given me the gift of saving some energy for me. Most days I can be assured that she has marshaled her time and energy during the day so that she has something left to give to me and our children at night. Often that means energy to talk about what has happened to each of us during the day. Sometimes that means energy to nurture me if my emotional tank is empty. Other times that means saving some energy to take a wheelchair walk or have some intimate time together.

"Third, Lynn has given me the gift of reciprocity. While she knows that I will do whatever I can to help our marriage and family stay strong during her CFIDS, I also need to know that she will reciprocate, that she will do her part. I know that she will contribute what she can. She continues to be the emotional hub of our family, listening, encouraging, motivating. She continues to manage our household from her couch, taking time to make sure each family member is on track.

"I don't mean to suggest that Lynn does all this every day or that she even does it well all the time. But over the seven years that she and Alisa have had CFIDS, it has helped me tremendously to know I can count on these things. It gives me emotional energy to do what I need to do to fill the gaps and keep us going."

Communicate Your Needs

Living with CFIDS demands different communication skills between husbands and wives. Jody Hurst reflects on the changes she has gone through in the years of her illness. "I really thought it would be better not to let my husband know how bad I felt. I tried not to worry him. Then a severe relapse made it impossible to hide anything from him. I realize now that if I had let him see more of what the illness was doing to me on the inside, he could have cautioned me more, and he probably would have seen the relapse coming faster than I did. By not telling him what was going on inside me, I took away his opportunity to minister to me. I thought I was doing a good thing for him by shielding him from my symptoms. We both have changed. I'm telling him more, and he's much more in tune to what I need."

If communication is important when one spouse has CFIDS, it's doubly important when both spouses are ill. "Our communication skills have been tested to their limits," says Shawn Fisher. "Gregg and I have learned that we continually need to inform one another how we are feeling. When I was first sick, I put on a smile and would try to act healthy. Then I would lose it and end up angry and crying. I would become angry at Gregg because I thought he should have been able to see how much pain I was in. It sounds so silly now. We, of all people, should know that most of the CFIDS pain doesn't show.

"We may think our pain and discomfort is obvious to the other person, but often it's not. So now Gregg and I ask each other questions. How do you feel this afternoon? What kind of things do you feel up to doing for the rest of the day? What are you thinking of? And what's important to you? Then we know what the other is feeling and what is important at the moment. It also gives us the opportunity to say that we're really hurting and need to rest and this is all we can handle."

Deepen Your Love for Each Other

As I listened to both CFIDS sufferers and their spouses describe the impact of CFIDS on their marriages, I sensed that out of the crucible of suffering God is forging a pure and uncommon love in many of these marriages. CFIDS forces the quality of married love to change. The love may no longer be propelled by feelings or excitement but by the *decision* to love. That kind of love may feel more like duty or hard work than love. But that *is* love. That is sacrificial love, the laying down of one's life for a spouse.

In reflecting on the impact of CFIDS on her married love, Hettie Kenny responds, "*Love* has become a verb, not a passive feeling. I listen, talk, pick up the slack, carry on, make do. I find myself doing a myriad of things I've never done before and really didn't expect to do at this point in my life: following ambulances, completing endless insurance forms, talking with each new doctor or technician after each new procedure. I now slip effortlessly into medical jargon in my everyday speech. As if this onslaught of changes were not enough, I find so little time to stop and think. My life's routines—now hopelessly splintered—still go on, though compounded by the need to be more than what I've ever had to be in the past.... I find that the emotional aspects of having a sick husband are far more difficult to deal with than the practical ones. I have learned to be flexible and tolerant, willing to do what needs to be done. It's what I promised to do when I married Tim, and it's what I will do forever."[4]

"Gregg and I have learned to develop an attitude of servanthood toward each other," adds Shawn Fisher. "We had to learn to appreciate what the other spouse does, no matter how little. He or she is also working with little reserve. We have had to learn to put the other person first. Gregg and I never allow ourselves to think of divorce because we are committed to each other and to working through any difficulties we have. We will stick with each other, no matter what. We will trust the power of God's love for us and his power to sustain our marriage."

Redefine Your Sexual Life

"I think our biggest struggle in our marriage is our sex life," laments Cathy Franco. "I had CFIDS when we got married, but I never expected that it would interfere with our sex life. But it has. In the first several years I was so sick that I didn't want to have sex. I seem to have lost my sex drive altogether. I wouldn't care if we never had sex again. Obviously, that is not a healthy attitude for our marriage. So we struggle. I want to be able to satisfy Ben, but my hormones seem to have shut down."

Like the Francos, many couples need to redefine their sexual life when one or both spouses are debilitated with CFIDS. Several couples share their thoughts and struggles with maintaining a healthy sex life while living with CFIDS.

Sarah Franklin, who has been married for over thirty years, shares these insights. "I found that CFIDS has definitely affected my libido. I've been comforted to read that other people have experienced the same response, but it's still a problem. I am able to enjoy sex from time to time and experience a climax, but I wouldn't care if I ever made love again. I'm just too tired. When Jim and I do make love and it's a wonderful experience, I think, *I ought to remember how good this is.*

"Jim is sensitive to my illness and has backed off from initiating sexual contact, which was good at first because it relieved some of the pressure for me. But now it's up to me to initiate when I feel well enough. I feel as if I must plan for his need, regardless of what I feel like. That is difficult for me and has led to some anger.

"I want to bring Jim pleasure, but it is such hard work. I decided this was as much a spiritual problem as a physical, sexual one, so I have prayed and asked for guidance. Many times in marriage the Lord has enabled me to lay down my body for my husband or our children, and I asked the Lord to help me truly minister to Jim in our sexual experience. Slowly the Lord has taken away my fear that I will feel worse for expending so much energy. Slowly I am learning to initiate times of intimacy, even when my own sex drive seems nonexistent. As a result of trusting God and choosing to minister to Jim, we have experienced times of deep closeness, pleasure, and peace—exactly what God has in mind for us."

Jim Franklin concurs, "God has helped Sarah and me to find a path through our sexual struggles. I found it was important to confess my anger and frustration to God and ask for help. And he has been faithful. I think it's also important to be aware that while a husband and wife are redefining their sexual lives because of illness, they are on guard not even to get close to any situation in which they could be tempted. We can respect our spouse's limitations and our marriage relationship by choosing not to use the illness as an excuse for infidelity of mind or body."

Helen and Don Gruelle both live with extreme fatigue, but they too have committed themselves to redefining their sexual life so that they could find meaning in the midst of the limitations. "We need to remind ourselves that intimacy is a closeness, a bonding that is more than the sex act. It's a hug or holding hands or intimate smiles or sharing the same thoughts. Romance may be scaled down from a romantic weekend away to an occasional rose, or popcorn on the couch while watching a movie. It's saying, 'I'd rather be here with you tonight—even though you're wiped out—than with anyone else.' Intimacy involves more than just commitment. It's conveying the feeling that your partner is worth being with and loving—even though he or she is sick. . . .

"A television movie several years ago portrayed a couple where the wife was terminally ill. She was in treatment and exhausted. I remember one scene where they were lying on their sides, her back to her husband, his arm around her. She said, 'I wish we could make love.' He held her close to him and said, 'We *are* making love.'"[5]

Helen and Don Gruelle put sexual intimacy high on their list of priorities. When they save energy to enjoy each other, they communicate that their relationship is important, even though it is severely limited. For example, Helen tells Don, "I've saved some energy to spend time with you tonight." If possible, they intentionally decide how they can use their energy to focus on each other and enjoy being together—whether or not that time ends in sex.

Keri and Jon Sanders, who both have CFIDS, share some of the lessons they have learned about coping with the effects of the illness on their sexual life. "For the first years we were ill, I found I had no sexual desire. I wanted to be involved sexually with Jon, but somehow my hormones were not functioning. In the beginning I blamed myself. Now I realize that it's probably a chemical thing. Most of my emotions were deadened for the first several years I was ill. Then in addition to feeling no sexual desire, I was more than 90 percent debilitated during the first several years of our marriage. I would find that the exertion of sexual intercourse would make me sicker for several days. This was not what we had thought our marriage would be."

Jon adds, "I felt like a failure as a husband. That was not easy for me to deal with. I understood in my head that Keri was in too much pain, but our sexual desires are such primal needs. I felt frustrated on two fronts: My sexual needs were not fulfilled, and I had a deep need to give Keri sexual pleasure. I blamed myself, too, thinking maybe I wasn't expressing my love verbally enough or maybe I wasn't cuddling her enough or helping her feel secure."

"At one point Jon and I also realized that some of the medication I was on had deadened my sexual desire," Keri continues. "After stopping one medication I had been taking for three years, I had a stronger sexual desire and felt more responsive. Jon and I were so amazed by the difference that we both cried. That response revealed to us how much pain we had been carrying. Here we had been struggling for years, wondering what we had been doing wrong, blaming ourselves. I still struggle with low sexual drive and lack of passion and energy, and that affects both of us differently. I have come to realize how important sexual expression is to Jon, so I have chosen to make that a priority in our relationship, even though my commitment is based more on intellectual and emotional desires than on physical, sexual desires.

"Several things have helped us through these difficult years. First, we share our feelings with each other. If Jon's angry or frustrated and struggling, he tells me about it. He'll say, 'I know it's not your fault, but I'm so frustrated. I didn't think our marriage would be this way.' He's very careful not to blame me, and I don't feel hurt because we consider this our problem, not my problem. We view it as another painful challenge that we need to face and deal with together. Sometimes I am just too sick to respond sexually to him, and he has come to accept that because we are both committed to our sexual relationship.

"Second, when Jon initiates sexual intimacy, I need to make sure I don't reject him. That doesn't mean I say yes all the time. I often can't. But we have found that if I initiate sexual involvement when I feel strong enough, then Jon knows I'm interested in him and he doesn't always risk making advances and feeling rejected. Or if he does initiate and I am not up to it, I have learned to say, 'I would love to respond, but I'm not feeling well right now. Let me try to get some good sleep, and I'll save energy for tomorrow afternoon.'"

Jon continues, "It's so helpful to me when Keri responds that way. She communicates that she wants to be sexually involved and that it's a priority for her. It's just that the timing isn't right. I can live with that. I can't live with no response. I need to know that Keri wants me, even if it can't be today or tomorrow."

"It's very healing and bonding when we can be involved sexually," Keri adds. "Jon has told me that he prays for me whenever we make love. That really touches me and frees me. I don't have to perform or meet certain expectations. I can give myself to him in whatever limited way I am able for that day."

Keri and Jon have decided to love each other and grow sexually in the midst of over a decade of debilitation from CFIDS, in spite of their weakness, in spite of their exhaustion, in spite of their pain. They have accepted that they are giving each other their best, even though their best still is very limited.

Get Counseling Help

Several couples I interviewed indicated that their marriages have suffered some potentially fatal blows during the years of struggling with CFIDS. A few spouses have found the disappointment with God so strong that they have abandoned their faith, bringing added grief and stress to their marriages. Other marriages have been weighted down with the sick spouse's despair and despondency or threats of suicide.

Many couples have wisely chosen to get counseling help, either together or individually. Steve Volkers, whose wife and five children have CFIDS, says, "Cyndi and I have relied on counseling to help us get through these difficult years. If it didn't cost so much, we would go for counseling more often, but the times we have gone have been essential for Cyndi and me. The counselors have helped us work on deeper communication skills so that we can survive these years. If we had not gotten counseling, the chances of failure in our marriage would have been much greater. The emotional help has been as significant as the medical help for the physical side of Cyndi's illness."

Don't be hesitant to get outside help. CFIDS is a destructive illness, but it need not destroy you or your marriage. If you think you and your spouse need counseling, but your spouse is not willing to go with you, go alone.

In their chapter "Sex When Illness Hits the Family" therapists Cliff and Joyce Penner suggest, "When the physical and emotional strain of illness begins to interfere with the *strengths* of our relationships, a third party is usually needed. No matter how great the marriage is and how satisfying the sexual life has been, no marriage can survive the endless stress that comes with a long illness. We need outside support and objectivity. A psychotherapist can guide us in working through the emotional problems the situation has stirred up. A counselor can assist us in expressing our hurts and needs in a way that enlists the other's care and love, rather than creating distance."[6]

Can We Have Children?

A final issue voiced by several couples living with CFIDS is whether or not they should consider starting a family. This section does not pretend to offer any definitive answers. Instead, it will share some insights and experiences various couples have had as they have faced this question.

Shawn and Gregg Fisher, who both have had CFIDS for over thirteen years, have wrestled with this question. "I think Gregg and I have been able to accept not being able to have jobs, not being able to finish our education, and not being able to be involved in ministry, but the children issue seems insurmountable. I feel that God made me to be a wife and mother. That has always been my deepest desire. Gregg also desperately wants children. Gregg and I always saw ourselves with a family of many children. The illness has made it impossible; we have had no choice. We have had enough trouble trying to feed ourselves; there's no way we could have taken care of a child. Even now a pregnancy would not be wise because I am taking medication, and that wouldn't be safe for an unborn child. It's just been very painful. When I turned thirty-five, I put a lot of pressure on myself. I thought every day about having children. It felt like torture. We can't speed up our healing. We can't make plans for financial security because neither of us is well enough to work. As much as we think and struggle and pray, any change is beyond our control. We've cried a lot of tears. We still hope for the future, but it has been one of the greatest tests of our trust in God." Shawn and Gregg have agreed to continue waiting, hoping for a time when they will be strong enough to be parents.

Other couples do not agree about the children issue. Jeff and Donna McCullough have had bitter fights about whether or not they should have children. "Donna can barely function as it is. What would life be like for both of us—or all three of us—if we added a child to that? I can't handle that at all."

Donna's perspective is different. "Yes, I have CFIDS, I have limits, but I've learned how to balance my life. I'm a very resourceful person. If I have a relapse that makes me too sick to take care of a child, we will call someone in to help. We would get through it. Jeff thinks I'll get sick all the time and throw this kid at him. But I won't. Even now I clean the house, do the cooking, run the errands. I would do anything to take care of a child." Years of counseling have not brought a satisfactory resolution to their disagreement. Donna has agreed not to have children, but only with great pain.

Mark and Nancy Fuller have different concerns. "We don't have questions about the ability to give birth to a child or care for a child because I don't have CFIDS," says Nancy. "However, we are concerned about whether or not Mark can pass on CFIDS genetically to our child. We are researching this side of the issue."

Dave and Carla Crosby reflect on their decision-making process before Carla became pregnant. After several miscarriages, Carla gave birth to a son in 1991. Although Benjamin was born with a low birth weight, he is an energetic, bright toddler. Carla and Dave have had to remain flexible and open to getting child-care help when Carla is crashing. "Dave and I had to pray about whether we could be parents, whether I could be a mother while battling CFIDS. When I first got sick, it was not an option to become pregnant; I was too sick, and I was on medication. After I had recovered a bit, we began to ask the question again. We never questioned whether I could love the child enough. We never questioned whether I could share Jesus with our child in a meaningful way. The question was a more practical one: How can I take care of a child if I'm in bed myself? How can I consistently discipline and train a child if I'm suffering from debilitating symptoms and unpredictable emotions?

"We talked about all kinds of options, including having someone come into our home to take care of both the child and me if that were necessary. We are grateful that it has never gotten to that point, but even as we are contemplating additional children, we have talked about the options again. Some days it's not at all easy to be a parent, but, with or without CFIDS, every parent can say that. CFIDS certainly complicates our parenting because I am still debilitated for weeks at a time. But we do not regret the decision and both are so thankful that the Lord has allowed us to be parents."

The stories in this chapter illustrate the unique ways each husband and wife are working to redefine their marriages to find meaning and joy in the midst of CFIDS. May their creativity, courage, tenacity, commitment, faith, and love spur you on to new levels of maintaining a healthy marriage.

Chapter 11
Understand Children with CFIDS

Adults with this disease have their lives thrown into turmoil. They lose their jobs, their homes, their children, and their self-esteem. But as horrifying as this disease is in adults, it is even worse in children. Children are the ones most cheated of their dreams. . . . The social, educational, and psychological consequences of children with CFIDS are dramatic and frequently irreversible. One can never relive the formative years.

DR. DAVID BELL, CFIDS RESEARCHER
AND CFIDS PEDIATRIC SPECIALIST

While it is hard for anyone to deal with CFIDS, it is particularly hard for the children who have CFIDS. They face the physical, emotional, relational, and spiritual pressures without the maturity that comes with age and life experience. Their debilitation prevents them from being involved fully in some crucial developmental years of their lives. Most of them are too sick to attend school or be involved in the activities that help children define their gifts and abilities. Instead, they spend years debilitated by fatigue, fever, swollen lymph nodes, pain, as well as neurological disturbances that leave many of them unable to read or concentrate.

Yet as I listen to the children with CFIDS, I find in them a depth of awareness and maturity that belies their years. While they feel all the losses, misunderstanding, and questioning that adult CFIDS sufferers feel, many of them have come to an unusual place of acceptance and integration.

This chapter will allow you to hear the voices of these children as they articulate what they experience living with CFIDS. Several of them became ill when they were nine years old; one was only five. The voices you will hear in this chapter include more females than males, not because males don't get CFIDS, but because the males were less willing to talk about their experiences. While most of the children have been ill for three or four years, a few have been ill for over ten years; one was newly diagnosed while I was writing this book. Some of the children in this chapter are the only members of their family to have the illness, while others have a parent who also suffers from CFIDS. Five of the children are from the same family; their mother also has CFIDS.

I wish you could have heard their voices as they talked with me about their experiences. One of them was too weak to talk for more than ten minutes at a time. Some of them cried as they recounted the physical and emotional pain they have endured. Others laughed as they described the absurd trails their doctors sent them on before they had an accurate diagnosis. Still others expressed the anger and bitterness they struggle with because of how people have treated them.

For the children who read this chapter, I hope these voices will help you realize that you are not alone and that you *will* make it, even though the road seems so long. For the adults who read this chapter, I hope these voices give you new understanding and compassion for the children who suffer with CFIDS, whether those children are your sons and daughters, nieces and nephews, grandsons and granddaughters or whether they are children in your classroom, youth group, or medical practice.

Grieving the Losses

Brooke Volkers started grieving her losses a month before she was diagnosed with CFIDS. For nine of her thirteen years, she has watched people in her family battle CFIDS. "I'm scared because it looks as if I'm getting CFIDS too. I have a doctor's appointment very soon, and I'm afraid she's going to say that I have it. I live with that constant fear. All the time. What scares me about getting a CFIDS diagnosis is that I can't say anymore that I don't have it, that I'm the healthy one in the family. To have to say, 'I have it too' is very hard. When the doctor said she wanted me to keep a diary of my symptoms because she wanted to start watching for CFIDS, I was scared. It brought tears to my eyes, just to hear her say I might have CFIDS."

Ann McErleane, who became ill with CFIDS four years ago, recalls the beginning of her illness. "One weekend I couldn't move my body or open my eyes. It felt as if a most incredible force was pressing me into the couch as I lay there helpless. I also had a most intense and painful headache, when I had never had headaches before. These symptoms persisted for a few days. I never before had felt anything even close to what I was experiencing, and I was scared. I eventually asked my dad to take me to the doctor. I was continually bedridden, hardly able to move. I would go from my bed to the couch, back and forth as a day's accomplishment.

"Later that summer I recovered a bit and tried to go to college in the fall, but in a few weeks all my symptoms came back, only to be accompanied by more. I now had cognitive problems. I could hardly read a page a night and couldn't concentrate in class. I fell severely behind in my classes. I felt completely helpless as this disease tore the life I once knew away from me."

"The hardest part of living with CFIDS," reflects our daughter, Alisa, who has struggled with CFIDS for seven years, "is accepting all the losses. The symptoms, pain, and debilitation are hard, but I have learned to live with those. I've lost the ability to have a social life, to be part of my friends' lives. In a way, I lost my self. For one year, when I was in a relapse, I lost my personality, my outgoing, people-person self. Because I was too sick to go to school, I became very introverted and a loner, which is the opposite of what I had been before I got sick. With that came the loss of friends and the loss of being able to be involved in sleepovers and other social activities. That led to my not knowing myself. Most teenagers find themselves in their teen years, but since I lived such a limited life, without being able to taste other things, I didn't know who I was. I lost part of my real self.

"If I were well, I would be involved in drama, music, speech, and gymnastics. When my brother was growing up, he had been able to be in a children's chorus and in school plays and had some great experiences growing up, like singing on a CD with the Chicago Symphony Orchestra and Choir. I have not been able to do any of those things, and that makes me sad. I know I have lots of ability in music and drama and sports, but I've not been able to get any of the training the other kids have had in classes and after-school activities.

"Another loss I feel is that while I was lying in bed so sick, I would think of all the things I wanted to do, like build a fort in the backyard, clean my room, or take up ballet. Inside I was excited, but my body wouldn't let me do the things my brain wanted to do. It's also hard to be the only child with CFIDS in my town, so people, kids and teachers, don't understand."

Craig Maupin, who became ill during his senior year in high school, agrees. "The hardest thing about living with this chronic illness is dealing with all the losses, with what I can no longer do. Before I got sick, I was physically active: I ran regularly, lifted weights, and played basketball. Only recently, after nearly eight years of illness, have I been able to begin some resistance exercises. I also lost my independence. I was looking forward to going off to college and beginning a program that would lead to a career. Now at age twenty-five, I have attended only a few weeks of college. In the first years, before I realized the power of this illness, I had tried college, but within two weeks, I had collapsed physically. I have not been able to return since then, and I have not been able to work at all. I've also lost the ability to maintain meaningful relationships. CFIDS really threatens relationships, and many of them become more painful than nurturing."

"The losses have been hard," admits Christina Volkers, who has struggled with CFIDS for nine years. "I've had to give up going to school, and that also means not being in choir, honor society, musical performances. If I had not gotten sick, I would be up there with my friends, singing in the school musicals. It's hard for me to go and watch the performances because I want to be part of it so much. I don't feel jealous of the kids, but I do feel sad that I can't be part of it. I finished school through the GED program, in which I studied for certain tests, passed them, and earned the general education diploma."

"I think I lost a sense of stability when I got sick with CFIDS," says Becky Moore. "Before I got sick I never doubted that God would take care of me. It never occurred to me that I'd get sick as a teenager. I figured that when I'm sixty, I might get a little heart disease or something like that. I just assumed that I would go to medical school, get a practice, and have kids. But now all of that is uncertain. I may not be well enough to go to medical school. I may have a relapse that would make me unable to function. Dealing with the unknown future is the worst part of this illness. I like to set goals and work to achieve them, but CFIDS has changed all of that.

"I also miss things that were essential in my life, like performing music. Before I got sick I was in chorus. I've always done a lot of music at school, and I miss that very, very much. That was my outlet for everything emotionally, stress, praise for God, everything. I loved that. I played violin an hour and a half or two hours every day. Now I can only remember those times."

Twelve-year-old Brooke Volkers misses not being able to be a normal kid. "I wish I could go out and play with my friends. But I have to go to bed early, at eight o'clock. It's hard for me to look out my window and see my friends out, having a good time, and I have to go to bed. I couldn't handle gym class at school today, so I had to sit it out. I could see my friends having a great time. I just had to sit because the pain was so bad."

Brooke's fifteen-year-old brother, Steven, misses sports. He was an active tennis player before a case of pneumonia spiraled into CFIDS four years ago. "I have always played sports—tennis, baseball, cycling—then suddenly CFIDS took all of that away from me. At first it was real depressing. Now I've gotten beyond the discouragement. Every once in a while I try to do some tennis, but even hitting a few balls against a wall makes me sick."

Although fourteen-year-old Amanda Volkers has been able to attend school a few hours a day, her CFIDS also limits her life. "School is top priority, and until I'm well enough to go to school full-time again, I can't be involved in anything like cheerleading or swimming. I was on the yearbook staff, but I had to quit because I got too sick. That was one of the hardest things I've had to do. But it was either give up that or the group in my church. I needed the Christian fellowship, so I dropped the yearbook.

"Another loss I felt was having a mother with CFIDS. That was hard for me to adjust to at first. She doesn't get up as early as I need to, so I had to learn to do a lot of things for myself. In the beginning I felt sorry for myself: Poor me, my mom is too sick to be up with me. But I've learned to do it. Mom gets up ten minutes before I leave for school to check me over and make sure I have everything I need. One year she was too sick to go to the mother-daughter social at our church, but another woman took me. At first I felt sad and disappointed about that, but then I realized that we are all going to have to bend a bit to get through this time in our family's life, with six of us sick. My mom bends over backward for us, so I decided I need to make some changes too."

Timmy Volkers, who became ill with CFIDS when he was five years old, has a growing sense of loss in his life. "When I was in kindergarten, I was able to go to school only half days. In first grade I felt a bit stronger and was able to go a bit more. For the past two years I've been at school about half-time again. In the winter I'm often in the hospital with pneumonia; then I'm out of school more. It's hard to go back when I've been out for a few weeks. I wonder if the kids will tease me or if I'll get sick again. I love school and get good grades, but it's just hard to get back in with my friends after I've been so sick. That makes me sad."

Nancy Masoner, who became ill with CFIDS when she was fifteen, felt her losses gradually. "Before I got sick, I was active in school. I liked biking, and I enjoyed life a lot. My losses came gradually, and I grieved them gradually. One thing that I grieved a lot about was not being able to read. At first I thought I was just tired. I didn't realize how CFIDS affected me cognitively. I would be pushing and doing schoolwork as soon as I got home until ten o'clock, and then spending my whole weekend doing schoolwork and getting only half of it done. Finally I was unable to go to school at all.

"I felt a deep sadness about losing things. It was hard losing my friends. At the beginning of my sickness I wouldn't see or hear from my friends for maybe a month. That loss hit me hard, and I wondered if I would ever have friends again. It was a terrible picture of what life would be like, not being in school. I struggled with this loss a lot. When other friends move or go away to college, I say, 'Lord, you've given me friends in the past, but I think this is it. I won't be able to have any more after this. I don't see how I can meet people.' Finally I realized I need to let go of needing friends and let the Lord fill that need in his way. When I was able to do that, I felt more peaceful. He always has given me surprise friends. For instance, since I've been sick, a group of girls has come to our house to have a small Bible study, and that has been a wonderful bonding experience for us.

"As I look back, I realize that I haven't lost anything that I would want back. The Lord has given me so much more than I have lost. I enjoy beauty more. I enjoy my parents; they're my best friends. I enjoy all of life more. I would love to be in school, but I'm loving learning at home. Although I've lost my ability to do all those things, I now can say that I enjoy life a lot more now. In George MacDonald's book *The Peasant Girl's Dream,* he says, 'One of the hardest demands on the obedience of faith is to do nothing. It is often so much easier to do something foolishly.' I'm learning the joy of obedience in the quietness of life."

"CFIDS is the disease of so many aspects, physically and emotionally," says Beth Waysek, who has been severely debilitated by CFIDS for four years. "It's a Pandora's box, full of emotions and potential land mines. Living with CFIDS is like having my life taken away, losing the ability to do what I used to, losing the ability to think clearly. Knowing that I may never get my mind back to where it used to be is a horrible thought.

"I have suffered major losses. Relationships with my former friends have changed. They call me with their problems because I listen, but their problems are so superficial that I become frustrated. My peers and I are headed in the same direction, but we are on very different tracks. I don't go to school, so I've lost that whole life, the academic challenge, the hanging out after school with friends, the prom—all of it. I don't think I've lost my identity. If anything, I have become more sure of myself. I've handled my losses with prayer, and that has helped.

"I had trouble with God in the beginning. I felt so alone. I couldn't understand why God was doing this to me. One night as I stood in my room, I was crying, and I screamed at God, 'I hate you. I just hate you for doing this to me.' Although I felt horrible for having said that and although I had to ask for forgiveness, I got out my deepest feelings. That was a spiritual turning point for me. I have never felt since then that I hate God. He can take my anger and frustration, and I know he has forgiven me. I try to tell him what I'm feeling on a regular basis now."

School Life with CFIDS

"I got sick in the fourth grade," recalls our daughter, Alisa. "So I finished elementary school and went through all of middle school while I was sick. I was too sick to attend school full-time, so I went a few hours a day to school and then had the rest of the classes tutored at home. The first year my mom taught me the afternoon classes, and for the other years, the school district provided a homebound tutor who came every day to help me with my afternoon classes. When I was in eighth grade, I had a severe relapse and was not in school for six months. The homebound tutor had to teach me all the classes then. That was the worst time of my life. I would lie on the floor on a quilt most of the day, lifting up my head every once in a while to do some studying. When the tutor came, I was often too sick to write or even talk some days. But we got through all the subjects, except for algebra, which another teacher helped me finish over the summer.

"I came out of that horrible relapse enough to be able to begin high school. I took only four subjects, and I was able to go to school for those classes about four days a week. I would come home from school and do homework and occasionally meet with a group to work on a group project for my advanced classes. But by the end of the school year, I was so sick that it would take me four days to bounce back from being at school for three half-days. I would come home from school, drop my books, and go to bed. I'm not sure how I got through those last two months. I probably should not have gone to school many of those days, but I couldn't bear the thought of needing to study during the summer or getting an incomplete or maybe not being able to graduate on time. The brain fog got so thick that I failed several tests, and I had never failed a test before. It really hit me when I failed the test on the Holocaust. I specialize in the Holocaust; I've read dozens of books about the Holocaust, but I failed the test. But my teachers were understanding because they knew I was a good student and not just trying to get out of work, so they adjusted my projects and gave me extensions."

Britta Magnuson became ill with CFIDS when she was in seventh grade. "In the early years of my illness, I was able to go to school off and on, but this year I haven't been able to attend at all. A flu shot in the fall of 1993 sent me into a relapse that left me housebound. I'm tutored at home. It's hard for me to do homework because I can't always concentrate very well on reading and other things like that, even though I like to read. My writing has suffered the most. I can't write very well when I'm feeling sick.

"One of my tutors teaches me algebra and biology, which I like. This year I'm taking chemistry. I also have taken three years of Spanish and hope to take a fourth. I haven't been able to do any sports, though. I definitely want to go to college. I think I might take a year off after high school though just to catch my breath. I have not had a full summer vacation for six years because my studies always need to go into the summer.

"When I first got sick, I was in a private Christian school about an hour's commute from our town. For the first few years I was able to keep up with the work, but as I got into the higher grades, the demands became greater. Also, because the school is small, it was not able to be as flexible as we needed it to be. So I have now moved to the public school in my town, and that seems to be working better for me."

Nancy Masoner, who was in ninth grade when she became ill, tried to stay in school. "I was not in school for about a month and then I was just in and out. Then I tried to go full-time, but that didn't work. Now I'm not in school at all because I can't read for more than about five minutes. Reading makes me very tired in my head, and my eyes burn. Also my brain doesn't process the visual and auditory stimulation of being in a crowd either at school or at church. Several months ago I couldn't even listen to books on tape, but now I can do that again. A tape or a lecture or a book on tape eliminates some of the stimulation. Writing even short notes drains me. I can do low-level math for short periods of time.

"At this point, I am not concerned about graduating from high school. I hope to take the GED tests. For the immediate future, my education may be limited to listening to the classics on tape and having a few questions to respond to. I'm just letting go of any college plans because there's no way I can go unless I begin to feel better."

Many children with CFIDS opt to take the GED, the general education diploma, to earn a high school diploma. "For the first six years I was sick," Christina Volkers relates, "I went to school part-time. When I was a freshman in high school, I became too sick to continue school. I had been in honors classes, but suddenly I was unable even to do any schoolwork at home. That's when we decided to do the GED, general education diploma. I studied the workbooks and prepared for the tests. I passed the tests and will receive my diploma when I turn eighteen."

Steven Volkers, Christina's brother, has been homebound as well. "A tutor comes to the house and teaches me algebra, world history, English, literature, and biology. My biology teacher has worked with many students who have physical or mental disabilities, so he designed the biology course for my needs and sent the work home for the homebound teacher. That made all the difference. Without that sensitivity, I would not have been able to complete a laboratory class at home."

So far, Amanda Volkers has been able to attend school four hours a day. "I get up early to go to school, come home at noon, and then sleep. When I go home at noon, my friends think I am the luckiest kid because I can go home. I look at it just the opposite. I think *they* are the luckiest kids because they get to stay for the whole day and don't have to go home because they feel so sick they can hardly hold their head up. When my brain fogs up and I have 'no-brain' days, it's very frustrating."

Schools willing and able to be flexible offer children with CFIDS the best opportunity to stay in school. Sharon Walk wishes her high school had been flexible. "The school insisted that I take a six-class day. It was a disaster! I got sicker and sicker. I went from going to school almost every day in November to being there one out of every three or four days in January. At the beginning I went home every day, ate, changed, and took a nap. By January, I had to put my head down and rest in my classes. Luckily my math teacher was very understanding and let me use his class to rest so I could get through the rest of the day. Most of the time I didn't think I'd ever make it to the bus in the afternoon. I had trouble opening my own front door when I got home, and I had to sleep right inside the front door to get up the energy to get myself to bed.

"The school kept insisting that I add another class to my day. It lasted two days. I survived the first. The second day we went to see *Hamlet*. I slept the whole time, on the bus, at the movie, at lunch back at school, waiting for my bus home, on the bus home, and as usual on the floor inside my front door. When I woke up the next morning, I couldn't move. I was ten times sicker than I had ever been before. All my old symptoms were worse, and new stuff came up. For the first time, I had problems with my memory and concentration. I couldn't judge distances and had no sense of time. I was so scared; my brain just wouldn't work. After two weeks my mom called my doctor and told her that I was going to have to leave school again. I never went back.

"I've changed a lot since then. I've grown up, I guess. I finished high school at home, and now I'm taking college classes by mail. I can do only one class at a time, but I really enjoy it. I want to be a counselor and work with chronically ill kids. I'm still very sick. I'm totally home-bound and nearly bedridden."

CFIDS Forces Changes

Ann McErleane, like Sharon Walk and most kids with CFIDS, discovered that CFIDS has changed her. "The kind of personality needed to recover from CFIDS is opposite of my personality. It seems as if every part of my personality is wrong for the healing. It has been very hard to live with CFIDS, but it has changed me in many positive ways. Even though I can't do the things my friends are doing, God has touched a place deep inside me, and I am growing.

"In the beginning I would have horrible nightmares because I was in constant turmoil, trying to figure things out. I remember one night while I was sitting on my bed, I was crying out of fear and praying to God. All of a sudden, as I looked out the window, the most intense, incredible shock hit me. I don't even know how to describe it. Almost immediately my tears of fear transformed into tears of joy. I began to feel an incredible joy for all that I had and all that I was given. I felt God's presence with me, accompanied by a peace and joy inside me too. I felt very comfortable, very safe, more than I had ever felt. I was overcome by the realization of all that I *do* have. I am much more at peace with myself through this whole experience, and I'm not afraid to be myself anymore.

"I feel as if the lessons I've already learned are so valuable to me, for the rest of my life. At first I was angry that all of this had to happen to me at such a young age, but now I feel privileged. Now, at my age, CFIDS has taught me many important things, and I have the rest of my life ahead to enjoy the benefits of this blessing."

"CFIDS has changed our family a lot," affirms Christina Volkers. "Of course it has done some horrible things to our family; six out of seven of us have CFIDS. But in many ways CFIDS has strengthened us. I was the first one to become ill, nine years ago. I don't know what I would have done without my family. Even before the rest of them got sick, they were understanding, but they have become even more understanding now that six of us share the same illness. They are totally behind me in all the decisions I have to make because of this illness.

"CFIDS has drawn our family closer together. Because of CFIDS many of our friendships have been shaken. We look to each other more for friendship and support than we would have if we had all been healthy. We stay home a lot more, so we spend a lot of time together. We know more about each other than the average kids know about their brothers and sisters. The five of us kids are at very different stages in our lives, and normally we would be going in five different directions. But instead, we're all here, home together, enjoying each other and getting to know each other better. We pull together. It's hard on Brooke, who was the only well kid for a while, to see the rest of us be so sick. But now that she has CFIDS too, we can comfort her the way she used to comfort us.

"When I was first sick, I felt that God had left me. I was too sick to go to church or meet with other young people. My faith was quite young at the time. But now that I am older, my faith has developed more strongly, and I no longer wonder whether God is with me. I *know* he is."

"Before I got CFIDS, I knew I was a Christian," recalls Steven Volkers. "But I didn't understand who God was. I had doubts earlier, but now I know he's there. God comforts me when I am sad at night. I love the Lord so much more now. When our family has had financial problems, we have prayed about it, and he has answered the prayers. One time someone sent us a $200 gift certificate to a department store. The gift came with no name. We knew God had prompted someone to do that.

"I don't have many friends because I have been too sick to go to school. But my brother and sisters have become my friends. We have a deep connection with each other. We help each other to cope. I'm glad we have this illness because we can't afford to be mean to each other. Sure, we fight now and then and get frustrated with each other, but mostly we have to help each other."

Like Steven Volkers, Craig Maupin has found that his ability to maintain relationships has been severely limited by CFIDS. "Like many people with this illness, I grew more and more introverted. I was a mild introvert before I got sick, but I am more withdrawn now. I find that I withdraw from any situation that would require an explanation of my illness or a commitment. It is hard to live with other people's expectations of me at a time when I can barely predict how debilitated I will be from one week to another. I don't like some of these changes, but they have been forced on me by CFIDS."

"CFIDS has made me stronger," asserts Becky Moore. "In many ways it has strengthened my self-esteem. I had weaker self-esteem before I got sick. I was really shy. I got teased a lot because we didn't have the money for me to dress like other kids. So I was really a very withdrawn kid. Now I'm really the happiest I've ever been with friends.

"At first I questioned my identity. I guess I identified myself by what I did: I played the violin or I loved to work with children or I loved to sing or I loved science or I liked to volunteer. When I got CFIDS, I questioned: If I don't do these things, Who am I? What am I worth? I was voicing that question to a friend one day, and she said, 'Well, you care about people.' So basically what's most important to me is my internal role, not anything that I do. I do something loving or I read a book or I try to learn something and I find some sort of worth in my day. I trust that God is working in my life, and I trust him for my future. In the end, I believe, it will work out.

"I like the way I am now. I don't know if I would ever want to go back. I don't like being sick. I would love to get up this minute and have a wonderful experience and be healthy, but I am also learning a lot right where I am."

Sharon Gray has experienced a similar acceptance during her four-year battle with CFIDS. "I cannot think of anything bad right now. I'm not satisfied with where I am; I'm not satisfied with being sick. But I'm not angry, and I know I'm not crazy. I'm more sane now than I have been in my whole life. I've been completely debilitated for most of the years that I've been ill. I'm beginning to regain some of my ability to function now, but that doesn't matter.

"I'm finding more strength than I ever knew I had. I know that I'm headed in the right direction now, and I'm not afraid any more.

God is the center of my life. I've always had faith in God, but at one point I was confused. When everything slapped me in the face, I realized that I needed God and had been ignoring him, because he had always been there. I guess I started thinking differently at the worst point of my illness.

"I remember one night in particular. I never wanted to end my life myself, but I was at the point that I really didn't mind if someone else did. That night I felt as if I had broken free from something. I felt God was telling me that he wasn't going to put me through anything that I couldn't handle and that he was there for me and that I was safe. From then on I have felt him with me now more than ever, and I don't know what I'd do if I hadn't realized that."

"I really feel that God has a purpose for my having CFIDS," Beth Waysek affirms. "I may never know what that purpose is, but the most important thing I can do is try to be accepting, pray about it, look for the good things, and hang on to those as hard as I can. I still see God as a loving God, even though I am going through a horrible time. My greatest fear is that I will never recover my mind and that I will not be able to support myself when I get older. My parents have assured me that they will take care of me as long as I need it, and that gives me comfort while I wait."

Kids' Coping Strategies

"When I was the sickest, I kept a journal," offers Alisa Vanderzalm. "I wrote about what I was feeling, my frustrations. Some of what I wrote were poems; other entries were intense ravings. Now when I read back over the journal, I can see obvious places that I have grown. I realize I used the journal to counsel myself.

"I can see that some of the pages are blotted with tears. I remember screaming into my journal when I finally came to grasp that this illness may be with me for the rest of my life, that it's not something I can ignore, that it will be a big part of my life forever. That journal gave me a lot of peace. It gave me a way of seeing importance in myself, a way to see myself grow.

"When I wrote in my journal originally, I was unaware of what was happening. I started it to record my life, as normal thirteen-year-olds do. But of course I wasn't having normal thirteen-year-old experiences. Instead of notes about boys and clothing, the pages were full of questions like, "If God is so loving and kind, why did he give me this illness?" with twelve pages of responses. The entries that went into that journal were the kind only someone with a debilitating chronic illness could write. I had the time, and I certainly had the problems. It was only later that I could look back, and on those pages, in black and white, I could see myself grow. It was pretty amazing."

"One of the major things that helps me cope with my illness is CFS Youth Outreach," says Ann McErleane. "CYO, a network for kids with CFIDS, was started by Sharon Walk, who also has CFIDS. Coming into contact with Sharon and other people with CFIDS—people who shared my needs and questions and feelings—was a major turning point for me to be able to cope with this. I wrote letters to the other members of CYO. That was pretty much all I could do for a while. The mail was the highlight of my day. Some days I'd be able to walk up and get the mail, and that was my whole day. I would respond to the letters in the evening. I don't know how I could have made it through without that base of support. It was a big help."

"Because I have been unable to read," adds Nancy Masoner, "I have to listen to books on tape. We get the tapes through our local library, which has access to the government's books on tape for the blind. Our library can get anything in the world, which is wonderful. If our library doesn't have a book I need, even if the book has never before been recorded, the librarian will send in a request and someone will record it. They have magazines and some newspapers on tape too."

"When I became sick as a nine-year-old," Alisa Vanderzalm describes, "I could no longer go out and do active things with my friends, so my mom helped me compensate by creating a world that my friends could come and enjoy quietly at my house. Several years before I became ill, a woman had made a wardrobe for one of my Fisher-Price° 'My Friend' dolls. My friends loved to come to my house to play with the dolls and the wardrobe. Mom suggested that I

224

use a wing of our third-floor attic loft to create a large dollhouse. We put carpeting on the floor and gathered all the doll beds, chairs, dishes, and miniatures we could find. Slowly over the years my friends and I have decorated six rooms that we made with cardboard separators lined with wallpaper samples. We hung curtains at the window, stocked the table with clay foods, and filled the bookshelves with miniature books, some of which I wrote myself. I made quilts for the beds and braided rugs for the individual rooms. My aunts added to my collection by sewing more clothes for the dolls, and other friends have collected more dolls at garage sales because the dolls are no longer manufactured.

"The doll house has served several purposes while I have been sick. First, playing in the dollhouse was a quiet activity my friends and I could do together while we sat or I lay on the carpet. While we dressed the dolls and rearranged the rooms, we would talk and catch up on each other's lives. Second, decorating the dollhouse gave me a place to express my creativity in ways that my friends could value and share. Third, the dolls became my friends too as I gave to each of them a personality and history. Even though I don't play with the dolls too much anymore, every time I climb up to the loft, I see beautifully designed rooms filled with dolls dressed in calico dresses and pinafores, reminding me that those first four years I was sick were not a total waste. I think young girls will enjoy my collection for many years to come."

"I try to stay hopeful," says Craig Maupin. "Many days I don't even think about my illness, even though I still am quite debilitated. I think I'm realistic. I have faced the fact that I may never recover fully from this illness, but I don't want to force myself to accept the illness completely. I want to continue to hope that at some point I will be able to function enough to go to college, get a job, and get married."

Several children mentioned that their moms had been most influential in helping them cope. "It's been wonderful to have Mom being sick, too, just to be able to talk and not feel as if I'm complaining," says Nancy Masoner, whose mother, Barbara, also has CFIDS. "She's been very understanding and thoughtful. She and my dad have worked hard so that we have a nearly normal family life even though we don't do any of the things we did before Mom and I became sick. We're so much closer now."

"I don't know if I would have made it this far without my mom," says Christina Volkers. "When I first got sick, my mom was healthy. When she would give me advice about how to cope with the illness, I would trust her just because she was my mom. Now that she has CFIDS, too, I trust her because she practices what she taught me. She depends on the Lord, and she has taught me how to do that too.

"In one of the early years of CFIDS I had continual severe head pain that would often land me in the hospital with seizures. At one point the doctors needed to give me an MRI to rule out brain tumors as the cause of the pain. I was terrified of the whole procedure. The night before the test, my mom stayed up with me because I couldn't sleep. She comforted me. I remember that she read the verse from Romans that says, 'Nothing can separate me from the love of Christ.' That verse has become one of my favorite verses since then."

Steven Volkers, Christina's brother, shares some of the same feelings toward their mom. "Mom keeps me motivated. When I get stuck, she gives me a pep talk. She doesn't let us sit around or watch television or neglect our homework. She tells us to sit out on the porch for a while and get a different perspective. Whenever I need her, she's there. When I turned thirteen, she gave me a cross to wear around my neck. She said that the cross was to remind me that she would always be there for me and that God would always be there for me. Whenever I feel discouraged, I hold on to the cross and remember that."

"My father has been the one to help me cope," says Ann McErleane. "I don't know where I'd be today without my father. He also was ill when he was a late teenager and went through many operations when he was a young man. Overall he's healthy and can lead a full life, but he knows what it's like to be sick, especially at my age. I feel he's taught me everything I know. He's just an excellent role model. He's always been there, and he's always understood.

"I had to realize how hard CFIDS is on my parents too. I don't think I did at first, and I'm sure I still don't understand completely. I think that it's important for me to learn. I need to have a respect for their feelings too. I think a lot of it was knowing they were completely helpless. I'm their daughter, and they couldn't do anything for me. Well, they could support me and take me to the doctor, but they couldn't fix my problem. All my parents' friends' kids were off to college and doing things that I should be doing. It hurt them to know that I couldn't be doing that too."

Sharon Gray also recognizes her parents' part in helping her cope. "I had been living on my own for a year when I first got sick. But when I became too ill to care for myself, my parents took me back into their home and have sacrificed time and money, just everything. They have given every penny that they've had and provided whatever I needed. I couldn't even list the many things that they've done for me, because there are just too many. It's just too much."

"God has helped me cope with CFIDS. He has been real to me in my illness," explains Christina Volkers. "Recently my mom was hospitalized for complications with her CFIDS. It was a stressful week because my grandmother was also in the hospital for a cancer operation. But God gave me a peace that everything would be okay. The week my mom was in the hospital, our church youth group had a special speaker. He spoke to us from his wheelchair about his disabling physical condition that at one point nearly killed him. During one hospitalization, when he was in a coma, his wife would pray for him every night before she left, asking God to send his angels to protect her husband while she was gone. After the man came out of his coma, he told his wife that every night he had seen and heard angels around his hospital bed. As he and his wife told the story to us that night, their faces lit up. I could tell they had had a powerful experience with God. Then the man said, 'I believe someone here tonight has a parent who is hospitalized, a parent who needs those angels. Let's pray right now.' My brother Steven and I were so shocked to hear him say that. He had no way of knowing that Mom was in the hospital. But our youth-group leaders knew. So they and all the kids surrounded us and prayed right then for the angels to surround Mom. It was incredible."

Many children with CFIDS say that their pets have helped them cope. Britta Magnuson's dog and cat have given her companionship during her six years, especially during times of relapse. Alisa Vanderzalm's pet rabbit, Midnight, spent many hours cuddled up on her body while she read books. Clover, Amanda Volkers' bunny, has been her confidante during her years of illness. "Whenever I get depressed, one of our family members brings Clover to me and says, 'Mandie, Clover is very lonely and needs someone to talk to.' I know that it's the other way around; I'm lonely and need a bunny to talk with. She always cheers me up, even when I'm at my worst and am crying from disappointment. Clover doesn't care whether I'm dressed up or in my pajamas, whether I've had a good day or a bad one. She is always there for me."

"The best way for me to deal with CFIDS," says Beth Waysek, "is a sense of humor. At some of the bleakest times in the early months, our family laughed hysterically. The day my parents paid $400 for a hot-shot New York specialist to tell us that I needed psychiatric help immediately or I would be institutionalized—that was his diagnosis before he asked about *even one* of the symptoms that landed me in his office—brought us to a crossroads. We left his office and sat in the hospital cafeteria. While my dad went to get the food, my mom and I started to laugh. We lost it. We laughed ourselves silly, almost made ourselves sick, broke right through the chair. But it felt wonderful. I said, 'I am not crazy. We're going to fight this. We're going to make it.' We regularly exercise our humor. We have the corniest jokes, but we are still sane. I know that without my sense of humor, I wouldn't be functioning at all today.

"That hysterical laughter was a great mother-daughter bonding time. When my dad came back with the food, he didn't know what had happened. At first he thought the specialist had been right, and maybe both of us needed to see a psychiatrist! Now that I'm housebound, Mom and I are together all the time. She knows best what I am feeling because she has seen it all. She can tell what I'm feeling by looking at me.

"I also found help from a Christian psychiatrist. After the circus I had been through to get a diagnosis, I needed to gain some perspective. I could discuss with her all my emotions, and we could pray together. She helped me sort out some of my friendships too. Many of the friends I had before I got sick didn't want anything to do with me anymore. Some of the rumors going around were, 'Beth has AIDS' or 'Beth is pregnant' or 'This is all in Beth's head.' I basically lost all my friends. I was very angry, and my parents were concerned that I might become bitter through all of this. So it was good to talk it out with the Christian psychiatrist."

Friends and CFIDS

As Beth Waysek's comments indicate, dealing with friends can be one of the hardest aspects of coping with CFIDS. Children with CFIDS face misunderstanding, rejection, neglect, and fear from their friends.

"Friends have been cruel," says fifteen-year-old Amanda Volkers. "One of my friend's parents is scared to have me be around her child. Sometimes when I've made plans with my friend, she cancels them at the last moment for some vague reason. I then find out later that her parents didn't want her to be with me because they think she might get sick. A lot of girls in my school say things behind my back. I know that all junior high girls do that, but when you're sick and already feeling out of it, it hurts even more. My friends in the girls' program at church have been important to me. They let me relax and be silly. I need that time to feel normal."

"When I first got sick, we didn't know what was wrong with me," relates Becky Moore. "My friends were concerned in the beginning, but then they couldn't figure out how to deal with me. Plus, I was just too sick to talk to them, so I totally lost contact. I didn't hear from them at all for a couple of months. One of my friends told me that the kids at school were saying, 'Becky doesn't want to come to school. She's not sick. She doesn't look sick. She just doesn't want to be here.' They're really kind, good people at heart, but they don't know how to be around someone who's sick. I've lowered and lowered and lowered my hopes, but they haven't been able to give the support I need. That makes me angry. I'd like to think that I'd be different if I were in their places, but I can't say that I would be. I don't know.

"After I got a diagnosis of CFIDS, I wanted people to understand the illness, so I passed out some brochures that explained what CFIDS is. As a result, my closest friends knew that I wasn't making this up. We can still talk occasionally. Every couple months we'll talk on the phone for an hour and really, really talk, because there is some sort of connection there. But they can't handle visiting me. I get my support right now from my friends with CFIDS. I write and talk to friends I've met through CFS Youth Outreach."

Sharon Gray, who lives in the Maine woods, hasn't seen her friends much since she's been sick. "My friends up here don't really come around that often. At this point the people I feel more connected to are people I don't even see. I feel as if I have more friends now than I've had in my entire life, even though I don't hang out with them. The person that I consider my best friend is someone I met through a letter. Ann got my address from CYO and wrote me a letter. It was just a short letter, but I knew the second I read that letter what was going to happen and who she was. Ann has been a gift that's come into my life when I needed her the most. I feel as if meeting her was in God's plan for me. I've never met anyone so much like me, someone with whom I feel so much connection."

As Timmy Volkers grows older, he finds his need for friends grows too. "When I was in kindergarten or second grade and was sick with CFIDS, it wasn't so bad because my mom and my brother and sisters would be my friends. But now I need my own friends, and it's real hard. When I'm at school and we go out for recess, my friends want me to play ball with them. I tell them I'm too sick to play ball, and they don't understand. They say, 'Well, play with us, and when you get too tired, sit down.' They don't know that I'm tired and sick all the time. Then when I go home from school early, they think I'm going home to play or whatever. They don't know that when I come home I have to rest for several hours. Having friends when you have CFIDS is hard."

Alisa Vanderzalm reflects on her seven years of living with CFIDS and its impact on her friendships. "When I got sick, I was in the fourth grade, and it seems friends weren't as important to me then as they are now. I went to school a few hours a day, so I saw the kids. They really didn't have a clue what was wrong with me, but they began to see that it was normal that I left school at noon. Sometimes they teased me, saying I had a kindergarten schedule, but we all accepted it. If I missed a few weeks because I had an infection on top of CFIDS, they would send me a card or sign a huge poster to let me know they remembered me.

"When I got to middle school, things changed. I started needing friends more, but the way to have friendships in middle school is to do things together. Well, I couldn't do things. I was happy if I was strong enough to make it to school a few hours a day. And in middle school, it's important to be carbon copies of everyone else. Because I had CFIDS and because I didn't go to school full days, I was different. Therefore, I was ostracized and made to feel very friendless. I became self-conscious, shy, unsure of myself. While that's common for most middle-school kids, I didn't have a lot of emotional strength at that point. I needed most of my strength just to live with the nausea, pain, and exhaustion I felt every day as I dragged myself from class to class. Then when kids said mean things, I would fall apart. I cried a lot in those years. The very people I needed to support me in those years turned their backs on me because it was uncool to associate with someone who was different.

"Now that I am in high school, friendships are built not so much on doing things together or on being just like everyone else but on what's inside. Even though I'm still in school only a few hours a day and even though I can't be with my friends at night or on weekends, we can talk on the phone and write each other. I need a few friends who are loyal, patient, and unflappable. And the Lord has blessed me with several incredible friends."

Advice to a CFIDS Teenager

Brenda Sheridan, a twenty-nine-year-old with CFIDS, looks back on her years of illness and speaks to teenagers with CFIDS. "I wanted to be a counselor or teacher someday, get married, and have children of my own. CFIDS changed a lot for me, but it also taught me a lot along the way and made me a stronger person. Today I am happily married to a loving, kind, and understanding man.

"There was a time when I felt worthless because I couldn't work. I know now that's not true. We all have worth. I thought I was a weak person because I wasn't physically strong. Now I know that's not true, either. We all have different strengths and weaknesses. I may not be strong physically, but I am a strong person. People fighting this illness have to be strong in their own way. CFIDS has given me compassion and understanding. My friends call me when they have a problem because they know I'll listen.

"Don't ever give up on love. That special person may be right around the corner. When the time is right, you'll find each other, even if you're not looking. Growing up, there were many times I wondered how I'd ever find someone. Would anyone ever love me enough to accept me with this disease? Was it just an impossible dream? I'd just like you to know that I found that special person. And you know what? The day we met, I wasn't even looking."

What CFIDS Children Need from Others

1. *Believe us.* Believe that we are sick, even though we look fine (at least when we are out in public, we look fine), even though we have a hard-to-diagnose illness that people don't understand. Our symptoms wax and wane, and we have little control over how we will feel from day to day. We are not school phobics or hypochondriacs.

2. *Trust us.* Most of us are responsible, bright, capable people. Before we got sick, most of us were honor students. Teachers need to trust that we want to be the excellent students that we once were, but we can't. Sometimes our brains fog over, and we can't remember even simple things. Nothing on the outside will indicate we feel this way. Just trust us when we say it's happening. Teachers need to trust us that we will follow through on our homework, even if we can't meet the normal deadlines. Trust that we are not using you or the system for our own gain.

3. *Help us trust you.* We need to know that you are for us and not against us. We need to know that you will be there for us. We need to know that you will not use this illness to punish us or to make an example to others. Youth-group leaders need to know that we struggle with our faith; sometimes we question whether life is worth living. Stay involved with us, even though we may not be able to come to youth-group meetings or activities. Help us maintain relationships with one or two kids from the group. We are often too sick to take the initiative, but we need to stay connected to our peers in the church. We need to know that we are still part of Christ's body during this rough part of our lives.

4. *Try to understand us.* We struggle with a powerful and complex illness. We won't bore you with all the details of what we know about our illness, but we need you to try to understand some of the unique dynamics of our illness so that when we need to say no to something, you won't be puzzled that we can't be involved.

5. *Accept us.* We don't expect you to understand us completely; we don't even understand ourselves sometimes. But accept that we are debilitated, and help us have as normal a life as possible. Accept that we will be sick some days and not others. Accept that we will be deeply discouraged at times. Accept that we are still the same people, with the same ideals and the same idiosyncrasies, even though our bodies happen to be fighting a virus and an immune-system dysfunction.

6. *Stay with us.* We are not going to recover tomorrow or next week or next month. We may not recover next year. Don't let that frighten you. We are not going to die, but we may have relapses and become quite a bit sicker. We have come to accept that, and we need you to accept that too. Commit yourself to stay with us for the long haul.

7. *Keep in touch.* Check in with us and let us hear the school gossip: Who's going out with whom, what teacher did what, what happened at this party. When we are housebound, you may be our only link to the normal world. Call us, even if it's for five minutes. Teachers, we need you to stay in touch. Communicate with

us, especially if we're out of school for long periods. Tell us what you expect from us.

8. *Be our friend.* Realize that we aren't always going to be able to go to a mall or to a movie, but we still have a lot to offer a friendship. In fact, sometimes kids with CFIDS can offer a deeper relationship because we are there to talk. Many of us have gone through some pretty rough things, so we are often more mature than the average kid our age. We have been forced to think about a lot of things, so many of us can offer deep spiritual awareness and insight into life and others.

9. *Put up with us.* When we are sickest, we can get very crabby. We don't mean to be crabby, but it takes so much energy to live with this illness. Remember that most often we are not crabby with you—it's the illness.

10. *Send us cards, letters, or notes.* If we are housebound or bedridden, communicate with us through the mail or the phone. Send us encouraging cards. Make us a tape of greetings from friends at school or from our youth groups at church. Make a videotape of a party or meeting you're having. Help us stay connected to your world. Leave us messages on our answering machines.

11. *Make us laugh.* Help us keep perspective by making us laugh. Send us cartoons or lend us funny videotapes. Tell us the funny things that have happened in your life.

12. *Encourage us.* Tell us when you think we are doing a good job of coping with this illness. We can't compete in sports or perform in drama or music, so we don't have the normal access to affirmation. Let us know that our strength, perseverance, and courage are important to you.

13. *Pray for us and with us.* More than anything, we need to know that you stand with us in asking for God's help as we struggle with all the losses and changes CFIDS brings to our lives. Let us know you pray for us, and pray *with* us too. Come to our houses and let us hear your voices as you pray for us.

Chapter **12**

Help and Advocate for CFIDS Children

The family struggling with CFIDS must function well. There needs to be good communication between parent and child, appropriate behavior control, and above all, trust.

DR. DAVID BELL, *THE DOCTOR'S GUIDE TO CHRONIC FATIGUE SYNDROME*

When our daughter, Alisa, became ill with CFIDS seven years ago, Bas and I found ourselves in uncharted territory in several ways. First, our daughter had never been seriously ill before. Second, our family had never had to deal with a chronic illness before. Third, we were our school district's only family that had a child with CFIDS. Fourth, the medical community did not seem to know much about CFIDS in children. Fifth, we knew no other parents who were in our shoes.

We are glad to say that at least the last two factors have changed. Several specialists have done serious work in the past few years to study CFIDS in children and to treat their symptoms. To Dr. David Bell, Dr. Charles Lapp, and others, we express our profound thanks and support. As the years have ticked by, we have found other parents whose children have CFIDS. As we have shared our stories, we have learned from each other and have encouraged each other. We hope that the following chapter will do the same for you.

In many ways the parents of children with CFIDS are alike: We share the pain, challenge, and commitment to stand by our children as they face a crippling and confusing illness that is misunderstood and difficult to treat. In other ways we are different. Some of us have one child with CFIDS, while others have as many as five children with CFIDS. Some of our CFIDS children are young; others are teenagers or adults. Some of us know about CFIDS because we also have the illness, while others know CFIDS only through what their children tell them, what they observe, and what they read.

The insights shared in this chapter in no way represent expert opinions. We all merely describe what we are experiencing as we move through the years with our children with CFIDS. Because each family situation and each child is different, our responses to their illness vary. But that's the point. We can learn from each other.

Losses and Changes

In many ways I think it has been harder for me to be the parent of a CFIDS child than to be a person with CFIDS, although it's hard to tell where one stops and the other begins. On the one hand, because I also have CFIDS, I have instant empathy with what Alisa feels and experiences, and that brings a richness to our relationship. On the other hand, I'm a normal parent who sees her child lose crucial stages of her life, and that brings pain and sadness.

Parents of children with CFIDS move through many of the same stages outlined in the early chapters of this book: grieving the losses, accepting the illness, making the changes in your own life and in the life of your child, and staying strong.

"Rog and I have grieved deeply for our daughter Chris, who was sixteen when she became ill with CFIDS," says Sharon Postma, who also has struggled with CFIDS for over a decade. "Twice Chris has been totally debilitated. We wondered several times if she would be able to live through the night. She has had no social life and has had to give up college plans. She is now twenty-three and normally would be living on her own, but with her continual setbacks she can't live alone. Family support is critical to her. Watching her be so limited is painful. I know I could not have helped her as effectively had I not also been sick."

Like Sharon Postma, most of us feel sadness as we watch our children fight pain and exhaustion when they should be fighting their opponents on a sports field. We see them crippled by illness when they should be bouncing through the carefree days of childhood. We see their minds hampered by brain fog when they should be sharpened in classrooms with their peers. We see them confined to beds and couches when they should be developing their self-image on the stage, in groups, or in leadership positions. We see them struggle with friendships when peer relationships are so crucial for their growth. We see them dependent on us when they normally would be trying out their wings.

As the years pass, we grieve that our children are not getting better, and we face the grim reality that they may never completely recover. We grieve deeply when they go into relapses. We grieve our own helplessness.

Linda Waysek recalls the grief she felt in the first months her fifteen-year-old daughter Beth was too sick to go to school. "Every day I would cry. I would sit at the kitchen table, see the kids walk down to the bus stop, and cry. Beth wasn't going to the bus stop the way everyone else was, the way she should have gone. Our other children, Eddie and Rebecca, would come downstairs and ask, 'Did Beth go to school today?' When I would say no, their shoulders would sag. It became a discouraging thing to hear that school bus every day. And after a while I wouldn't open the shades anymore because I didn't want to see the other kids go by. It was horrible."

Steve Volkers grieves his son's losses. "It hurts to see Steven anxious about going back to school. For the past two years he has been able to start each school year, but within weeks, he becomes too sick to stay in school. He has spent most of his last two years working with home tutors. Now as he looks at another year of high school, he has the normal preschool jitters, but he also feels so alone. He has been out of the social flow for two years, and that increases his anxiety. It's tough for him, and I feel his losses too."

"It has been hard for Steve and me to watch our sick children at times become so despondent that they wanted to die," shares Cyndi Volkers. "We have observed that their level of despondency is directly related to how deeply disabled they are by CFIDS or by how long they have been out of life's flow. None of our children wanted to die because of the pain or the symptoms of the illness itself. Instead, they saw heaven as a welcome relief, a place where they would have the freedom to be normal, healthy kids. When Christina was in elementary school, one of her friends died from cancer. Both girls had enjoyed riding their bikes. During the last months before the friend's death, she spoke often of wanting to ride her bike in heaven. That's how our children have seen it too. Because of their intimate relationship to Jesus, they see heaven as a safe and inviting place."

Parents of CFIDS children grieve the losses not only in their children's lives but also in their own lives. We lose our own dreams for our children. We lose some of the dreams we had for our families. Two years before Alisa and I got sick, Bas and I had decided to spend our vacations for the next six years exploring the country with our children. Those years would be our family's "golden years," years when both our children would be free during the summer and able to enjoy family time together. For two years we were able to do that, taking our camping equipment and exploring our country's cities, national parks, historical sites, and natural wonders. We found those times to be rich in discovery, laughter, and togetherness as we read books aloud in the car, studied the various sites and people we would visit, and sat around the campfire each night. We lost the rest of those years to CFIDS.

Parents of CFIDS children lose their own space. Barbara Masoner expresses what many of us have felt. "I miss being alone. Before Nancy and I got CFIDS, I would paint in a private studio, which was for me a place of solace. I loved being able to be alone, listen to music, paint, and be totally immersed in that world. I have nothing really like that now. Now Nancy and I are at home all day together, and we've had to adjust to having our time and personalities overlap. Don't misunderstand me. Nancy and I like each other a lot, and we've become very close during these years of illness, but I don't have my house to myself anymore. Time alone is pretty much nonexistent.

"We've also lost our privacy. Most teenagers spend more and more time out of the house, but Nancy has been here with Dave and me. I miss our privacy. That's very difficult. But the positive side of the situation is that Nancy has had a greater opportunity to see Dave and me as an adult couple. She's seeing how it works. She and I have some natural opportunities to talk about the insights that the Lord had given me as a wife, to be vulnerable and share my faults with her."

Bas and I felt some of the same things. During the time we normally would have children out of the house, Alisa was with us often twenty-four hours a day. It isn't normal for an adolescent to be home all the time, an adolescent who needs to separate, who needs to individuate at this time of life. We wondered if our child would develop abnormally because she was with adults all the time and not with her peers.

Another mother adds these comments. "I have to confess that I became resentful of my sick daughter. I was frustrated with her sleep patterns. She can't get to sleep very well at night, so although she goes to bed about ten or eleven o'clock, she doesn't fall asleep until two o'clock in the morning. Then she needs to sleep later in the morning, which means I have to tiptoe around and make sure I don't wake her. I've adjusted to it now, but I remember my growing frustration."

"Looking back on the many years of mothering children with CFIDS," reflects Cyndi Volkers, "I wonder if I did the right thing by not allowing myself the gift of personal space. Because of our children's very real physical and emotional needs, I felt I needed to be available at all times. After I became ill with CFIDS, too, I allowed the children to visit me in my room, crawl up on the bed to cuddle, no matter how sick I felt. Because of the unfair curve CFIDS has thrown into their young lives, I felt driven to fill all their needs as well as I could. Meanwhile I short-changed my own physical, emotional, and spiritual well-being. I now realize that it may have helped *all* of us if I had enforced a private time or a people break for a few hours every afternoon."

The adjustments for parents of adult children with CFIDS have been great as well. One set of parents, close to retirement age, took in their single daughter who became ill with CFIDS when she was in her late twenties. She was completely bedridden the first two years and needed home care for two more years before she was strong enough to leave home again and go back to school part-time. That was not in the script either for the parents or for the daughter, who had lived on her own for many years before getting CFIDS.

Another mother and father moved across the country to care for their son and daughter-in-law, who both had CFIDS for five years. Although their son has improved some, their daughter-in-law has gotten worse. The situation is now so intense that every resource the parents have—emotional, physical, spiritual, and financial—is focused on helping her survive.

One couple has four young adult children with CFIDS; at one point three of the children had moved out and started life on their own. Thinking they were moving toward an empty nest, the parents put their house on the market and were looking to buy a one-floor condominium. But during the past year the three children who had previously moved out all had relapses and returned home to live with their parents. These parents are beginning to wonder whether their children will need continuing care from them during their adult years. The parents may never have an empty nest.

One parent who also has CFIDS said, "Some doctors have told people in our support group that the only way to recover from CFIDS is to do aggressive rest therapy. They suggest that the CFIDS sufferer's only goal should be to get better. They should rest whenever they need to and severely limit their activity. For me as the parent of a CFIDS child, that's impossible. Some days I feel very resentful that some people in the support group have basically quit their lives to get better. I don't have that option."

After facing and grieving the losses, we gradually come to a point of acceptance. This is the way life will be, and we will make the best of it. We make the necessary changes and commit ourselves to our child's wholeness in the midst of a broken situation. In doing so we become models for the CFIDS child as well as our healthy children of how to face adversity and how to integrate the illness into our lives.

As we attempt to be effective parents of our children who have CFIDS, we can give them several gifts: our trust, our support and encouragement, our love, our commitment to their growth, our commitment to bring balance to their lives, and our commitment to protect them and advocate for them.

Gifts We Can Give Our Children

Trust Your Child

One of the most important gifts we can give our children who struggle with CFIDS is our trust. This trust involves knowing your child, believing your child, and communicating effectively.

The trust factor is crucial in the early days of the illness, especially during the weeks and months before a diagnosis is made. Linda and Ed Waysek's experience with their daughter, Beth, is all too typical of what parents face in the early months. "We knew Beth was sick, that something was desperately wrong, but no one seemed to know what it was. We shuttled from doctor to doctor, specialist to specialist, but no one seemed to have believable answers to explain the exhaustion, mental impairment, nausea, loss of mobility, dizziness, and fever that reduced her to a very sick child. Some doctors told us she was school phobic; others told us she had psychiatric problems. While we were tempted to believe the professionals, whom we were paying for their best judgment, we also knew Beth. We knew she loved school and had no reason to use an illness to avoid the experience. We knew she was not suffering from some neurosis. We knew she spoke the truth, that when she said she was feeling a certain symptom, it was the truth. We didn't discount what the doctors were telling us, and we didn't stop trying to find out what was wrong. But we knew our daughter, and we believed her. Our instincts proved to be right."

Our situation with Alisa was easier than the Waysek's situation. I became sick with CFIDS before Alisa did, so that by the time she started to report symptoms, I knew what she was talking about. When she described the pain in her throat in her colorful way, with phrases like "cauliflower stuck in my throat" or "coral in my throat," I knew the swollen throat that made it hard to swallow, as if something were stuck midway down; I knew the rawness that felt as if coral had gouged my throat. Despite the fact that doctors could not explain her sore throats—she didn't have strep or mono or other throat infections—I knew they were real. Alisa's symptom cluster is different from mine, but we had enough overlap that I never doubted our nine-year-old when she reported what she was feeling. Because I could trust her and because she communicated her symptoms truthfully, Bas and I could confidently help her explain her situation to doctors and school personnel.

I have great respect for the parents who do not have CFIDS themselves. They truly have to trust and believe their children. I would hope that even if I had not had CFIDS, Bas and I would have trusted Alisa, but we know we would have had many more doubts and frustrations. The fact that the symptoms vary from one day to the next, that they can wax and wane from hour to hour is most frustrating. As Linda Waysek says, "The symptoms change from day to day. Beth and I laugh about it. It's almost a dial-a-symptom kind of thing. One day it may be the head pain and cognitive problems, the next the nausea and muscle pain, the following day the dizziness or all the above."

The unusual dynamics of CFIDS can be very frustrating to parents if they don't know their children and don't know the effects of CFIDS. It's imperative for parents to read reliable information about CFIDS, especially as it relates to children.[1]

Trust also becomes an important factor as the child gets older and makes more of his or her own decisions. When Alisa was first sick, at ages nine and ten, we made most of the decisions for her—treatment options, what activities she would be involved in, how much activity she could tolerate—because she didn't have the resources to do that. But as she gets older, she needs to make more of those decisions herself. As she does, she learns her limits—physical, emotional, relational, mental, and spiritual. She is learning the consequences of pushing too hard or of expecting too much from herself or of spending too much emotional energy on negative things.

It's not easy to watch Alisa make decisions. We sometimes can see a crash coming before she can, or we can anticipate the consequences of some activity. But we need to let her make those decisions. Many times she does not set healthy limits. She's driven by her need to be normal, to be involved, or to be in school when perhaps she should be pulling back, when her body is screaming with symptoms. Finally she crashes and then is too sick to do anything for several days. But she is learning. And when I am tempted to criticize her for her decisions, I need only to think about my own decisions. I'm a forty-seven-year-old person, and I frequently make poor decisions about my energy, and that's after seven years of practice. I have to realize that if it's hard for adults to find the delicate balance, then it's much harder for adolescents and children, who by nature want to pull out all the stops. So we advise, trust, and learn what to demand and expect of our child.

Barbara and Nancy Masoner found another interesting dynamic at work in their relationship as they both struggle with CFIDS. "I found it difficult to watch Nancy be sick, and I reacted in a strange way. I pushed myself to overdo, thinking that I would show her that she could go to church or she could read a little bit or whatever. I was trying to prove to her that we could do more than we felt we could do. The whole thing backfired. Not only could Nancy not respond, but I got sicker because I was overdoing. My journal reveals some of my thoughts during that time. 'Lord, you have shown me that I don't really understand Nancy or appreciate how hard she does push to do whatever she does. If I allow myself to realize the depth of her disability, I subconsciously become more obsessive and obsessed to show what I can do and what I think she could do. My obsessive performing is fear more than anything. I fear her sickness. She feels bad, I overdo. I get angry. But I'm afraid. I fear the permanence of this situation. I don't trust you, Lord. I'm afraid that you won't work this awful CFIDS time for our good.' That was a tremendous insight. I was able to back off after that and let her do less than I was doing and let myself do less. As I reflect on that time, I realize that the Lord is working this awful CFIDS time for our good."

Encourage and Support Your Child

"The best gift I can give my child with CFIDS is summarized in three words: Encourage, encourage, encourage," says Sharon Postma. "That means I try to understand her, empathize with her, let my anger go. That means I accept her for who she is right now, not for what she could have been without CFIDS. That means I give her my time, my hugs, and other expressions of love. That means I do special things for her and praise her for even the little things.

"I have felt like a full-time psychologist during the years Chris has been sick. God has given me an enormous amount of wisdom and understanding in this situation. Sometimes I need to listen for hours as she talks through what she's dealing with. But I feel that's one way I can support her. I take her seriously and stay with her until she has worked her way through a stormy situation. We have drunk countless cups of tea together in the night, when neither of us can sleep.

"But I look at Chris now, six years later, and I see growth. She has a healthy sense of humor and an increased sensitivity to the needs of others. She's very mature. She has gone through so much pain and disappointment—not only with my illness, but also with her own—that she can look at other people going through hard times and really empathize."

Encouraging our children through the hard times is a great gift we can give to them. People with CFIDS have so little emotional reserve that discouragement can easily overwhelm them and threaten their perspective. Alisa, who feels things intensely and articulates them with equal intensity, has experienced some very deep despair. She trusts me enough to share that despair with me as she sobs out her questions or anger or lack of hope. It's painful for me to watch her go through those times, to listen to her piercing questions and pain.

When Alisa is very sick, it takes every ounce of emotional energy she has just to go from one day to another. She often collapses emotionally, overcome by hopelessness. One night during a particularly sick week, she lost it. She was distraught and very angry with God. She sat on my bed and sobbed and shouted at God for over an hour. Then she felt such guilt at what she had said to him that she couldn't even hold up her head. I knew that easy answers and pat phrases had no place in that situation. Besides, I had no easy answers. So I held her and rocked her until her body stopped shaking and until she settled down. I assured her that God could handle all of her feelings, that he knew how hard it was for her to cope with this illness, and that he would not reject her for what she had said. I held her in my arms that whole night because I wanted to demonstrate on a physical level that no matter what she says to God, no matter how despondent she feels, he will still hold her and never, ever let her go.

Guard Your Child's Self-esteem

"Children with CFIDS have to endure a lot, not only physically but also emotionally as they face doubt and insensitivity from other people," says one mother. "Each insensitive comment is a blow to their self-esteem. After having been too sick to be in school for several weeks, our daughter returned to school somewhat shaky, only to be greeted with 'How nice of you to stop by for a visit' from one of her teachers. She also had to face the rumors that she had been in a mental institution for several weeks. The staff heard the rumor, but they did nothing to squelch it. As parents, we need to do all that we can to prevent that insensitivity. Let's have the school be open with the students about the kids' illness. Our kids are in a Christian school. Let's have the school pray for them as they do for any other person who is struggling with illness. We need to boost our children's self-esteem whenever we can. We can help them develop coping skills, help them find things they *can* do, help them see themselves as valuable."

"We have fought to guard Calen's self-esteem on every front," says Karen Lang, who also has CFIDS. "Calen is remarkably self-assured for a young man who's gone through what he has. He not only has had CFIDS for six years, but he also has serious learning disabilities. We have set up situations that will enhance his self-esteem and not undermine it. One of our decisions involved keeping Calen in his Christian school, even though it can't offer him a lot of special programs. At the Christian school Calen is surrounded by people who may not understand CFIDS, but they understand Calen as a person and are supportive and flexible. The school taught the other students at a very early age that Calen has learning disabilities but that doesn't make him any less a human being. And if Calen can't read very well, then God probably has given him a special talent, and it's their role to help him discover what that is. His peers in his class stand in the gap:

They read to him or help him with oral testing or correct his papers. They accept it. 'Oh, Calen can't read well, but, boy, can he play base-ball.' Calen goes just a half-day to the school, and he does other classes through a tutor. The socialization and support at the school are essential to him. He has remarkable self-esteem."

Commit Yourself to Your Child's Growth

The Langs, like many parents of children with CFIDS, are committed to their child's growth. Their commitment expresses itself in the choice to drive a forty-mile round trip and pay full tuition to a Christian school so that Calen can attend a few classes there because that's where his social network is, that's where he can grow, that's where he can find wholeness.

One family's commitment to their child's growth led to leaving their church, where they had been members and leaders for over twenty years. Some church members' inability to accept their child's condition and the inability of the youth group to handle their child's illness led the family to another church. "Changing churches was one of the hardest things we've done, but we needed to do it. We need to be at a place that helps us stay spiritually strong. This illness is devastating. We need other Christians who are supporting us, praying for us, encouraging us, challenging us—all of us, our child with CFIDS as well as us, the primary caretakers."

"When we talk with our five children and ask them how they have come to accept their lives with CFIDS and not be bitter," says Steve Volkers, "they say to us, 'Mom and Dad, you always taught us to emphasize the positive. You have never overlooked the negative aspects of this illness. You have let us cry and be angry about CFIDS, but you also taught us never to let the negative side weigh us down so that we can't function. You have shown us how to look for the positive aspects, accent them, use them to grow on, and make the good parts bigger.'

"I see our kids acting on that perspective. For instance, when Steven, our older son, gets discouraged about how many of his teen years have been colored by CFIDS, he thinks of our younger son, Timmy, who has been sick since he was five years old. Steven says, 'At least I had those years. I'm grateful for the good years I did have.' He could be saying, 'Look what I've lost. How horrible.' When I ask him why he's not saying that, he responds, 'Well, that kind of attitude isn't helpful. It will only make me lose ground and keep from moving ahead. Yes, it is horrible, but I'm going to make it.'

"It's heartwarming to hear our kids say that we have taught them the importance of emphasizing the positive. With so many people sick in our family, I often feel as if we are just trying to survive, to get through this day or that crisis or this hospitalization. I'm a pragmatist by nature. I'm not always aware of the gifts I'm giving my children. I have tried to be responsible, both at work so that I can provide financially for my family and at home. I assess what needs to be done and try to do it. Cyndi is the frontline person to help the kids with most of their illness-related feelings and problems. I try to do the practical things: shopping, laundry, playing board games with the kids, making sure I get the family out once in a while so that they feel somewhat normal, helping our children have some fun in the midst of their debilitation. I don't think about it too much. But it's reassuring to hear our kids reflect that in the midst of all the survival tactics we have also taught them some valuable life skills."

Dave Masoner has seen the years of his daughter's illness as a time to spend more time with her and focus on her growth. "I have new opportunities to nurture Nancy and exhibit the Lord to her because she is homebound with her CFIDS. Last year, when she was able to go out a bit, we had a birthday dinner together, and we had a wonderful time. Realizing that I am committed to her growth, she once asked me to listen to a tape of a program she had heard on the radio. I ordered the tape and listened to it. The tape was about a guy who learned to pray with his daughter alone before she went to bed. So Nancy and I have been doing that for a few years now. And she just glows after we pray. That little bit of time, thirty seconds to a minute, of asking the Lord to bless her sleep and protect her or of praying for a future husband for her gives her such security and blesses us both."

Committing ourselves to our children's growth also means that we continue to discipline our children, even though they are debilitated by CFIDS. That's not easy. "It's hard to know when to push and when to back off, when to expect from my sick child what I would expect from any child her age and when to let go of any expectations," says Linda Waysek. Again it helps to know our children. If our children exhibit negative behavior that needs to be dealt with, we can't wait until they recover from CFIDS to take care of some of those things. If we sense our child using the illness as an excuse to indulge in negative behavior, then we need to address that. But we must remember that the illness sometimes exaggerates our children's weaknesses too. We must use discernment when we discipline our children. It's wise to wait until a child bounces back from a crash before talking to him or her about the need to change behavior and set limits.

Compensate for the Losses

One of the significant ways Bas and I have committed ourselves to Alisa's growth during her years of CFIDS is by compensating for the things she has lost. As parents we are the guardians of our child's whole person, not only her physical well-being but also her emotional, relational, mental, and spiritual well-being. Our goal is to keep a balance in her life.

When CFIDS robbed Alisa of her ability to take drama classes and be involved in drama clubs, we worked to balance that loss by renting videos of classic dramas, by getting videotapes of her school's drama performances, and by taking her to a few major theatrical productions. That wasn't easy. We would rest up for days ahead of time so that we could sit during a three-hour performance of *Les Miserables*; then we would crash for days afterward. Alisa will tell you we almost cried when the theater elevator was not working and we had to climb four flights of stairs to get to our seats at *The Secret Garden* on her last birthday. She was so nauseated several times that we thought she was going to lose her food. We can laugh about it now, well, almost, but we thought we weren't going to make it. But ten years from now Alisa will remember the magic of the drama production and music, and we hope she will forget how sick she was.

Alisa has already described the doll room we made so that her friends would be eager to come to spend time with her, even though they were all used to doing active things with Alisa before she got sick.

When Alisa looks back on these years, we hope she will look at the rooms she has designed and realize that she may not have been able to be in art classes, but she could express her creativity in a fantasy place that her friends could enjoy with her.

When she couldn't be involved in any groups at church, we arranged for a particularly sensitive and compassionate young woman to come to our house once a week to spend some time with Alisa. They did quiet needlework together and talked about things that mattered to them. When Alisa couldn't be involved in her friends' lives, we visited a local church's library and brought her stacks of books to read about people her age. When she was too sick to read, friends brought her books on tape or videotapes of children's classics.

Balance is the key. When Alisa is feeling particularly out of the social flow, we allow her to go to a birthday party or to a sleepover. Sometimes that means she is sicker for a week, but we have to judge that helping her stay emotionally and socially balanced is the most important thing for that week.

A few times we've had to force some balance on her. One week after watching Alisa's being cooped up in the house, Bas felt she needed to get out. When Alisa resisted, he decided to "kidnap" her. He carried her to the car, put her quilt, pillow, and rabbit with her in the backseat, and took her for a ride. We ended up at a sandwich shop an hour away. He put my parka over her flannel nightgown and escorted her to our booth. The three of us tried to pretend that everything was normal, that Alisa was not dressed in her nightgown and slippers. We giggled over our food that night, and we've giggled about that scene many times since then.

"One of the things we have tried to compensate for in Nancy's losses," says Dave Masoner, "is in the area of dating. She's just too sick to be involved in that part of life right now. We as parents can model a godly marriage relationship, and we can also fill in the gap sometimes. I have taken Nancy out on 'dates.' I hold the car door open for her, seat her at the restaurant—things that aren't considered to be politically correct right now, but things she and I enjoy. We talk about a variety of things, including what male-female relationships are all about. We have helped Nancy host a Bible study for young women her age as well as a prayer group of college young people."

Advocate for Your Child

One of the major gifts we can give our children with CFIDS is to advocate for their needs. That advocacy means representing them, explaining their situation, and, if necessary, fighting for their rights with the medical community, the school district, school personnel, as well as friends and family.

The need for one father to advocate for his daughter has changed him. "I'm generally a quiet, compliant person, but since our daughter has had CFIDS, I have learned to be aggressive, to be tenacious. Probably the toughest thing for me to deal with has been the response of the church and public schools to our daughter's illness. And probably the church more than the public schools. It's been very disappointing, and I have really struggled with that. I've talked with our pastor and talked with some of the elders and friends in the church. They say, 'Well she looks great. She doesn't look sick.' Or a man up the street says, 'If you had faith, you'd be better.' I've tried to protect our daughter from this kind of assault by intervening. Although the church has not ministered to our daughter, God has. And that's important for me to realize. I won't always be able to advocate for her, but God loves her more than anybody on earth does. If I can keep that focus, I won't walk around with a chip on my shoulder, with expectations that haven't been reached."

Education and CFIDS

By far the most important area of parental advocacy for children with CFIDS is the educational system. As David Bell says, "Numerous factors are involved in the difficulties faced by the school-age child with CFIDS, including severity of the illness, time lost from school, the degree of cognitive problems (ability to think clearly), the flexibility of the educational program, family functioning, and the child's ability to cope."[2]

Dave Masoner, who has taken on that role of educational advocate in their family, says, "I was surprised to find that the people in the schools are really not advocates, especially if your child doesn't have any mental disability. I had to gain a lot of the information on my own, and I had to become a very, very strong advocate. I called the NICCYD, the National Information Center for Children and Youth with Disabilities. Finally I got the school's attention, and they set up an IEP meeting (individualized educational program). They tried to tell me that they couldn't do anything for Nancy because she was too smart. It was one of the most frustrating processes I've ever been involved in. But I have some ideas now, and I'm going to go back and explore the transition program under the ADA, the Americans with Disabilities Act. Children who don't have a high school diploma and who are under age twenty-one are guaranteed help with a transition into the world of work or education or wherever their goals are. These people have wonderful information, are accommodating, and are very aggressive.

"Nancy is too sick right now to consider much of anything, but we will stay on the trail of getting her some help when she gets strong enough. At this point we are trying to give her an education at home. Nancy is content with that. If she never goes to college, that will be fine with her, but she wants to learn. And we're trying to avail ourselves of programs on the Discovery Channel and other educational programs. Our church library has videos about church history, history, and the arts. So we're trying to do what we can do, and possibly that will ultimately evolve into an external degree of some kind. This year Nancy hopes to be involved in a college Bible study group just so she can be interactive with people her age."

Ruth Magnuson has also needed to become an advocate for Britta. "I learned that our town's school system is required by law to pay for our daughter's tutors, even though in the beginning she was not enrolled in the public school. She is a town resident, and that qualifies her for these funds. Many parents aren't aware of the city and state laws that would benefit them, because the cities and states do not disseminate the information. I had run for school committee twice in our town, so I had learned a lot of the regulations and laws. I was involved with people who had problems, and I would check things for them. I never dreamt that I would be using the special-education laws for my own daughter. The laws are fairly clear for children who have a learning disability or a severe handicap that is noticeable. But CFIDS is so unusual. In the fine print, the state allowed for severe illnesses and catastrophes like accidents. And that's where we fit."

"Beth has been home from high school for two years," says Linda Waysek. "We have a homebound tutor. It's been hard, but it was either that or have these horrible relapses. She would try to go to school for a while, but she would get sicker. It just wasn't working. At one point when she was at school, she lost her mobility and got stuck in the stairway; she couldn't go up, and she couldn't go down. That was the last straw.

"The tutors have worked well with Beth. Math calculations and computation have been particularly difficult, only increasing the cognitive problems she was having. The history and English tutor would have to read aloud the questions to Beth because something happened between her brain and her hand. She would orally answer with the right response but would mark the wrong answer with her pen. It was a day-to-day thing. Some days she's sharper than others, but we always know that any additional exertion could cause her to crash."

Our daughter, Alisa, has been blessed with an understanding school system at this point. We have worked hard on that. I have worked to communicate, to meet with people to help them understand. Each year Bas and I meet not only with the guidance counselors, but I also meet with each teacher Alisa will have. The activity of those initial weeks of school puts a great strain on my body, but I feel that the investment is worth it.

Before I meet with each teacher, I send a letter explaining Alisa's situation.[3] I know that most of the letter won't sink in or that the teachers will forget much of what is in it, but I hope they will keep it in their files for later use. Then I meet with each one of them, assuring them that Bas and I will work with them in any way that we can to ensure a smooth year for Alisa and for them. Every two or three months I send each of them an update of Alisa's condition from our perspective at home. If she regresses, I send a note earlier. I feel it is important for them to know that even though Alisa may be perky in their classes, she is often sick every afternoon and most weekends. I use the update letters as an opportunity to thank the teachers for their extra work and kindness on Alisa's behalf. Having been a high school teacher, I know that dealing with a special-needs child in the midst of a heavy class load takes extra energy and effort. Midway through the school year, I also write a letter to the principal, expressing our appreciation for the way the guidance staff and teaching staff are helping our daughter get through the year.

When Alisa first became ill with CFIDS, I tutored her when she was too sick to be in school, thinking certainly she would recover the following week. Before her second school year with CFIDS, her pediatrician said to me, "I know you have a teaching degree and are qualified to teach Alisa, but I don't think it's wise. Not only do you need to safeguard your own health, but you also need to be strong enough to be a mother, nurse, and encourager to a sick child. Someone else can tutor Alisa, but no one else can be her mother." That was sound advice, and we are glad we took it.

Middle school was hard in many ways. Not only was Alisa quite sick, but she also was going through the normal early teen developmental stages. Plus the academic load was less flexible, and she had to deal with some disbelieving and insensitive teachers. Children are at a tough stage in their development in middle school, often forming their identity by ridiculing anyone who is different. Alisa's own identity was not yet well developed enough to withstand some of the pressure, and she was often in tears after a few hours in school.

High school, so far, has been a better experience. She has some incredibly faithful friends, and her self-esteem has soared. With the consent of the school's guidance department, Alisa takes only a half-load of academic classes. In her first year of high school, three of those classes were advanced-level classes, so she still works hard, but she occasionally has a weekend with no homework. She needs that break, which she hasn't had for five years. In previous years she had worked every weekend, every break, every summer vacation because she was always behind. This way she has some bounce-back time. Her second year she has opted not to take as many advanced-level classes so that she has more time to recover on the weekends. She may need to take summer classes or take a fifth year to finish high school, but our focus now is maintaining a balance that will allow her to be in school a few hours a day at least a few days a week.

A parent who has done extensive work as an educational advocate for children with CFIDS is Karen Lang. Lang, who also has CFIDS, began her work as an advocate for her son, Calen. Lang writes about their family's experience with the educational system in "Calen's Story: A Child's Journey Through CFIDS," which appeared in the Winter 1994 issue of *The CFIDS Chronicle*. Calen was in a private, Christian school when he became ill with CFIDS. Researcher and CFIDS specialist Dr. Daniel Peterson, Calen's doctor, recommended home schooling provided by the local school district so that Calen could recuperate. But the loss of his social network at his Christian school left Calen withdrawn and reclusive. The Langs and Dr. Peterson agreed to have Calen be involved in baseball, a sport that would give him social contact without demanding a great deal of physical exertion. The school district balked, insisting that if Calen was well enough to play baseball, he was well enough to be in school. They did not feel they needed to serve Calen's needs any longer. However, after meeting with five school officials, the district agreed to Calen's need for socialization and continued to provide the home schooling.

However, the next year the district refused to provide the home schooling, insisting that those services were available only on a short-term basis. When Lang asked what services were available for their son, she was told that maybe another district could provide better services. Following that advice, Lang explored options with other districts but was told they were not willing to pay for services that the local school district should provide. At that point Lang "called the legal and special education departments of the California State Department of Education to find out what Calen's rights were. I was told that he was entitled to receive educational services at home if his medical problems prevent him from functioning normally in a regular academic environment. I was also told that if the district drags its feet in responding to our request for services, I should ask for a due process hearing, to be conducted by independent legal counsel, at the district's expense.

"Empowered by this information, I called the assistant superintendent and told him, . . . 'You should be advised that I have been in touch with the legal department at the State Department of Education and I know what Calen's rights are. He is protected by PL 94–142, Section 504 [the Education of All Handicapped Children Act of 1975].'" The school official contacted the Centers for Disease Control and learned that the disabilities Calen had as a result of CFIDS did, indeed, make him eligible for Section 504 services.

Lang shares several suggestions for parents working with school districts on behalf of their children with CFIDS. "Approach the district with an attitude of cooperation but with the knowledge that your CFIDS child is entitled to special services under Section 504 of PL 94–142.

"Don't be afraid to get tough if you need to. Remember that the student has the benefit of the doubt if there are any problems. He/she is eligible for a number of different services. Some, the district may not know about, and some it may hope you won't find out about. Services include access to counseling, physical therapy, social work services, transportation (if needed), and a variety of mechanical aids such as calculators, computers, and tape recorders so that disabled students can function more easily and on a more equal basis with nondisabled children at their grade level. Ignorance of what is available, lack of time, and lack of money may be the district's concerns, but your child's academic and emotional growth and development are yours. Keep in mind that you are negotiating your child's future.

"Don't hesitate to contact either the assistant superintendent in charge of student services or the district superintendent if you find you are getting nowhere with their lower-level representatives.

"Gather as much information as you can before dealing with the district so that you are prepared to counter arguments in the event that your child is initially ruled ineligible for district services.

"Contact the National Information Center for Children and Youth with Disabilities (NICCYD), P.O. Box 1492, Washington, DC 20013, 800/999–5599. NICCYD is an organization that provides resources for specific questions (CFS is in its database), referrals to other organizations, packets, and lists of publications. I received a free packet that included a copy of the Americans with Disabilities Act of 1973, with revisions since then, including PL 94–142, and an explanation of Section 504, the part that applies to CFIDS kids. It has been a valuable resource.

"Protection and Advocacy, Inc. is another excellent resource. It is a nonprofit federal agency that provides a variety of free legal services for the disabled, including Section 504 children. The organization has regional offices—check the business white pages in the phone book for the telephone number or the listings under the Department of Health and Human Services in the Federal Government section.

"Finally, do not forget that your state Department of Education has important resources and information. When I told the assistant superintendent that I had been in touch with the legal branch of the State Department of Education about Calen's rights, the change in his approach was remarkable.

"Above all, believe your child. Be prepared. Be empowered by the information and support services available to you. Be diplomatic but firm in your dealings with representatives who may be ignorant or stubborn in their views. Be aware of experts who warn of behavior problems. Be willing to share what you learn about working the system with others who follow."[4]

Karen Lang has recently been appointed to The CFIDS Association of America's public policy advisory committee (PPAC) and is working with the U.S. Department of Education to determine CFIDS children's eligibility for special services under the IDEA, Individual Disability Education Act. She and her colleagues are optimistic. The CFIDS Association of America will make information available to its readers when the study is completed.

Developmental Adjustments

I hesitate to include this section because most of these issues are still a puzzle to me. We all know that parenting any child requires much wisdom and prayer. Parenting a sick and debilitated school-age child presents challenges we are not sure how to handle. Then, when that child is also moving through what for him or her may be the period of greatest internal growth and development—adolescence—the task seems overwhelming; it's nearly impossible to discern which behavior and attitudes are the result of the illness and which are the results of normal adolescent development.

I offer the following observations not as an expert but as a parent who has listened to several dozen children and other parents talk about their experiences with CFIDS. I've asked Cyndi Volkers to share some insights too, since her experience as the mother of five children with CFIDS has allowed her to see the effect of the illness on children from ages five to nineteen.

Young Children

On the one hand, CFIDS children from ages five to ten find it difficult to maintain peer relationships. Most of their friendships exist within organized group activities: school, sports, clubs, Sunday school classes, and other small-group activity. When CFIDS moderately or severely limits young children's ability to be involved in these activities, the children lose many of their friends. On the other hand, young children are more content than older children to be alone or have a parent or sibling fill the friendship gap.

"I found it was very important for Timmy to feel emotionally safe in a classroom," says Cyndi Volkers. "When he was out of school for several weeks at a time, which often happened in his first few grades of school, it was hard for him to make the transition back to the classroom. If he knew the teacher would protect him emotionally by not letting the kids tease him or ask too many questions about why he was gone, he was more ready to go back. Several times when he returned to school from an absence, the teacher invited me into the classroom to help her with a project for a half hour, giving Timmy a chance to see me while he got adjusted to being back in school. As soon as we felt he had settled in, she thanked me for my help with the project, and I would leave. As Timmy got older, that transition became easier for him."

Fears in young children with CFIDS tend to be more about the immediate symptoms and the immediate losses than fear about the future or questions of why they are sick. Some young children with CFIDS have expressed fears that they are going to die.

More than the older children, the young children with CFIDS need advocacy; they need parents, teachers, and medical professionals to intervene for them. "When Timmy was in first or second grade, I could explain to the adults in his world what his illness involved. However, it was very hard for him to explain his illness to other people, especially his peers. They had no idea how sick he felt when he came to school, how sick he became when he was at school, and how long it took him to recover from sitting at his desk for a few hours a day. They had no idea how often he cried because he couldn't be in class with them. I offered to go in and talk with his class, but he was uncomfortable with that. He is open to having his doctor, a young male, come to talk to his class, so we may try that."

Needs of males and females differ at young ages. Males tend to build self-esteem in areas of physical activity, whether that be organized sports or wrestling with a sibling. Cyndi Volkers comments, "Steve had to learn how to be a father to sons who couldn't do the normal father-son things, like biking, hiking, playing ball, wrestling. The typical father-son activities were out of the question. Steve has had to learn to play board games or to play with Matchbox® cars while Timmy lies on the floor. Similarly, it has been hard to find boys who will play with sick boys and form relationships. I have consulted with the local centers that serve children with cancer, cerebral palsy, and arthritis, but I haven't come up with anything satisfactory. I've concluded that I can't expect young children to change their play habits or level of activity for a sick child."

Early Adolescents

CFIDS children between the ages of ten and fifteen find the loss of friendships to be more difficult than it was when they were younger. As children get older, they are less content to have parents fill the social gap; they need other people, outside people. Again, if CFIDS children are in school only a few classes a day or unable to be in school at all, then their opportunity to form a social network is severely limited.

Early adolescence is a time of major physical, emotional, and social change. Children's bodies and emotions grow and change at alarming rates, leaving them sometimes overwhelmed at what's going on inside them. At this age most children enter middle school or junior high school, where they deal with peers who can be cruel and insensitive as they form their own identities, often at the expense of other people. Early adolescents need to be like everyone else.

Children with CFIDS go through these changes with an illness that threatens their self-esteem, their metabolism, their hormonal balance, their major social sphere. CFIDS children are different. They are absent from school for long periods of time; they can't participate in most extracurricular activities; they have a "weird" illness.

It appears that CFIDS affects the metabolism of adolescents. "Children in our CFIDS support group are like two ends of the spectrum," reflects Cyndi Volkers. "Either they lose lots of weight, which four of our children have done, or they gain weight, which one of our children has done. Our older son, who was twelve when he became ill with CFIDS, went from one hundred thirty pounds down to as low as ninety pounds. He is slowly gaining back the weight, but at sixteen, he is still only a little over a hundred pounds. The female early adolescents in the CFIDS support group found this weight issue to be a major struggle in their ability to maintain positive self-esteem."

Parents' need to advocate at this stage is greater in the school situation because the number of people who interact with their child more than doubles from elementary school. Middle-school teachers tend to be less involved than elementary-school teachers in the lives of individual students. One mother commented, "When my daughter returned to school after a short relapse, the teacher announced to the whole class: 'If you're going to be in and out of school, you may as well not be in my class because you won't pass anyway.' He wasn't willing to deal with her individually, so he chided her in front of her peers. This is not what this child needed on her first day back after a tough relapse."

The females in a CFIDS support group for children have discovered that they face another problem in this life stage: menstrual abnormalities. All the adolescent females in the group were taking hormone supplements because their menstrual flow did not stop on its own. They also discovered that nearly all of them felt more weak and sometimes fainted during the first week of their period. Menstrual problems seemed magnified by CFIDS.

Older Teenagers

As children with CFIDS reach the ages between fifteen and nineteen, several significant changes take place. They are much more willing to talk about their illness with peers, doctors, school officials, and other adults. They find that as they enter high school, their peers are less critical and cruel. No longer needing to build self-esteem by putting down other people, their peers are able to affirm them and value ways in which they are different. In this stage, CFIDS children assume more responsibility to negotiate with teachers, tutors, peers, and other adults.

Once again, however, the CFIDS males suffer from losing their major arena for building self-esteem: sports. "Even when Steven is able to attend our church's youth group, he feels left out," says Cyndi Volkers. "The activities the boys do for bonding are all active: hiking, volleyball, rock climbing."

Obviously, the teenagers who are out of school altogether find it hard to maintain friendships because they are totally out of the social flow. Several of these teenagers have found deep friendships with other sick teenagers, especially other teenagers who have CFIDS. They find each other through organizations like CFS Youth Outreach.

The teenagers who are able to be in school part-time often find two or three close friends who will take the effort to understand their illness and help them cope. Alisa has several loyal friends right now. When she is absent, they take more detailed notes so that she can photocopy them later. They call to fill her in on school social life, and they understand when she can be with them only part of a night on which they have planned a sleepover.

Many teenagers with CFIDS find it hard to relate to their healthy peers, who seem less mature, somewhat sheltered, and sometimes even spoiled. Many of these peers have not lived with physical and emotional pressures. Many have not watched their families almost lose their house as a result of the financial pressures of living with chronic illness. Many of them have not had to cling to the Lord with the tenacity that the CFIDS teenagers have learned to do.

I feel hopeful as I listen to older teenagers talk about their years with CFIDS. Many of them have reached an amazing level of integration, of accepting the illness, of giving it an appropriate place in their lives, and of carving out a satisfying life in the midst of their debilitation.

As you watch your child suffer from CFIDS, give your child trust, love, as well as support and encouragement. Guard your child's self-esteem, and commit yourself to your child's growth. Compensate for the many losses your child experiences, and above all, advocate for your child whenever necessary.

Epilogue

The stories shared in this book are not over.

One mother and daughter have experienced increased brain dysfunction. One of the women has had a double mastectomy as a preventive measure to stave off the growth of breast cancer, which had ravaged her mother.

The battle with CFIDs continues for many families. Since I wrote these chapters, some people have gone into deep relapses. One of the couples has separated, unable to bear the stresses the illness placed on their marriage.

But many others have experienced marked levels of recovery. Two of the women have returned to part-time work. Several of the older teenagers have been able to take a few college courses. And two of the men have returned to full-time work. That's encouraging for us all.

The past year has been most difficult for our family. In the same ten months that I found myself gaining more and more ability to function, Alisa lost ground. A chemical imbalance in her brain led to a depression so severe that she lost all hope and perspective. Several months ago she took an overdose of medication, hoping to end her struggle. The months following her attempted suicide were filled with more doctors' visits than we would care to count, as well as a hospitalization for crisis stabilization. As we walked through those months, every statement and assumption made in this book came under fire. Once again we felt tested to the limit. But we remain resolute. We choose to have hope, even if—.

While we fought to keep Alisa alive, we had no guarantees. For now, the Lord has chosen to spare her life. We are grateful. But we do not assume that the storms are over for Alisa or for our family. I said in an earlier chapter that the only fatal symptom of CFIDS is suicide. For us, CFIDS has become a life-threatening illness. So once again we place our lives in the Lord's hands, trusting his goodness.

Epilogue

While the people in this book have tried to paint a realistic picture of their struggles, they do not want to leave you without hope. If you also battle with CFIDS, remember that CFIDS is a manageable illness. Remember also that you are not alone. Several million people walk in the valley with you. Above all, remember that Christ walks with you in the valley, comforting you, leading you, teaching you, and healing you. Take his hand and allow him to give you strength in your weakness.

Find the Help You Need

LEARN ABOUT CFIDS

Patient Networks

The CFIDS Association of America, Inc.
P.O. Box 220398
Charlotte, NC 28222-0398
(800) 44-CFIDS (800-442-3437)
(900) 896-CFID (900-896-2343) (Information line; charge per
minute); transcripts available
FAX (704) 365-9755

Services:
1. The CFIDS Information Line (900) 896-CFID (900) 896-2343)
   (charge per minute)
2. *The CFIDS Chronicle*
   * Quarterly journal of advocacy, information, research, and
     encouragement for the CFIDS community
   * Includes book reviews, "Ask the Doctor" column, bulletin
     board, paid advertisements, educational materials (bibliogra-
     phy and order form)
   * Special issues on current research and current treatment options
   * Back issues of *The CFIDS Chronicle* available for purchase
3. Brochures:
   * "Physician's Honor Roll"
   * "Support Network Sheet"
   * "Chronic Fatigue Syndrome Is a Real Disease"
   * "Chronic Fatigue and Immune Dysfunction Syndrome:
     A Guide for Persons with CFIDS"
4. Cost: Membership is $30 annually.

National Chronic Fatigue Syndrome and Fibromyalgia Association
3521 Broadway, Suite 222
Kansas City, MO 64111
(816) 931-4777

Services:
1. "Heart of America News" newsletter
   • Peer-reviewed, scientifically accurate information
   • Includes government updates, "Ask the Doctor" column,
     support services information, educational materials list
2. Information Packets:
   • General CFS Information Packet
   • CFS Patient Information Packet, spiral-bound
   • Physician Information Packet, spiral-bound
   • CFS "How to Be a Phone Contact" Information Packet
   • CFS Support Group Start-up Information Packet
   • Bibliography 1980–Present for Chronic Fatigue, CFS,
     HHV–6, and Fibromyalgia, spiral-bound
3. Brochures:
   • "Chronic Fatigue Syndrome, the Thief of Vitality"
   • "Chronic Fatigue Syndrome: A Pamphlet for Physicians"
   • "Neuropsychological Rehabilitation: Suggestions/Techniques
     for Assisting CFS Patients"
   • "Social Security Disability Benefits Information for CFS
     Patients"
   • "A School Guide for Students with CFS"
   • "CFS and School Success"
   • "Chronic Fatigue Syndrome in Men"
   • "Chronic Fatigue Syndrome in the Work Place"
   • "The Americans with Disabilities Act: CFS and Employment"
   • "Coping Skills: How to Maintain Your Equilibrium in the
     CFS Balancing Act"
   • "A Guide for Physicians When Considering a Diagnosis
     of Chronic Fatigue Syndrome in Children"
   • "Understanding the Emotions Surrounding CFS"

4. Educational Tapes
5. Cost: Membership is $15 annually.

CFIDS Foundation
965 Mission Street, Suite 425
San Francisco, CA 94103
(415) 882–9986

Services:

1. "CFIDS Treatment News" publication
2. Treatment bulletins
3. Telephone counseling
4. Referrals, training, and advocacy

Government Agencies That Provide Information

U.S. Department of Health and Human Resources
Public Health Service
National Institutes of Health
Bldg. 31, Room 7, B 50
Bethesda, MD 20892

Will send a copy of "Chronic Fatigue Syndrome, Spring 1993," an inclusive booklet that contains a compilation of reports written on everything from the history of CFIDS to research being done, to CFIDS in children and the elderly and more.

Centers for Disease Control
Division of Viral Diseases; Mail Stop A32
1600 Clifton Road, NE
Atlanta, GA 30333
(404) 639-1388
(404) 332-4555 (hot line; CFS is #7)

National Institute of Allergy and Infectious Diseases
Office of Communications
9000 Rockville Pike
Building 31, Room 7A32
Bethesda, MD 20892
(301) 496-5717

California Legislature Senate
Public Employment and Retirement Committee
Senate Publications
1100 J Street, Room B-15
Sacramento, CA 95814
(916) 327-2155

Will send 52-page booklet "Chronic Fatigue Syndrome and Application for Disability Retirement Benefits 610-S" for a cost of $5.95.

BIBLIOGRAPHY
Publications About CFIDS
Books About CFIDS

Allen, Tara. *Shadow & Light: The Voice of CFIDS.* Charlotte, N.C.: The CFIDS Association of America, 1993.

Bell, David S., M.D., *The Doctor's Guide to Chronic Fatigue Syndrome: Understanding, Treating, and Living with CFIDS.* Reading, Mass.: Addison-Wesley, 1994.

Berne, Katrina H. *Running on Empty: Chronic Fatigue Immune Dysfunction Syndrome.* Alameda, Calif.: Hunter House, 1992.

Berne, Katrina H., Ph.D., *CFIDS Lite: Chronic Fatigue Immune Dysfunction Syndrome with 1/3 the Seriousness.* Order from BHB Communications, 761 E. University #F, Mesa, AZ 85203. 1989.

Bolles, Edmund Blair. *Learning to Live with Chronic Fatigue Syndrome.* New York: Dell, 1990.

Feiden, Karyn. *Hope and Help for Chronic Fatigue Syndrome.* New York: Prentice-Hall, 1990.

Fisher, Gregg Charles, with Stephen Straus, M.D.; Paul R. Cheney, M.D., Ph.D.; and James Oleske, M.D. *Chronic Fatigue Syndrome: A Victim's Guide to Understanding, Treating, and Coping with This Debilitating Illness.* New York: Warner Books, 1987.

Kenny, Timothy P. *Living with CFS: A Personal Story of the Struggle for Recovery.* New York: Thunder's Mouth, 1994.

Wood, Terri Mosely. *Life in the Slow Lane: Coping with Chronic Fatigue Syndrome.* Madison, Tenn.: Woodshed Press, 1989. To order this book, send $9.95 per copy, plus $2.50 per-copy shipping charge to Wood-shed Press, Inc., 605 Vantrease Road, Madison, TN 37115.

Tapes About CFIDS

Berne, Katrina, Ph.D. *Chronic Fatigue Syndrome: For Those Who Care* (one audiotape). Order from The CFIDS Association of America, Inc., P.O. Box 220398, Charlotte, NC 28222-0398. Cost: $10.00.

Berne, Katrina, Ph.D. *Chronic Fatigue Syndrome: Information, Relaxation/Healing Exercise* (one audiotape). Order from The CFIDS Association of America, Inc., P.O. Box 220398, Charlotte, NC 28222-0398. Cost: $10.00.

Chronic Fatigue Syndrome: A Real Disease, with Charles Lapp, M.D. (90-minute videotape) . To order, call or write: Greensboro CFS Foundation, Inc., 10 Wild Partridge Court, Greensboro, NC 27455; (800) 597-4237. Cost: $19.95, plus $3.00 for shipping within the USA or $7.00 for shipping to Canada.

Lives in Limbo (46-minute videocassette). To order, call (800) 366-6056. Cost: $29.95, $19.95 additional tapes. All proceeds go to The CFIDS Association of America to fund CFIDS research.

Living Hell: The Real World of Chronic Fatigue Syndrome (1-hour videotape). To order, call (800) 577-4747. Cost: $29.95 for individuals; $19.95 for organizations.

CFS: Unraveling the Mystery (4-part video from CNN's Newsource). Order from The CFIDS Association of America, Inc., P.O. Box 220398, Charlotte, NC 28222-0398. Cost: $12.00.

Bibliographies About CFIDS

Berne, Katrina, Ph.D. Well-researched bibliography and resources in the appendixes of her book *Running on Empty: Chronic Fatigue Immune Dysfunction Syndrome.* Alameda Calif.: Hunter House, 1992.

Feiden, Karyn. See Appendix B and Appendix C in her book *Hope and Help for Chronic Fatigue Syndrome.* New York: Prentice-Hall, 1990.

National Chronic Fatigue Syndrome and Fibromyalgia Association publishes "Bibliography 1980-Present on Chronic Fatigue, CFS, HHV-6 and Fibromyalgia" ($3.50).

Walders, Vaille. *CFIDS Pathfinder to Information, 1993.* To order this 54-page, extensive bibliography, send $12.95 to CFIDS Pathfinder, P.O. Box 2644, Kensington, MD 20891-2644 or call (301) 530-8624.

Find Support
Support Groups
How to Find a Support Group
- Write The CFIDS Association of America for their state-by-state list of support groups

What to Look for in a Support Group
Look for a group that
- Disseminates information
- Provides empathy and identification
- Directs people to effective medical professionals
- Provides advocacy
- Provides support if you don't have a loving and supportive family

How to Start a Support Group
- See Appendix B in Katrina Berne's *Running on Empty*
- Write for "CFS Support Group Start-up Information" packet from the National Chronic Fatigue Syndrome and Fibromyalgia Association ($6.00)

Support Groups by Mail

CFS Adult Uplift
c/o Candy Feathers
648 Coop Road
Bell Buckle, TN 37020

(Send legal-sized, self-addressed, stamped envelope.)

International Fatigue Syndromes Share and Prayer Chain Ministry to Those Living with CFS/CFIDS/CEBV/ME/FMS/PVMS

c/o Janet Bohanon
919 Scott Ave.
Kansas City, KS 66105

(Cost: Freewill donation)

CFS Youth Outreach
c/o Sharon Walk
14 Shetland Road
Florham Park, NJ 07932–1813

(Cost: $15.00 membership fee)

A Newsletter for Couples with CFIDS
c/o Rita Ellison Frankie
735 West Main
Homer, LA 71040

(Cost: $5.00 subscription fee for quarterly newsletter)

Books About Fatigue

Bell, David S., and Stef Donev. *Curing Fatigue: A Step-by-Step Plan to Uncover and Eliminate the Causes of Chronic Fatigue.* Emmaus, Penn.: Rodale Press, 1993.

Gruelle, Helen (a person with CFIDS). *Horizontal in a Vertical World: Living with Long-Term Fatigue.* To order Gruelle's book, send $7.95 to Fatigue, 2012 Trailee Court, Roseville, CA 95747.

Reisser, Paul. *Energy Drainers, Energy Gainers: Solutions to Chronic Fatigue.* Grand Rapids: Zondervan, 1990.

Tournier, Paul. *Fatigue in Modern Society.* Atlanta: John Knox Press, 1973.

Books About Living with Chronic Illness

Dion, Susan, Ph.D. (a person with CFIDS). *Write Now: Maintaining a Creative Spirit While Homebound and Ill.* To receive a print copy, send a self-addressed and stamped (one 29-cent stamp and four 32-cent stamps) 6" x 9" (oversized) envelope. To receive a desktop publishing format (Macintosh and Microsoft Word 4.0), send a 3.5" (DD or HD) and self-addressed, appropriate-sized return mailer with correct postage. Send requests to S. Dion, 432 Ives Avenue, Carneys Point, NJ 08069.

271

Donoghue, Paul J., and Mary E. Siegel. *Sick and Tired of Feeling Sick and Tired: Living with Invisible Chronic Illness.* New York: W.W. Norton, 1992.

Maurer, Janet R., and Patricia D. Strasberg. *Building a New Dream: A Family Guide to Coping with Chronic Illness & Disability.* Reading, Mass.: Addison-Wesley, 1989.

Moench, Cynthia L. (a person with CFIDS). *Binding Up the Brokenhearted: A Handbook of Hope for the Chronically Ill or Disabled.* Joplin, Mo.: College Press Publishing Company, 1991.

Penner, Clifford and Joyce. "Sex When Illness Hits the Family," in *A Gift for All Ages: A Family Handbook on Sexuality.* Waco, Tex.: Word, 1986.

Register, Cheri. *Living with Chronic Illness: Days of Patience and Passion.* New York: Free Press, 1987.

Strong, Maggie. *Mainstay: For the Well Spouse of the Chronically Ill.* Boston: Little, Brown, 1988.

Tengbom, Mildred. *Why Waste Your Illness? Let God Use It for Growth.* Minneapolis: Augsburg, 1984.

Van't Land, Marcia. *Living Well with Chronic Illness.* Wheaton, Ill.: Harold Shaw, 1994.

Wheeler, Eugenie, G., and Joyce Dace-Lombard. *Living Creatively with Chronic Illness: Developing Skills for Transcending the Loss, Pain, and Frustration.* Ventura, Calif.: Pathfinder Publishing, 1989.

Strength in the Midst of Suffering
Books

Bartalsky, Kathy. *Soaring on Broken Wings.* Chicago: Moody, 1990.

Bell, Steve, and Valerie Bell. *Coming Back: Real Life Stories of Courage from Spiritual Survivors.* Wheaton, Ill.: Victor, 1992.

Biebel, David B. *If God Is So Good, Why Do I Hurt So Bad? An Understanding Look at the Journey from Pain to Wholeness.* Colorado Springs: NavPress, 1989.

Bridges, Jerry. *Trusting God, Even When Life Hurts.* Colorado Springs: NavPress, 1988.

Carmichael, Amy. *You Are My Hiding Place.* Minneapolis: Bethany, 1978.

_____. *Rose from Brier.* Grand Rapids: Zondervan, 1989.

Chesto, Kathleen O'Connell. *Risking Hope: Fragile Faith in the Healing Process*. Kansas City, Mo.: Sheed & Ward, 1990.

Christenson, Evelyn. *Gaining Through Losing*. Wheaton, Ill: Victor, 1980.

Craig, William Lane. *No Easy Answers: Finding Hope in Doubt, Failure & Unanswered Prayer*. Chicago: Moody, 1990.

Davis, Verdell. *Riches Stored in Secret Places*. Dallas: Word, 1994.

Dobson, James. *When God Doesn't Make Sense*. Wheaton, Ill.: Tyndale, 1993.

Dravecky, Dave and Jan. *When You Can't Come Back*. Grand Rapids: Zondervan, 1992.

Elliot, Elisabeth. *A Path Through Suffering: Discovering the Relationship Between God's Mercy and Our Pain*. Ann Arbor, Mich.: Servant, 1990.

Ferguson, Sinclair. *Deserted by God?* Grand Rapids: Baker, 1992.

Hansel, Tim. *You Gotta Keep Dancin'*. Elgin, Ill.: David C. Cook, 1985.

Kreeft, Peter. *Making Sense Out of Suffering*. Ann Arbor, Mich.: Servant, 1986.

Lucado, Max. *On the Anvil: Thoughts on Being Shaped in the Image of God*. Wheaton, Ill.: Tyndale, 1994.

Means, James. *A Tearful Celebration: Hope for Those Who Grieve*. Portland, Ore.: Multnomah, 1985.

Mehl, Ron. *Surprise Endings: Ten Good Things About Bad Things*. Portland, Ore.: Multnomah, 1993.

Nelson, Alan E. *Broken in the Right Place: How God Tames the Soul*. Nashville: Thomas Nelson, 1994.

O'Conner, Elizabeth. *Cry Pain, Cry Hope: Thresholds to Purpose*. Waco, Tex.: Word, 1987.

Patterson, Ben. *Waiting: Finding Hope When God Seems Silent*. Downers Grove, Ill.: InterVarsity, 1989.

Pippert, Rebecca Manley. *Hope Has Its Reasons: Surprised by Faith in a Broken World*. San Francisco: HarperCollins, 1989.

Reighard, Dwight (Ike), with Martha Maughon. *Treasures from the Dark*. Nashville: Thomas Nelson, 1990.

Schaeffer, Edith. *Affliction*. Old Tappan, N.J.: Revell, 1978.

Shaw, Luci. *God in the Dark: Through Grief and Beyond.* Grand Rapids: Zondervan, 1989.

Slater, Michael. *Stretcher Bearers: Practicing and Receiving the Gift of Encouragement and Support.* Ventura, Calif.: Regal, 1985.

Stoop, Jan, and David Stoop. *Saying Goodbye to Disappointments: Finding Hope When Your Dreams Don't Come True.* Nashville: Thomas Nelson, 1993.

Stowell, Joseph. *The Upside of Down: Finding Hope When It Hurts.* Chicago: Moody, 1991.

Strauss, Lehman. *In God's Waiting Room: Learning Through Suffering.* Chicago: Moody, 1985.

Tada, Joni Eareckson. *Diamonds in the Dust.* Grand Rapids: Zondervan, 1993.

Walls, David. *Finding God in the Dark: Rays of Hope for Life's Difficult Days.* Wheaton, Ill.: Victor, 1993.

Wangerin, Walter, Jr. *Mourning into Dancing.* Grand Rapids: Zondervan, 1992.

Wise, Robert L. *When the Night Is Too Long.* Nashville: Thomas Nelson, 1990.

Woodson, Meg. *Turn It into Glory.* Minneapolis: Bethany House, 1991.

Yancey, Philip. *Disappointment with God.* Grand Rapids: Zondervan, 1990.

————. *Where Is God When It Hurts?* Grand Rapids: Zondervan, 1990.

Tapes

Elisabeth Elliot, *Suffering Is Not for Nothing,* available from Ligonier Ministries, Box 547500, Orlando, FL 32854, or call 1-800-435-4343. Available in three-cassette audio series or two-cassette video series.

Books on tape are available through your state libraries and the Library of Congress. Ask your reference librarian for a copy of the brochure "Library Services for the Blind and Physically Handicapped." Call 800-424-8567 or 202-707-9275 for more information.

Children and CFIDS

Books and Brochures About Children with CFIDS

NICCYD, the National Information Center for Children and Youth with Disabilities

P.O. Box 1492
Washington, DC 20013
(800) 999–5599

NICCYD gives referrals, packets, and lists of publications, including a copy of the Americans with Disabilities Act of 1973, PL 94–142, and an explanation of Sec. 504, the part applying to CFIDS kids.

Brochures available from the National Chronic Fatigue Syndrome and Fibromyalgia Association

- "Chronic Fatigue Syndrome: A Pamphlet for Physicians"
- "A School Guide for Students with CFS"
- "CFS and School Success"
- "Coping Skills: How to Maintain Your Equilibrium in the CFS Balancing Act"
- "A Guide for Physicians When Considering a Diagnosis of Chronic Fatigue Syndrome in Children"
- "Understanding the Emotions Surrounding CFS"

Bell, David S., M.D., *The Doctor's Guide to Chronic Fatigue Syndrome: Understanding, Treating, and Living with CFIDS*. Reading, Mass.: Addison-Wesley, 1994.

Sample Letter for School Personnel

Dear faculty and staff,

For the past seven years, our daughter, Alisa, has been debilitated by a viral/immune-system illness called chronic fatigue immune deficiency syndrome (CFIDS). You may have read about the illness in the November 10, 1990, *Newsweek* cover story, or you may know someone who has CFIDS.

School history with CFIDS

Crippling fatigue, low-grade fever, swollen lymph nodes, nausea, joint and muscle pain—to name a few of her ongoing symptoms—have made it necessary for Alisa to spend several hours each day off her feet, allowing her immune system to regroup. For the first four years of her illness, Alisa was able to attend school half days and do the rest of her work from a couch with the help of a homebound tutor. In eighth grade Alisa suffered a severe relapse

275

that left her bedridden. At that point her doctor at Children's Memorial Hospital sent us to Dr. David Bell at the Harvard Medical School. Dr. Bell, the leading specialist for children with CFIDS, put her on medication that has brought back some of her ability to function, but she still is debilitated. Last year Alisa was able to attend school four periods a day, although she had twenty absences during each semester.

Although this illness sounds horrible, it is manageable. CFIDS is not fatal, and it is not progressively degenerative like MS or lupus. Although there is currently no cure for CFIDS, doctors can treat some symptoms with prescription drugs. However, the most effective treatment is rest—active, planned rest. With rest, the overactive part of the immune system stops dumping toxic chemicals into the body, allowing some symptoms to subside. The symptoms don't leave; they just settle down so the body can function with less pain.

Alisa and school

Despite these handicaps, Alisa has stayed at grade level and has remained on the high-honor roll most terms. You will find her to be a conscientious student who will take your class seriously and make up homework she has missed. However, her illness may force her to miss some classes, and at times she will not have assignments ready on time. She wants to be in school and finds it very hard to miss out on what's going on in class.

As you can imagine, this situation places a great deal of stress on an adolescent. Because Alisa expends a lot of her emotional energy just coping with the physical dynamics of her illness, she has very little emotional reserve for dealing with the many other stresses of adolescence. But she copes well. She certainly has her times of despair, when she loses all hope of ever feeling normal again, but for the most part she is positive and works toward health. Alisa is a sensitive person and may cry easily when she feels a conflict because of her illness. For instance, she wants to do "what is right." But doing what's right for the rest of the class—being in class every day, meeting every deadline, doing an excellent job—isn't always realistic for her in her present situation. This creates an inner conflict for her. On the one hand she wants to downplay her illness, not expecting any special treatment or any attention because of it. On the other hand the reality of her illness means she needs to be treated somewhat differently. As an adolescent, that conflict is hard for her to handle. Alisa also tends to be a perfectionist and expects a lot from herself, often not making good judgments about what will be the consequences of her intensity.

When you see her, she will look normal, at times even bouncy. But that doesn't last long. Her body has only a few good hours in a day, and then the symptoms begin to mount.

You can help in several ways:

1. Flexibility. Alisa may not be able to be in class every day. Work with her to maximize her learning. If in your class it would help her to know the assignments for the week so that she can keep up even if she's home, then arrange for her to get that list at the beginning of each week. (Some teachers photocopy their lesson-plan book.)

2. Discernment. If she's absent from your class and has makeup work to do, help her discern what in your estimation is essential to do and what is nonessential and can therefore be skipped. An occasional backlog of makeup work can prevent her from bouncing back from a crash. If you're open to extending a deadline, let her know that.

3. Communication. As a family, we want to be as helpful and cooperative as we can. If you see problems arising or if you become frustrated by the situation with Alisa, please call us. Take the time to reassure Alisa. She gets discouraged often and needs to hear from you that things are going to work out.

Our experiences so far with the school have been very positive. If you have questions about how teachers have handled Alisa in the past, talk with the teachers with whom we worked last year.

Thank you for taking the time to read all of this. We have found that a little understanding goes a long way.

Sincerely,
Bas and Lynn Vanderzalm
(Phone numbers)

Books for Children to Enjoy

Series by Sigmund Brouwer: Accidental Detectives series and Winds of Light series (Victor Books).

Series by Madeleine L'Engle: Austin Trilogy and Wrinkle in Time trilogy (Dell).

Series by L. M. Montgomery: Anne of Green Gables series, Emily series, The Story Girl series (Bantam).

Series by Janette Oke: Canadian West series, Women of the West series (Bethany House).

Books by Patricia St. John: Include characters that live with illness (Moody).

Series by Jane Sorenson: Jennifer Green series and Katie Hooper series (Standard Publishing).

Series by Hilda Stahl: Best Friends series (Good News), Elizabeth Gail series (Tyndale), Kayla O'Brian Adventure series (Good News), Prairie series (Bethel), Sadie Rose series (Good News), Teddy Jo series (Tyndale), Tyler Twins series (Tyndale), Wren House Mystery series (Cook).

Series by Bodie and Brock Thoene: Zion Covenant series, Zion Chronicles series, Shiloh Legacy series, Saga of the Sierras series (Bethany House).

Series by Laura Ingalls Wilder: The Little House on the Prairie series (HarperCollins).

Books That Became Friends

Anderson, Ken. *Bold As a Lamb: Pastor Samuel Lamb and the Underground Church of China.* Grand Rapids: Zondervan, 1991.

de Vinck, Christopher. *The Power of the Powerless: A Brother's Legacy of Love.* Grand Rapids: Zondervan, 1990.

Dravecky, Dave, with Tim Stafford. *Comeback.* Grand Rapids: Zondervan, 1990.

Carson, Ben, with Cecil Murphy. *Gifted Hands: The Ben Carson Story.* Grand Rapids: Zondervan, 1990.

Dodds, Elizabeth D. *Marriage to a Difficult Man: The "Uncommon Union" of Jonathan and Sarah Edwards.* Philadelphia: Westminster Press, 1971.

Elliot, Elisabeth. *A Chance to Die: The Life and Legacy of Amy Carmichael.* Old Tappan, N.J.: Revell, 1987.

Henry, Marie. *The Secret Life of Hannah Whitall Smith.* Grand Rapids: Zondervan, 1984.

MacDonald, Gail. *Keep Climbing.* Wheaton, Ill.: Tyndale, 1989.

Pierson, Arthur T. *George Müller of Bristol.* New York: Baker and Taylor, 1899.

Roseveare, Helen. *Living Holiness.* Minneapolis: Bethany House, 1987.

Schaeffer, Edith. *The Tapestry: The Life and Times of Francis and Edith Schaeffer.* Waco, Tex.: Word, 1981.

Senter, Ruth. *Beyond Safe Places: Trusting God Through Life's Risks.* Wheaton, Ill.: Harold Shaw, 1992.

_____. *Seeing God in the Ordinary Places.* Grand Rapids: Zondervan, 1990.

Smarto, Donald. *Pursued: True Story of Crime, Faith, and Family.* Downers Grove, Ill.: InterVarsity, 1990.

Taylor, Kenneth, and Virginia Muir. *My Life: A Guided Tour.* Wheaton, Ill.: Tyndale, 1991.

Taylor, Mrs. Howard. *The Triumph of John and Betty Stam.* Chicago: Moody, 1935.

Van Stone, Doris, and Erwin W. Lutzer. *No Place to Cry: The Hurt and Healing of Sexual Abuse.* Chicago: Moody, 1990.

Wilson, Dorothy Clarke. *Granny Brand.* Chappaqua, N.Y.: Christian Herald Books, 1976.

Notes

Introduction

1. "The name CFIDS was suggested by Dr. Seymour Grufferman, at a conference in 1987, to distinguish the illness from the common, garden-variety fatigue with which it is so often confused." David S. Bell, M.D., *The Doctor's Guide to Chronic Fatigue Syndrome: Understanding, Treating, and Living with CFIDS* (Reading, Mass.: Addison-Wesley, 1994), 93.

2. Dr. J. Van Aerde, "The Other Side of the Fence," *The CFIDS Chronicle* (Spring 1992): 11.

CHAPTER 1: What is Wrong with Me?

1. Summarized from the working case definition published in the *Annals of Internal Medicine* 1988:108:387–89 and summaries printed in the *North Carolina Family Physician*, the official publication of the North Carolina Academy of Family Physicians, vol. 43 (Winter 1992) and "Diagnosing a Disease," *Chicago Tribune*, 21 October, 1990.

2. David S. Bell, M.D., *The Doctor's Guide to Chronic Fatigue Syndrome: Understanding, Treating, and Living with CFIDS* (Reading, Mass.: Addison-Wesley, 1994), 148–49.

CHAPTER 2: Understand CFIDS

1. To obtain these sources of information, see the "Find the Help You Need" section at the back of this book.

2. "A Guide to CFIDS," *The CFIDS Chronicle* (Winter 1994): 57.

3. David S. Bell, M.D., *The Doctor's Guide to Chronic Fatigue Syndrome: Understanding, Treating, and Living with CFIDS* (Reading, Mass.: Addison-Wesley, 1994), 101.

4. Timothy Kenny, *Living with Chronic Fatigue Syndrome: A Personal Story of the Struggle for Recovery* (New York: Thunder's Mouth Press, 1994), 192.

5. Bell, *The Doctor's Guide to Chronic Fatigue Syndrome*, 8.

6. For fuller explanations of the nature and role of these viruses, see Bell's book *The Doctor's Guide to Chronic Fatigue Syndrome*.

7. Bell, *The Doctor's Guide to Chronic Fatigue Syndrome*, 109.

8. Ibid., 25.

9. Ibid., 137.

10. Dr. David S. Bell, interview on *Good Morning, America,* February 16, 1994.

11. Sherry Chapman, as quoted in Tara Allen, ed., *Shadow & Light: The Voice of CFIDS* (published for limited distribution by The CFIDS Association, 1993), 26.

12. Daniel Peterson, M.D., as quoted in Tara Allen's *Shadow & Light: The Voice of CFIDS,* IV.

CHAPTER 3: Grieve Your Losses

1. Thomas English, "Skeptical of Skeptics," *JAMA* vol. 265, no. 8 (February 28, 1991): 964.

2. Walter Wangerin, Jr., *Mourning into Dancing* (Grand Rapids: Zondervan, 1992), 222.

3. Timothy Kenny, *Living with Chronic Fatigue Syndrome: A Personal Story of the Struggle for Recovery* (New York: Thunder's Mouth Press, 1994), 141.

4. Robert S. McGee and Pat Springle, *Getting Unstuck* (Houston: Word, 1992), 119.

5. Charles L. Whitfield, M.D., *Healing the Child Within* (Dearfield Beach, Fla.: Health Communications, 1987), 85.

CHAPTER 4: Make Physical Changes

1. Tim Hansel, *You Gotta Keep Dancin'* (Elgin, Ill.: David C. Cook, 1985), 102, 109.

2. Verdell Davis, *Riches Stored in Secret Places* (Dallas: Word, 1994), 57.

3. Terri Mosely Wood, *Life in the Slow Lane: Coping with Chronic Fatigue Syndrome* (Madison, Tenn.: Woodshed Press, 1989).

4. Quoted in Tara Allen, ed., *Shadow & Light: The Voice of CFIDS* (published for limited distribution by The CFIDS Association of America, 1993), 3.

5. Helen Gruelle, *Horizontal in a Vertical World: Living with Long-Term Fatigue* (self-published book; see order information in the "Find the Help You Need" section of this book), 73.

6. Cynthia Moench, *Binding Up the Brokenhearted: A Handbook of Hope for the Chronically Ill or Disabled* (Joplin, Mo.: College Press Publishing, 1991), 97.

7. See the list of books under the "Strength in Weakness" heading in the "Find the Help You Need" section at the back of the book.

8. Terry Waite, *Taken on Trust* (New York: Harcourt Brace & Company, 1993), 117.

CHAPTER 5: Find Emotional Balance

1. Terri Mosely Wood, *Life in the Slow Lane: Coping with Chronic Fatigue Syndrome* (Madison, Tenn.: Woodshed Press, 1989), 60.

2. Terry Waite, *Taken on Trust* (New York: Harcourt Brace & Company, 1993), 142.

3. Helen Gruelle, *Horizontal in a Vertical World: Living with Long-Term Fatigue* (self-published book; see order information in the "Find the Help You Need" section of this book), 46.

4. Robert L. Wise, *When the Night Is Too Long* (Nashville: Thomas Nelson, 1990), 95.

5. Tim Hansel, *You Gotta Keep Dancin'* (Elgin, Ill.: David C. Cook, 1985), 94.

6. Gruelle, *Horizontal in a Vertical World*, 54–55.

7. Matthew 6:34.

8. Psalm 118:24.

9. Maggie Strong, *Mainstay: For the Well Spouse of the Chronically Ill* (Boston: Little, Brown and Company, 1988), 102–19.

10. Waite, *Taken on Trust*, Foreword.

11. Susan Schmall, Ph.D. "Coping—A Study," *The CFIDS Chronicle* (Spring 1992): 13–14.

12. J. B. Phillips, *The Price of Success: An Autobiography* (Wheaton, Ill.: Harold Shaw, 1984), 196.

13. Ibid., 197, 201.

14. Ibid., 200.

15. Lamentations 3:21–25.

CHAPTER 6: Accept Changing Relationships

1. Helen Gruelle, *Horizontal in a Vertical World: Living with Long-Term Fatigue* (self-published book; see order information in the "Find the Help You Need" section of this book), 71–72.

2. Cheri Register, *Living with Chronic Illness: Days of Patience and Passion* (New York: Free Press, 1987), as quoted in Helen Gruelle, *Horizontal in a Vertical World*, 55–56.

3. Terri Mosely Wood, *Life in the Slow Lane: Coping with Chronic Fatigue Syndrome* (Madison, Tenn.: Woodshed Press, 1989), 48–49.

Notes

4. For information about CYO, see the "Find the Help You Need" section at the end of the book.

5. Psalm 55:12–14, author's paraphrase.

6. John 9:1–3.

7. 1 Peter 2:21–23.

8. *Mourning into Dancing* (Grand Rapids: Zondervan Publishing House), 1992, 175.

CHAPTER 7: Choose to Trust God

1. Deuteronomy 30:11, 15, 19–20, italics added.

2. John 10:10.

3. Ibid.

4. John 8:44.

5. See Genesis 22.

6. James 1:2–4, PHILLIPS.

7. 2 Corinthians 1:3–5.

8. See Philippians 4: 6.

9. Jeremiah 29:11.

10. Robert L. Wise, *When the Night Is Too Long* (Nashville, Tenn.: Thomas Nelson, 1990), XV.

CHAPTER 8: Maintain Spiritual Health

1. Psalm 56:8 TLB.

2. Robert L. Wise, *When the Night Is Too Long* (Nashville: Thomas Nelson, 1990), 119.

3. Job 42:5.

4. Mildred Tengbom, *Why Waste Your Illness? Let God Use It for Growth* (Minneapolis: Augsburg, 1984), 110.

5. Ibid., 111.

6. 1 Peter 4:12.

7. Wise, *When the Night Is Too Long*, 192.

8. Elisabeth Elliot, "The Terrible Truth," from *Suffering Is Not for Nothing*, available on audio and video tape from Ligonier Ministries. See the "Find the Help You Need" section for ordering information.

9. Ibid.

10. Elliot, "Offering," from *Suffering Is Not for Nothing*.

11. 2 Corinthians 12:9–10, paraphrase by J. B. Phillips.

12. Tim Hansel, *You Gotta Keep Dancin'* (Elgin, Ill.: David C. Cook, 1985), 96.

13. 2 Corinthians 12:9–10, *The Message*, paraphrase by Eugene Peterson.

14. Chaim Potok, *The Chosen* (Greenwich, Conn.: Fawcett, 1965), 265.

15. Timothy Kenny, *Living with Chronic Fatigue Syndrome: A Personal Story of the Struggle for Recovery* (New York: Thunder's Mouth Press, 1994), p. 214.

16. Romans 5:3–5.

17. Helen Gruelle, *Horizontal in a Vertical World: Living with Long-Term Fatigue* (self-published book; see order information in the "Find the Help You Need" section of this book), 94.

18. "Lord's Day 1" of The Heidelberg Catechism, as found in the *Psalter Hymnal* (Grand Rapids: CRC Publications, 1987), 861.

19. Available from Ligonier ministries. To order, see the information in the "Find the Help You Need" section at the back of the book.

20. Available from Hope for the Heart, Dallas, Texas.

CHAPTER 9: Voices from the Valley

1. Tim Hansel, *You Gotta Keep Dancin'* (Elgin, Ill.: David C. Cook, 1985), 142.

CHAPTER 10: Maintain a Healthy Marriage

1. Twila Paris, "Up Close," *Today's Christian Woman* (Sept./Oct. 1993), *128*.

2. Terri Mosely Wood, *Life in the Slow Lane: Coping with Chronic Fatigue Syndrome* (Madison, Tenn.: Woodshed Press, 1989), 88.

3. Helen Gruelle, *Horizontal in a Vertical World: Living with Long-Term Fatigue* (self-published book; see order information in the "Find the Help You Need" section of this book), 38.

4. Timothy Kenny, *Living with Chronic Fatigue Syndrome: A Personal Story of the Struggle for Recovery* (New York: Thunder's Mouth Press, 1994), 208, 215.

5. Gruelle, *Horizontal in a Vertical World*, 19–20.

6. Clifford and Joyce Penner, "Sex When Illness Hits the Family," *A Gift for All Ages: A Family Handbook on Sexuality* (Waco, Tex.: Word, 1986), 195.

CHAPTER 12: Help and Advocate for CFIDS Children

1. See the "Find the Help You Need" section at the back of the book.

2. David S. Bell, M.D., *The Doctor's Guide to Chronic Fatigue Syndrome: Understanding, Treating, and Living with CFIDS* (Reading, Mass.: Addison-Wesley, 1994), 77.

3. See the sample letter in the "Find the Help You Need" section.

4. Karen Lang, "Calen's Story: A Child's Journey Through CFIDS," *The CFIDS Chronicle* (Winter 1994): 1–6.